AF304781

Pipeline

Pipeline

Human trafficking in Italy
Elena Perlino

Schilt Publishing

The desire for a better life, to escape the poverty and desperation here, is stronger than anything else. Here prostitution is a business, or rather the business. No one is shocked by it. The local papers call the routes travelled by the sex slaves the 'pipeline'. And to tell the truth there is not much difference between the girls and the oil: both mean big money.

Giuseppe Carrisi, *La fabbrica delle prostitute*,
Newton Compton Editori, Rome, 2011

The images in this book were shot over the past eight years in the Italian cities of Rome, Turin, Naples, Palermo and Genoa, all of them major hubs of Nigerian trafficking to Europe.
The same scenario can be found in many other European cities, as the phenomenon has spread radically over the last twenty years.

The reportage was inspired by my seeing African women wearing handkerchiefs as skirts, lining major commuter routes into Turin even on the coldest winter mornings. It turned out that these women were mainly from the Edo State region, in the south of Nigeria. Their clan does not control Nigerian women working in the countryside as heavily as one would expect, since the control is based on psychological and emotional pressures rather than physical ones. This made direct interaction possible and allowed me to enter into their lives. The fact that I am a woman too may have played a role in gaining their trust. Faith, one of the first women I met, spent five years on the streets working as a prostitute every day. In the hope of creating a better life back home, she ended up finding herself with a debt of sixty thousand euros, to be paid back to the illegal organization that planned her trip from Nigeria for Europe. The last time we met, her sister in Nigeria had just died while in labour at 22 years of age. Her nephew is now seven months old and dependent on the money she sends back regularly.

The relationship between the trafficked women and their exploiters can
be paradoxical. How can anybody accept that a friend or even your sister
can turn out to have been your exploiter for years? One wonders how
women can sit next to each other at the Pentecostal church, participate
in the same weddings and enjoy the same local markets or nightclubs.
Women accept this though as the normal order of things, as part of the
surviving game. Coming to Europe is a dream to escape the Nigerian
nightmare, but the price to be paid can be high. Over five hundred
Nigerian women killed over the last ten years bear witness to that.

Two parallel lives are being lived: one in Italy and one in Benin City.
The lucky ones manage to send money home, allowing a three-storey
house to be built, and the whole family to be sustained. The construction
work starts and stops as the money trickles in. As Isoke Aikpitanyi, a
former victim of trafficking, stressed: 'In Nigeria it doesn't matter
where the money comes from, as long as it comes.'
Trafficked women sometimes end up becoming traffickers themselves,
or drug dealers. Evil and good can no longer be clearly distinguished.
After being exploited, women start to exploit others themselves. The
roles have become interchangeable parts of an endless chain.

Elena Perlino, July 2014

Giuseppe Carrisi
La fabbrica delle prostitute

Newton Compton Editori, Rome, 2011

[…] At night you can only imagine Benin City. Most of the city is in darkness, because there's no power. The only lights run on generators. For those who can afford them. The only things that work are the "internet cafés", which are packed with young people day and night. […] Everyone wants to go abroad, to the "promised land" they all dream about, and pursue at any cost. And it is what the girls dream of, first and foremost. All the girls in Benin City want to go abroad.

[…] The desire for a better life, to escape the poverty and desperation here, is stronger than anything else. Here prostitution is a business, or rather *the* business. No-one is shocked by it. The local papers call the routes travelled by the sex slaves the *pipeline*. And to tell the truth there is not much difference between the girls and the oil: both mean big money.

"Nigeria is paying the price for a total lack of industrial diversification" reads an article on the site "PeaceReporter". "The country's economy is based entirely on oil […]. Revenues from the extraction of crude oil (destined above all for the American market) have not benefitted the population due to the inadequate distribution of the wealth generated, which remains […] in the hands of government officials.

But why has Benin City, of all places, the symbol of what the Nigerians themselves call the "south south" of the country, become the "factory" of prostitution? Why do its women and girls, dreaming of a better life, systematically end up trapped in a perverse, inhuman system with no way out?

"You'd need to experience what it's like to get up in the morning and have nothing to eat, go through your day and have nothing to eat in the evening" says father Jude Oidaga, a Jesuit priest from Benin City. "No work, no petrol, no soap to wash with… you'd need to experience what it's like to struggle to survive, to be able to understand what drives these girls to leave at any price. But the responsibility for this situation must be sought at higher levels: in the corrupt, ineffectual institutions and governments, and unjust, discriminatory international policies […]"[11].

[…] Most of the women involved come from the south of the country (apart from Benin City, the other cities most affected by the phenomenon are Lagos, Akure and Ondo), from recently urbanised areas, with a Christian and animist culture, and they are already uprooted from their tribes. They shun traditional values to buy into the Western world's "modern" model of well-being, consumerism and emancipation. Selling your body doesn't seem such a serious thing abroad (in Nigeria prostitution is a crime). Europe, with its wealth and its opportunities, is like a promised land for these girls. What they don't see is the life of slavery that awaits behind the dream.

[…] To understand the phenomenon of prostitution in Nigeria, we must necessarily take voodoo into account. […] "The deal between the interested parties is struck in the presence of a voodoo priest," explains Cristina Jomir, "and if the woman who "borrows" the money does not pay it back she is threatened with death or madness or some other calamity. To take the oath, the victim has to give the priest some kind of guarantee – fingernails, hair, blood, photographs or personal items – that will be returned when the money is paid back. She then has to drink bitter kola or water extracted from corpses from the chest for the idols[…]. Nigerian groups have always used magic and fideistic rituals, which, together with the ethnic connection and the influential lobbies in their home country, represent a strong binding factor and a powerful form of intimidation"[18]. In recent years these magic rituals have been reinstated and reinvented by con artists and self-styled *babalawos* who exploit common belief in these practices to ensnare women and girls seeking to emigrate.

[…] Currently there are two "routes" to Italy: the luckier women, those in possession of genuine passports and visas, set off from Lagos to travel to France and Belgium, and from there to Italy, going through

Accra in Ghana. However most do the journey overland, following the same route: from Lagos or Benin City in Nigeria, through Ghana and Niger to Libya, Algeria or Morocco (or even Sudan or Mali), and then on to Spain, France and Italy, their final destination.

[...] During the trip, the women stop off at the so-called "halfway houses", in places like Kano and Sokoto, on the border between Niger and Nigeria. They usually spend short periods of time in these places, in housing found by the traffickers, but sometimes it can be a question of months. There they are separated from their initial contact (the "brother"), who hands them over to other men who will take them through Libya. Up to this point the trafficked girls have not yet been forced into sexual acts, and do not yet realize the fate that awaits them.

After Kano and Sokoto, the women are taken to Zinder, in Niger, where they wait for trucks travelling to Tripoli. [...] The next leg is Duruku, three weeks across the desert from Zinder. [...][29]

[...] Once in Libya, usually Tripoli, the Nigerian girls are usually forced to enter a prostitution ring. This is when Libyan traffickers, the epicentre of the transnational criminal organisation, enter the picture. They are the girls' passport to Italy: to get them embarked without any hitches there has to be a Libyan to interface with the local police forces that patrol the coasts.

Before the sea crossing, however, the girls spend long periods of time in brothels in Tripoli and the surrounding area, "paying back" the cost of their trip. "The length of time they have to spend in these brothels is determined [...] by the traffickers themselves", highlights the report by the cooperative "Be Free", "[...] and varies according to how long it takes to organise the crossing, the weather conditions and when the brothel madam sends the money to pay for the trip".

"[...] There were more than 30 girls in the house, all Nigerian, and all forced into prostitution before being sent to Italy. I was there for about four months and I had to have sex with an average of five men a day. There were fixed prices: 1.5 dinars with a condom (that the client had to provide), 2 dinars without; we took the money and then had to give it all to H. He always brought us the clients and told us what to do. We could never refuse to have unprotected sex: if we didn't do it, we were kicked and beaten with chains and other things. Violence was the order of the day ". [...]

[...] In recent years the routes have changed, in response to the push-back policies introduced by Italy[40]. Trafficked Nigerian women, and migrants in general, are increasingly coming ashore on the coasts of Calabria and Lazio, as well as Puglia and Sardinia. And Libya continues to be the "bridgehead" for those attempting to enter Europe. Both economic migrants and asylum seekers turn to Libyans to organise the most difficult part of the journey, namely entering the Schengen area, at an affordable price.

[...] A key role in prostitution rings is played by Nigeria's so-called "secret cults". These mafia-like "confraternities" have a strong code of silence and use voodoo and tribal initiation rites. Members, who have to pay membership fees, owe total loyalty to the leader and accept any punishments dealt out: beating, whipping, being slashed with a machete [...][44]. As well as the prostitution racket, the "cults" are involved in various other kinds of extremely violent criminal activities, from drug trafficking to fraud to armed robbery.

[...] After a police operation in Naples the "confraternities" disappeared, but the niche they left vacant was soon occupied by much more violent gangs, including "Black Axe" and the "Vampires". In 2003, after a double stabbing in Turin, the existence of numerous other Nigerian cults with chapters throughout the country came to light. [...] Since then, Turin has been viewed as the "capital" of Nigerian organised crime, and in particular the "headquarters" for the "secret cults". [...] The criminal activities are divided between different ethnic groups: trafficking is almost all in the hands of Ibo organisations, while fraud and computer scams are handled by Yoruba groups[51].

6   *F. Gatti, Fuga dall'Africa: in viaggio con i clandestini*, in "Corriere della Sera", 23 December 2003.

11   A. Pozzi, *Mai più schiave*, Editrice Missionaria Italiana, Bologna 2008, in http://www.webdiocesi.chiesacattolica.it/cci_new/.../222/schiave.pdf.

18   C. Jomir, *Donna, Fede, Crimine: la drammatica traviata della prostituzione nigeriana*, in http://issuu.com/rivistacriminale/docs/1_2008_criminalita_femminile, 26 January 2010

29   Be Free, a social cooperative that combats trafficking, violence and discrimination, *Dossier sull'esperienza di sostegno a donne nigeriane trattenute presso il C.I.E. di Ponte Galeria e trafficate attraverso la Libia*, in www.befreecooperativa.org, 2009

40   On 30 August 2008, Italy ratified the Treaty of Benghazi, better known as the Italy-Libya "friendship treaty", which entailed joint control of the Strait of Sicily, with the aim of containing flows of illegal immigrants from North Africa. Following the examples of Spain and Malta, Italy also stepped up push-back operations at sea. Prior to that, in August 2004, the Italian and Libyan governments had signed an agreement to the effect that Tripoli was to receive immigrants sent back from Italy, reinforce the country's southern border with Niger and repatriate foreigners entering Libya illegally.

44   *Torino, capitale del "cultismo" nigeriano*, "Redattore sociale", 7 May 2008

51   Nigeria is in third place internationally in terms of the number of its citizens arrested abroad (Senato della Repubblica – Camera dei Deputati, XIV legislatura – Disegni di legge e relazioni – Documenti, p. 167). In 2009 more than 30,000 Nigerian citizens were arrested and expelled by the Libyan government. This was made known by the Nigerian national news agency NAN, which released an interview with the Nigerian ambassador in Tripoli. According to the ambassador, 90% of those arrested were young people, apprehended by the police for crimes of varying gravity, but mainly prostitution for the women, and arms dealing, drugs and passport fraud for the men, as well as the more common charge of robbery.

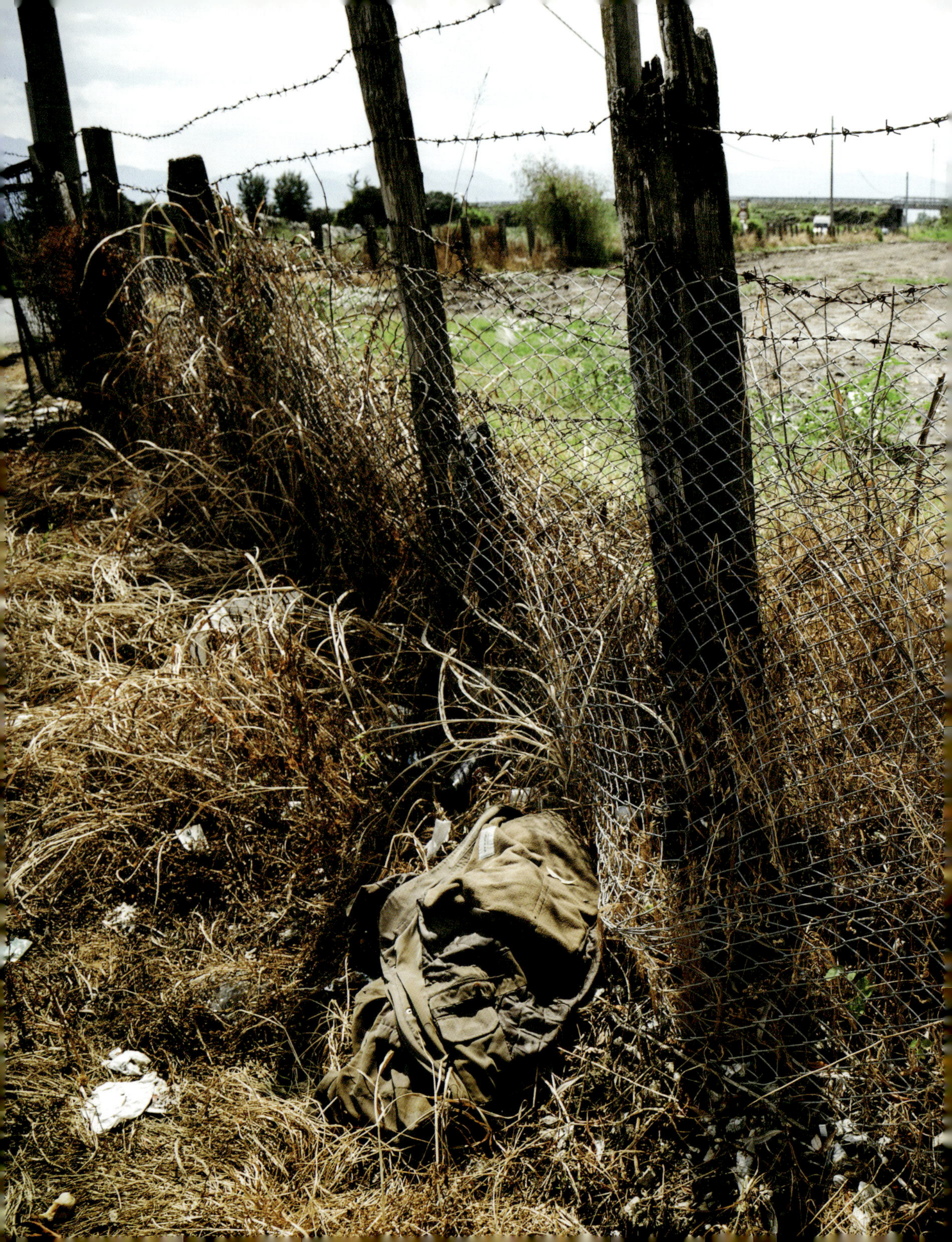

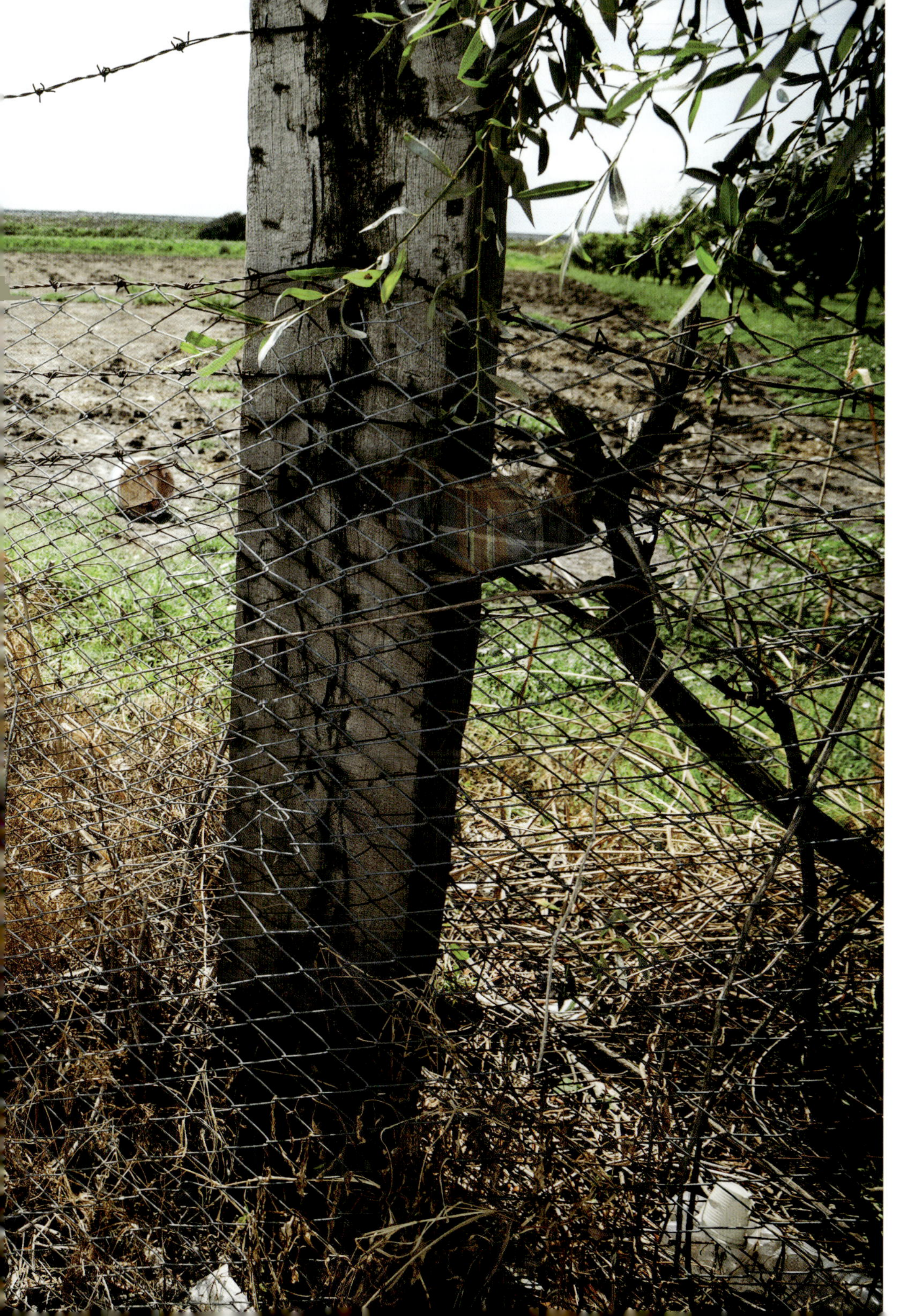

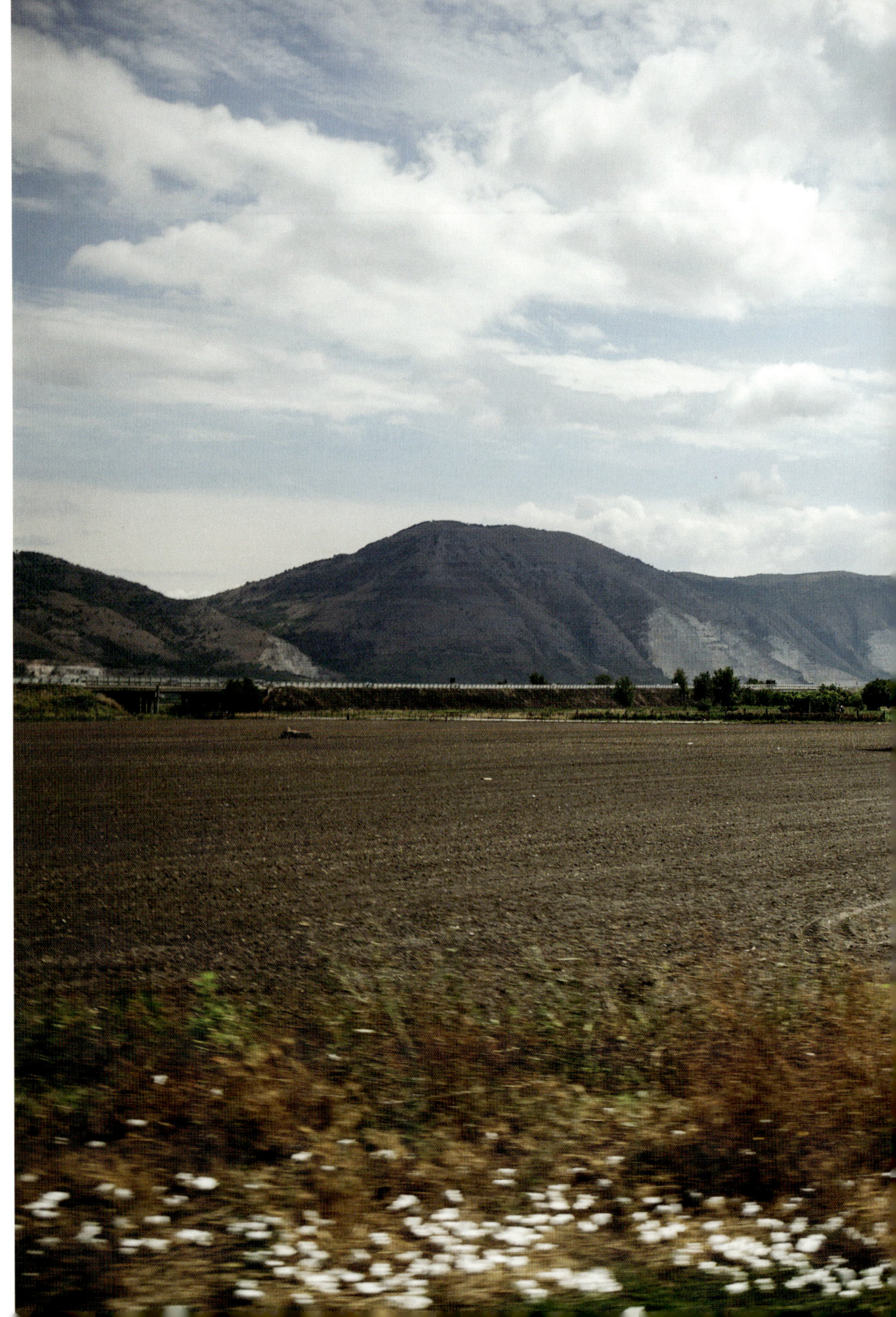

14

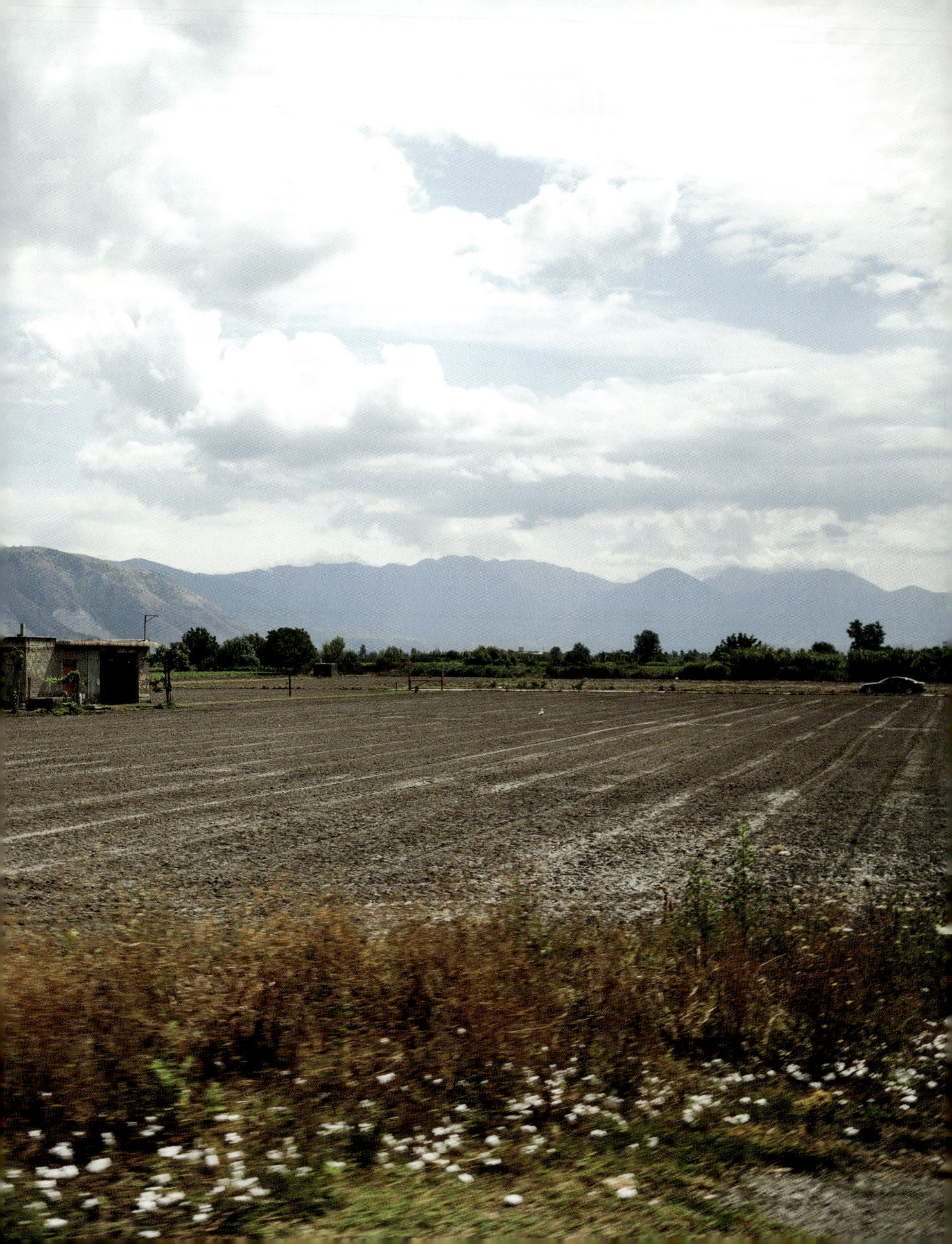

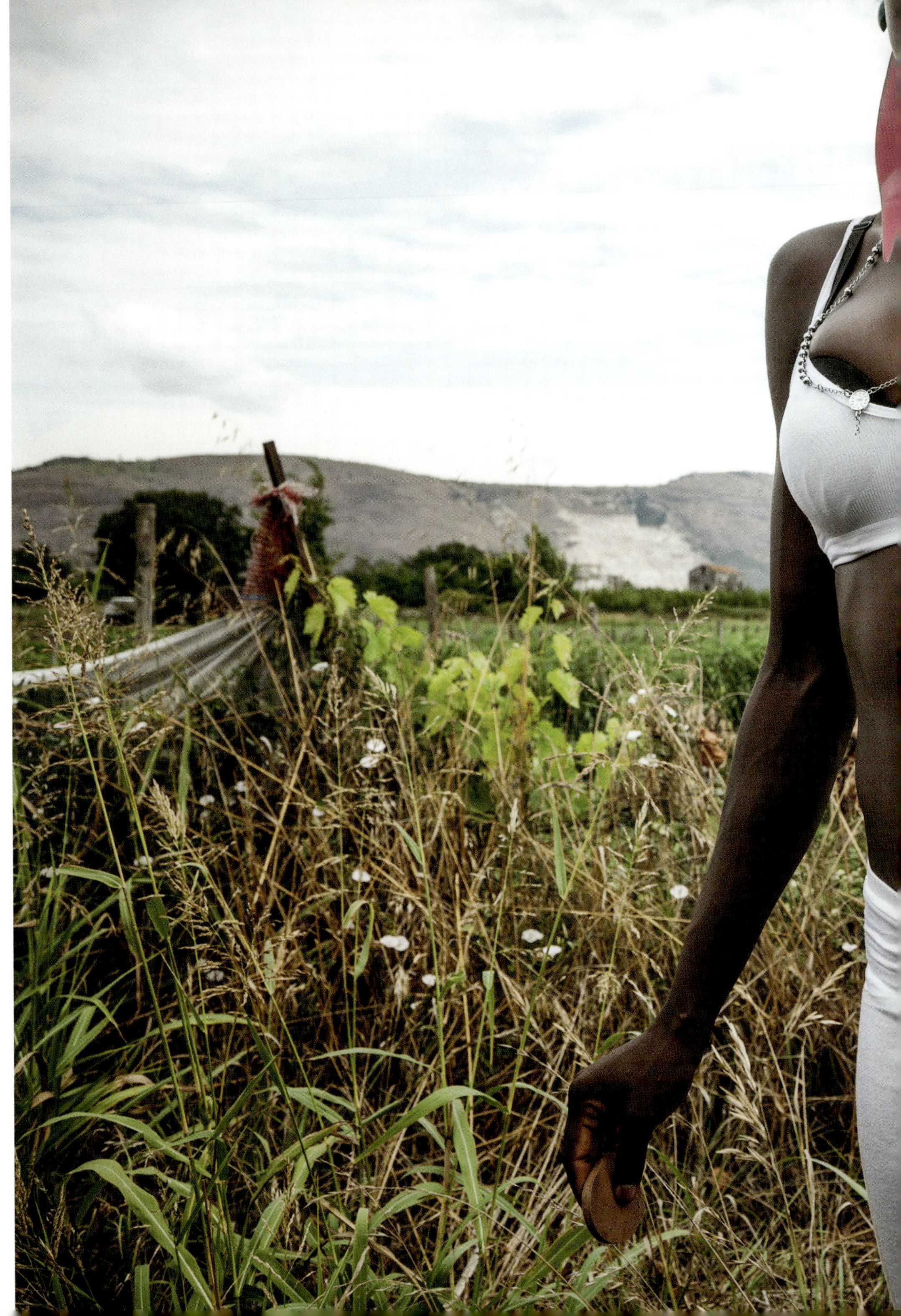

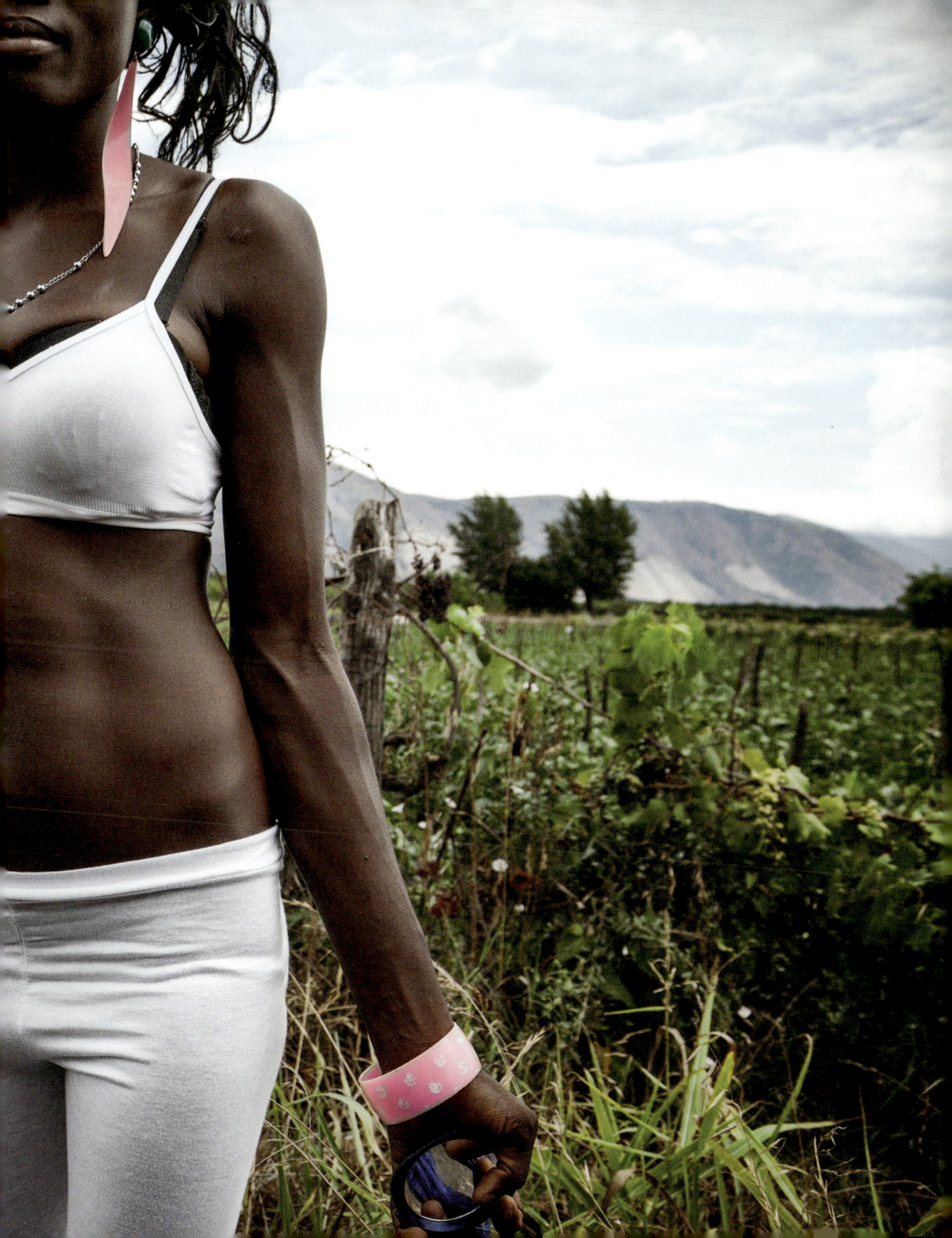

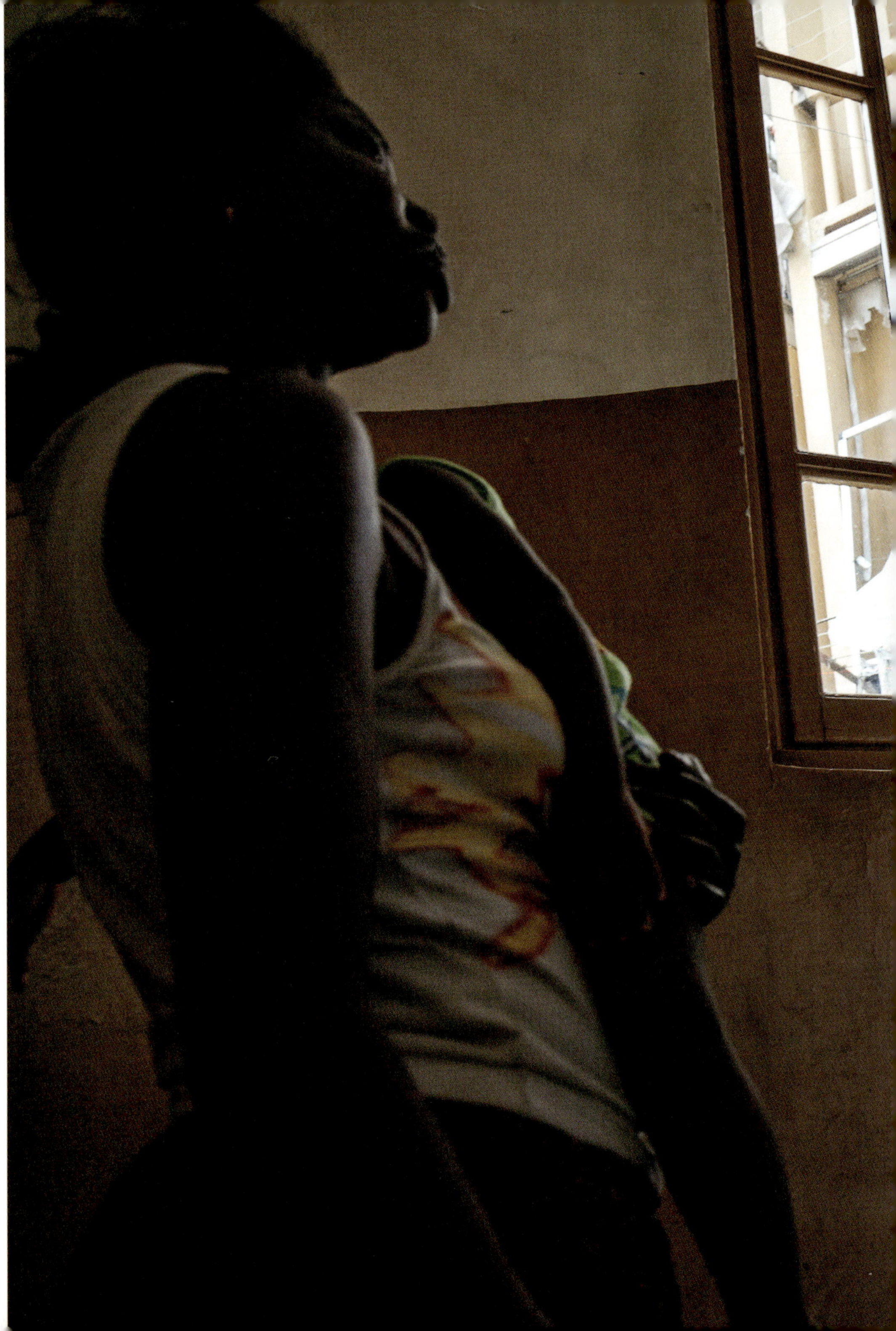

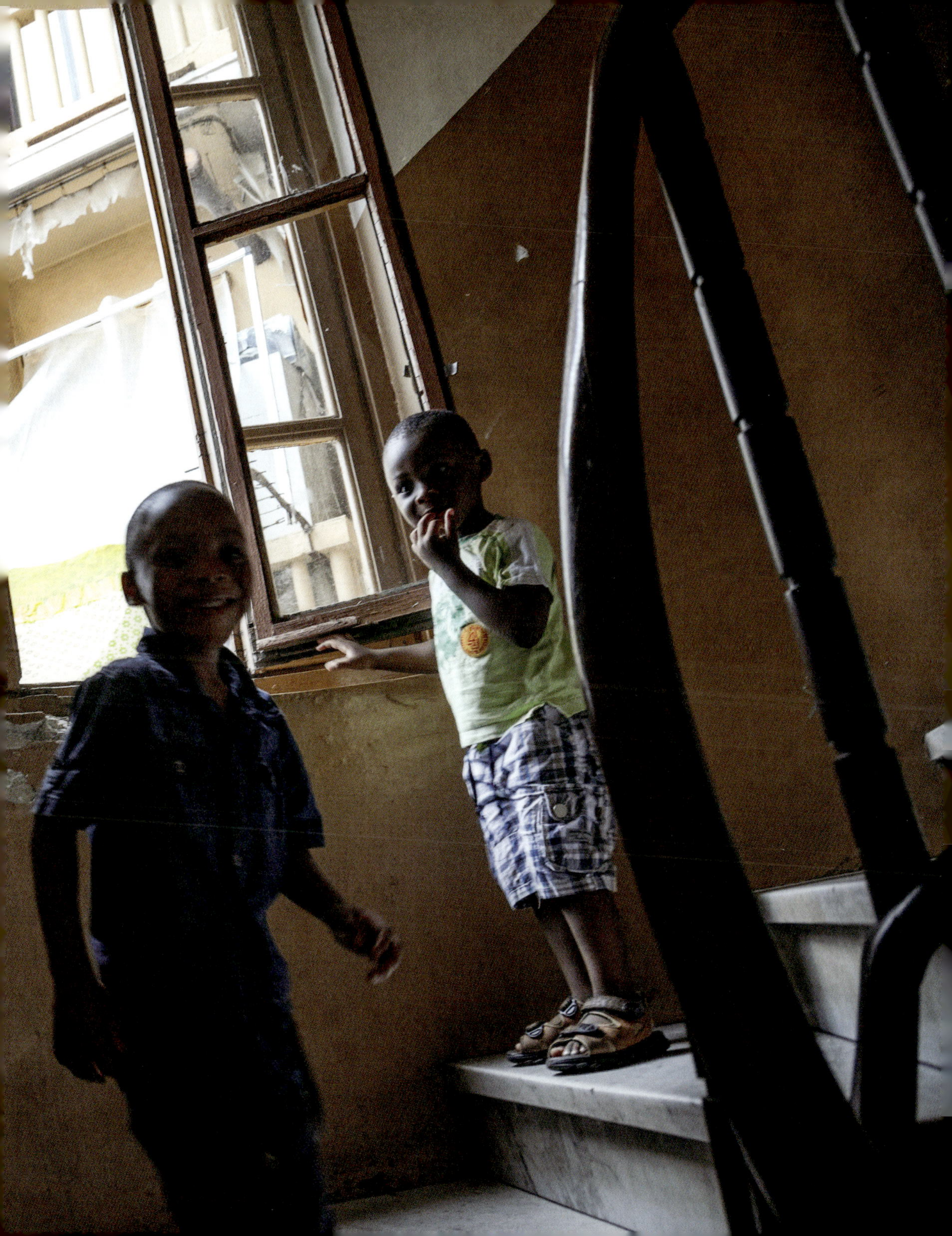

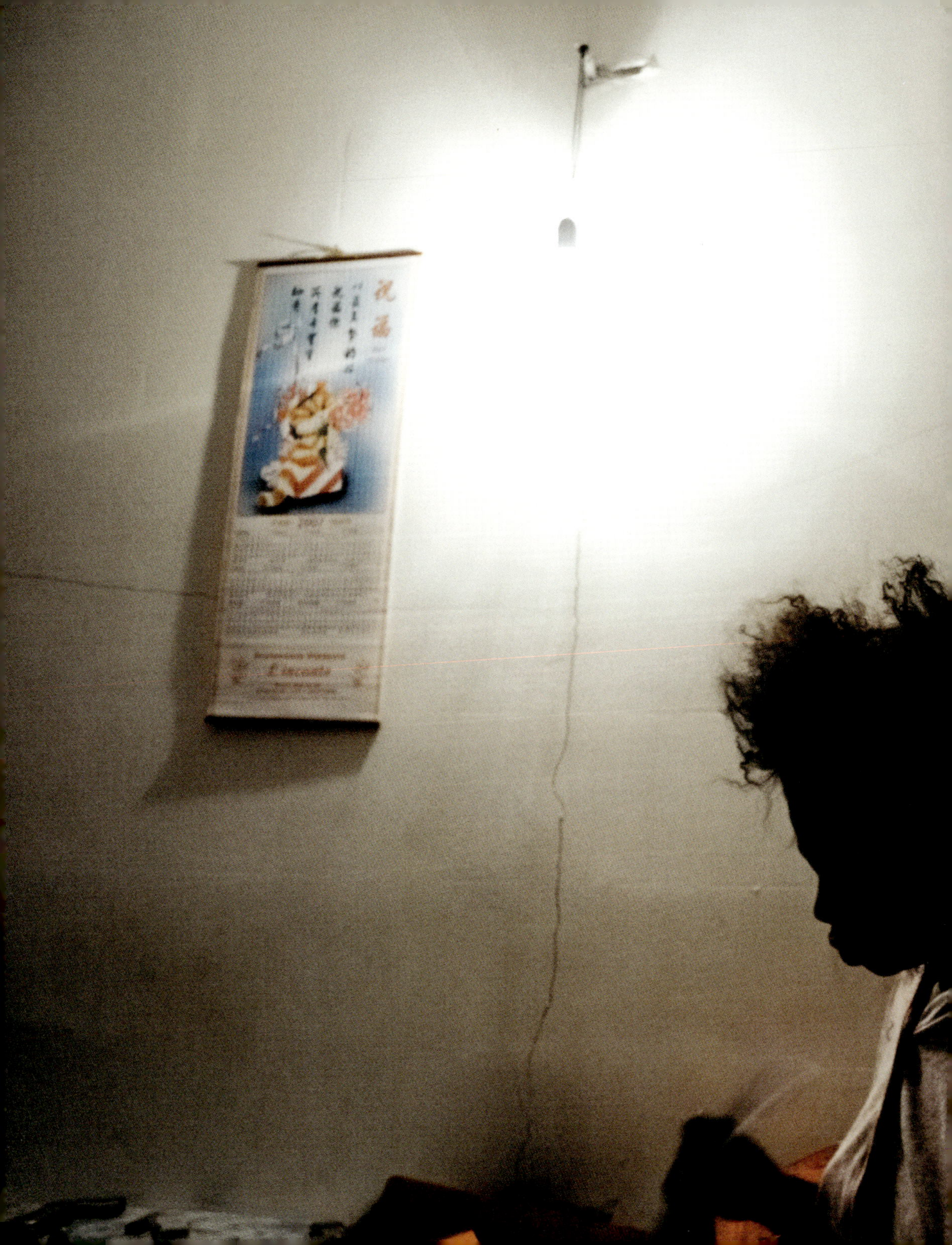

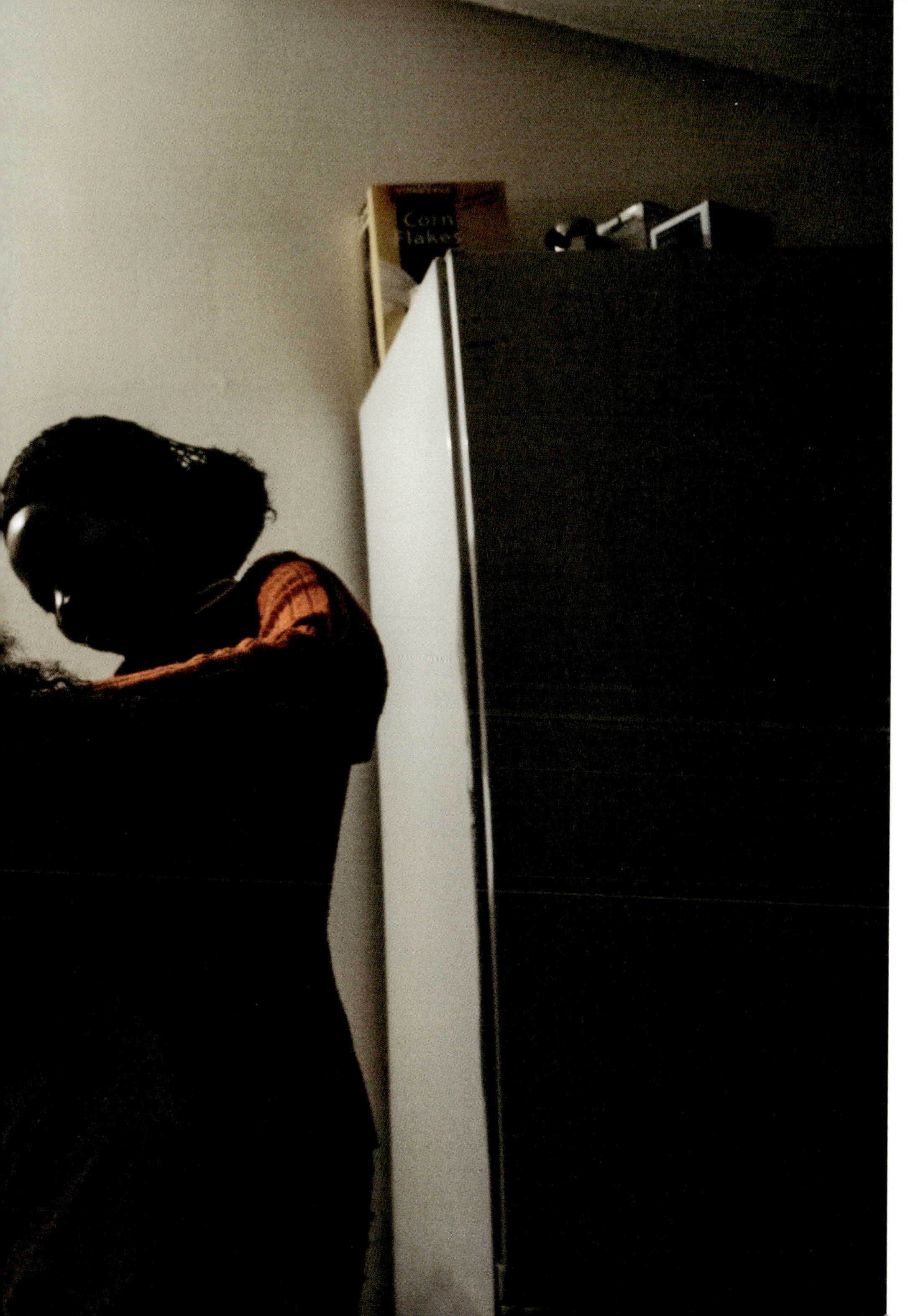
Corn
Flakes

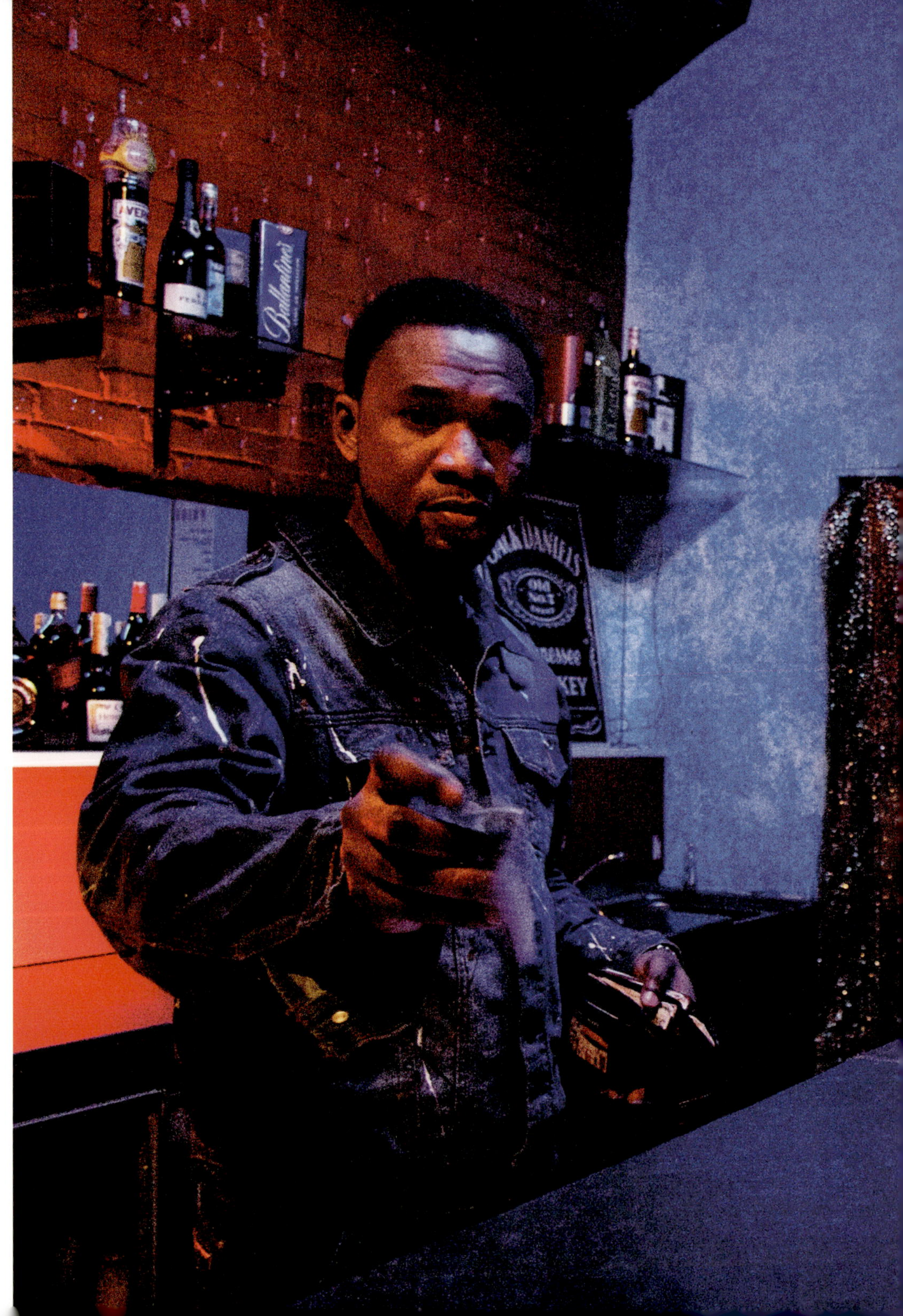

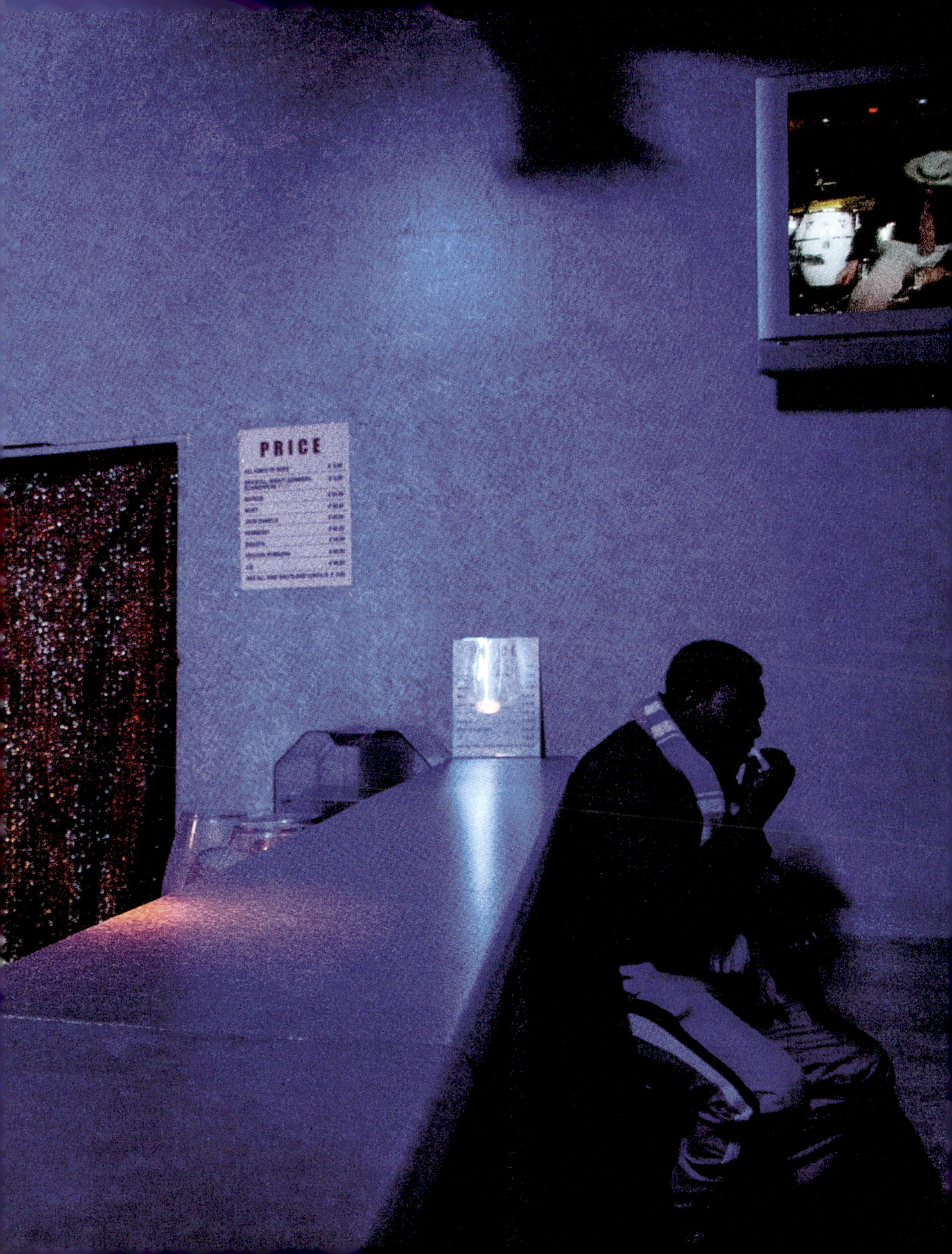
PRICE

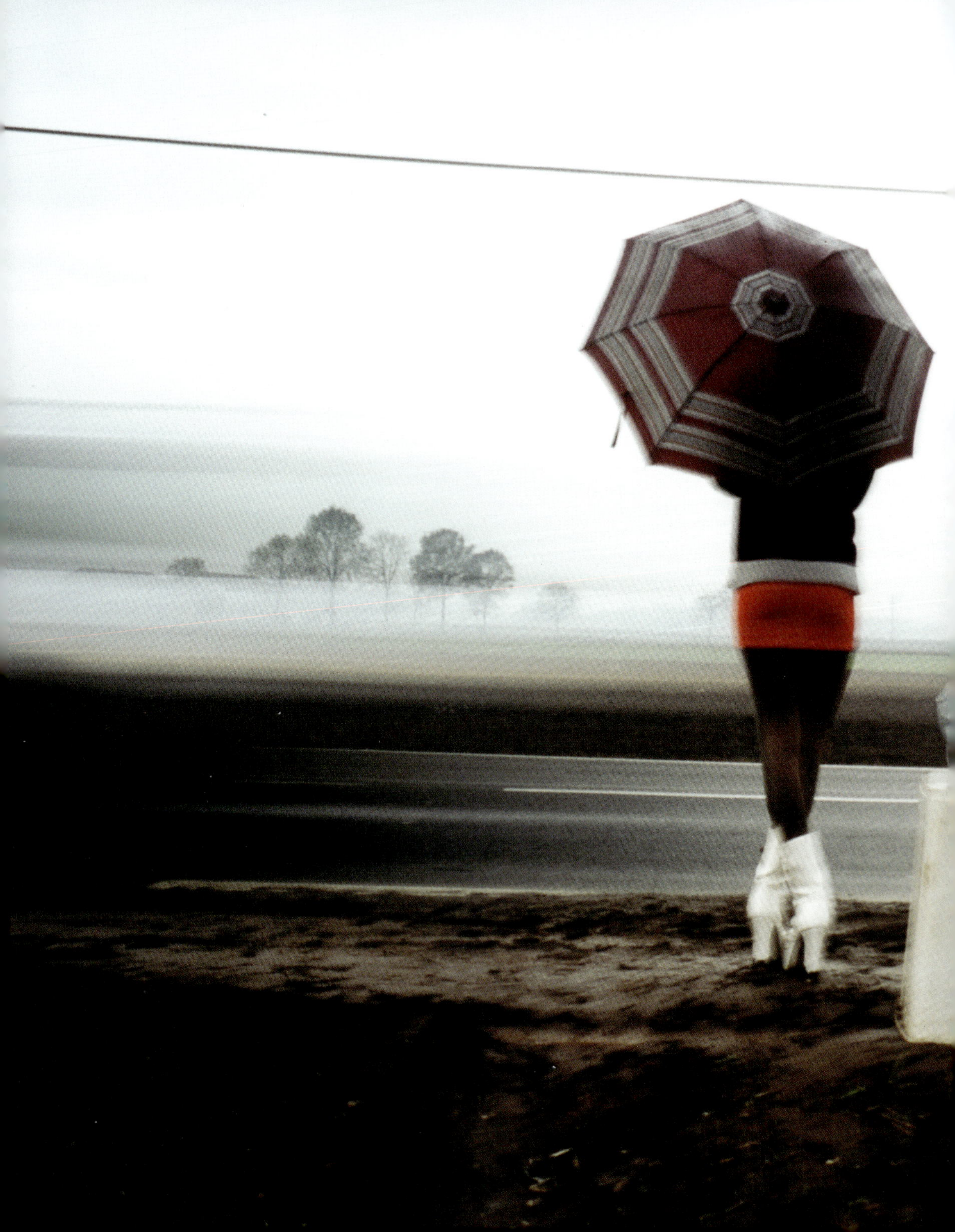

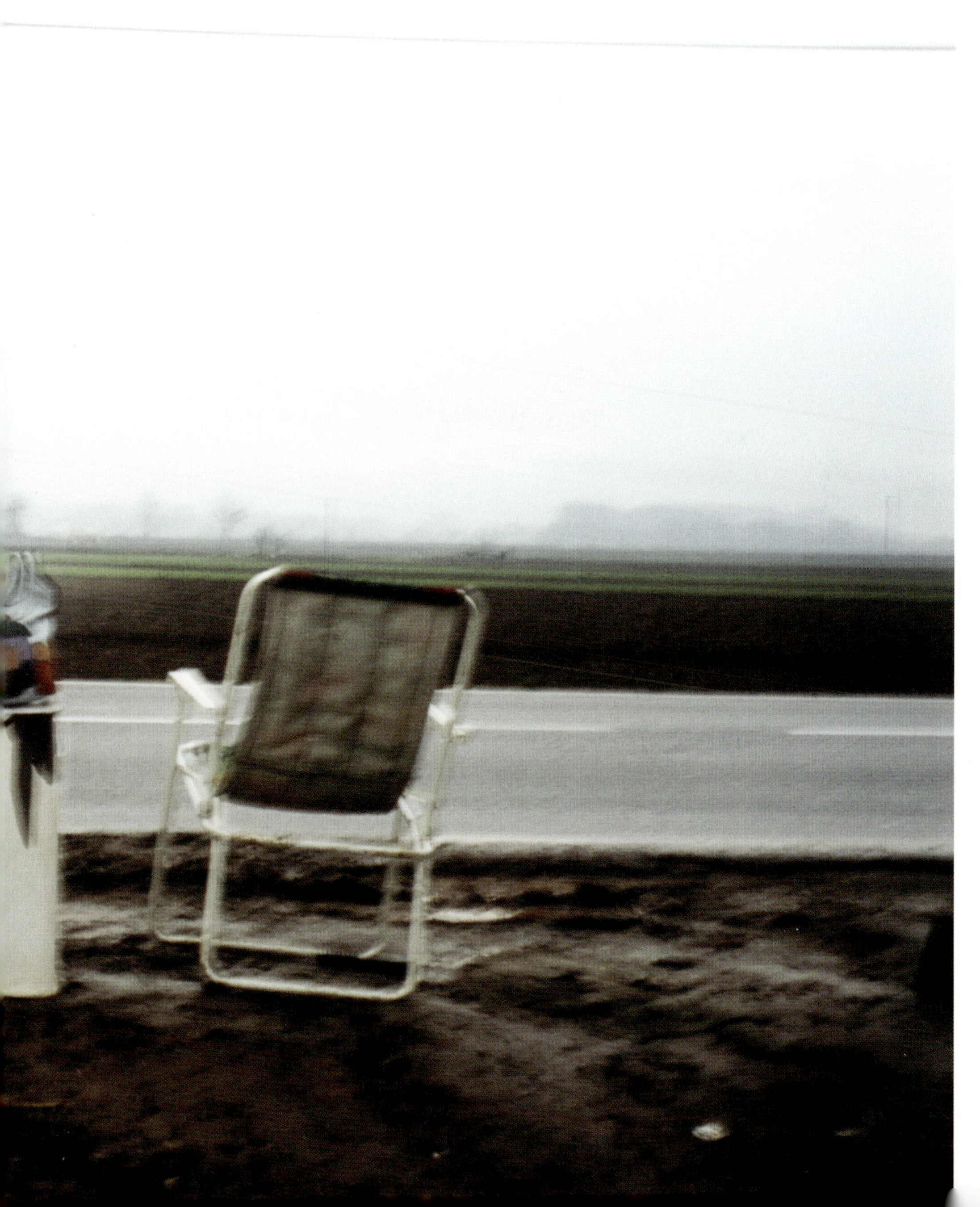

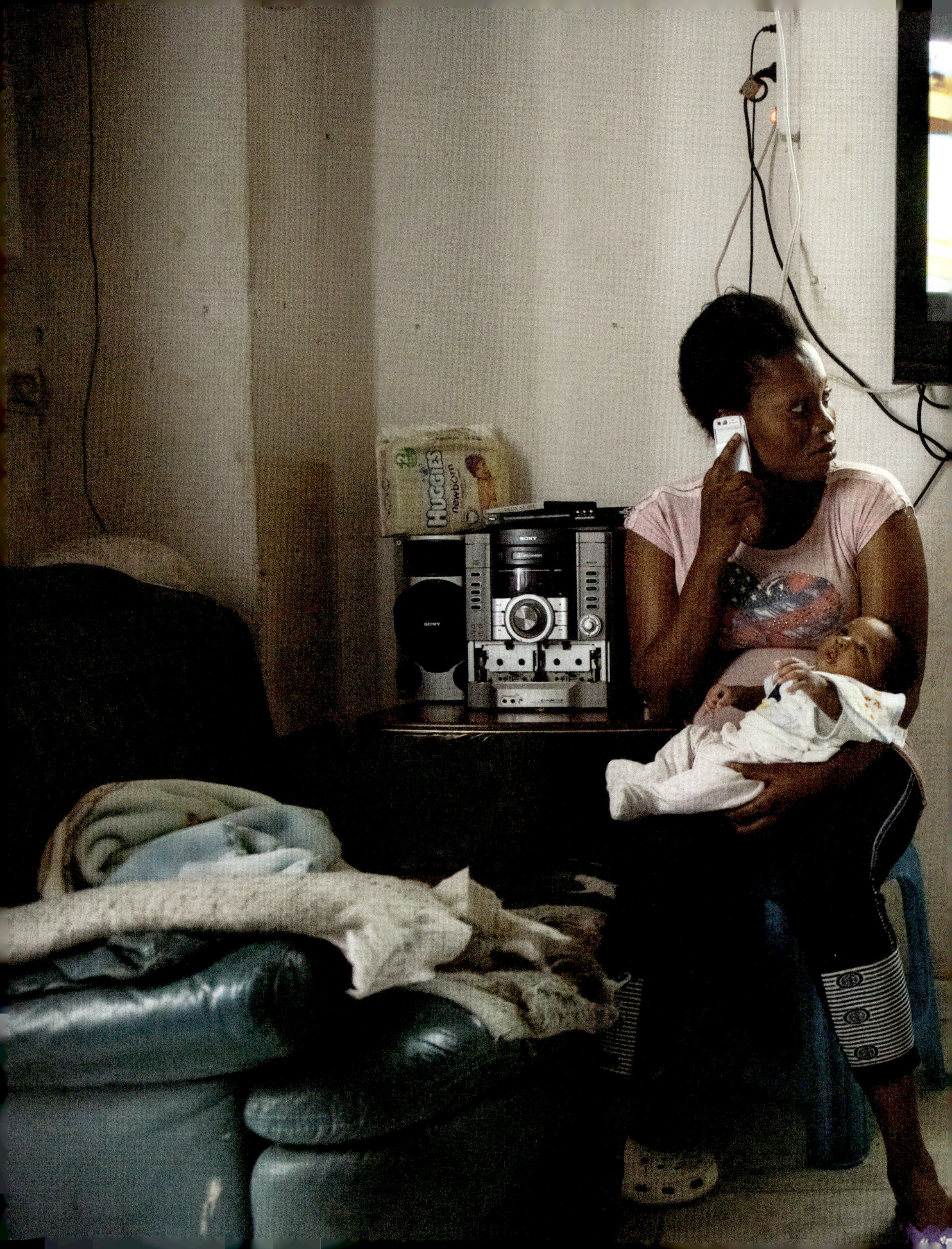

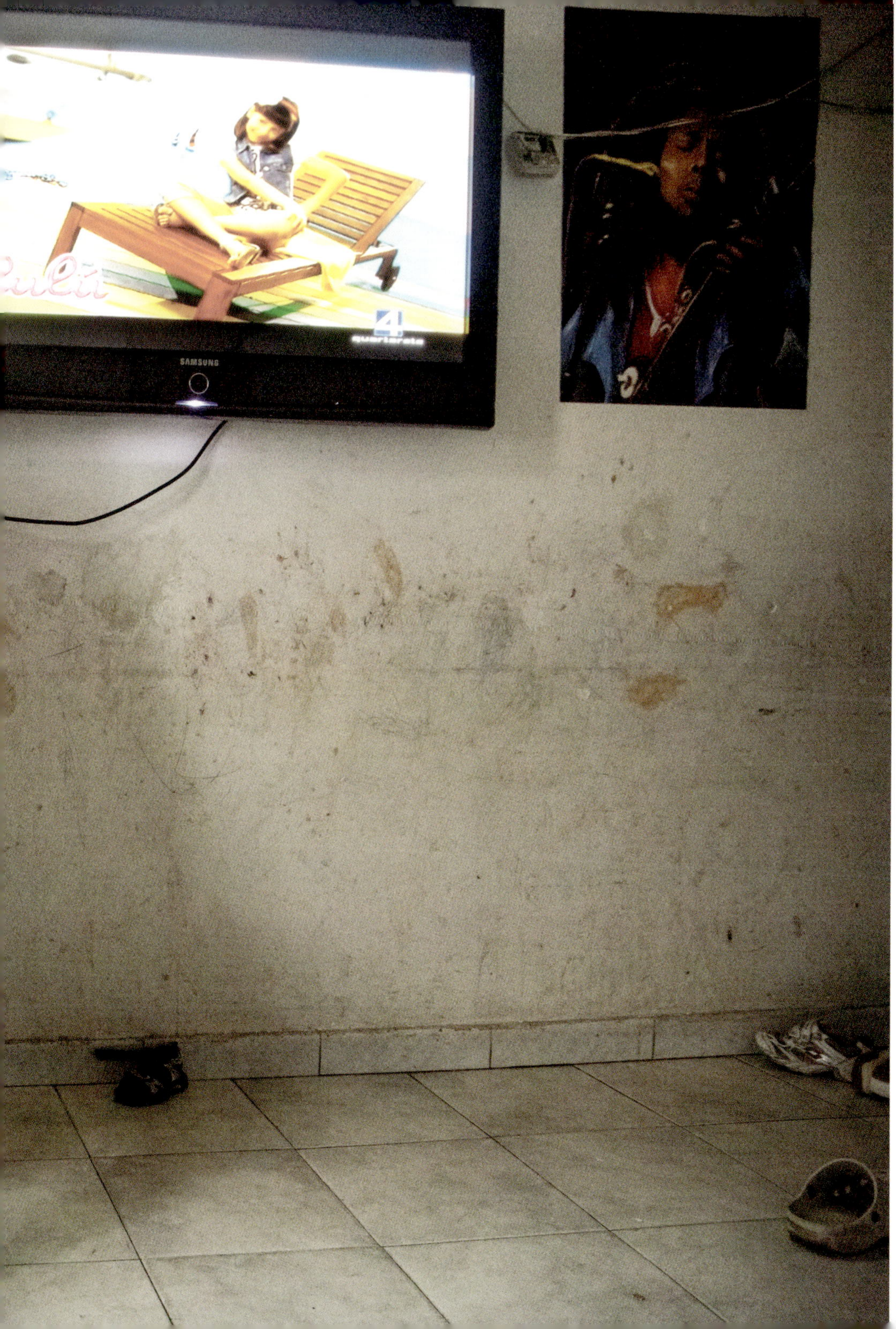

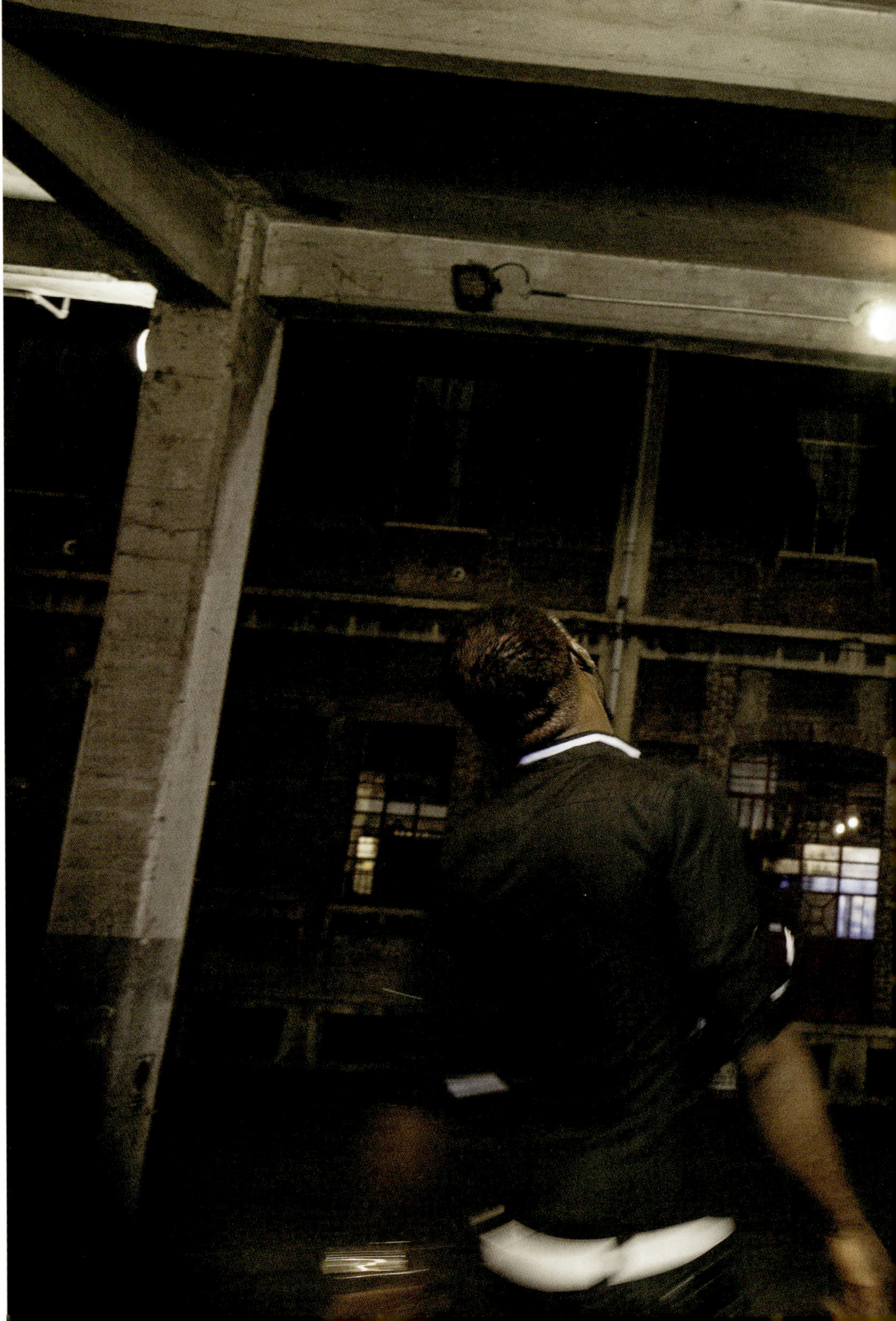

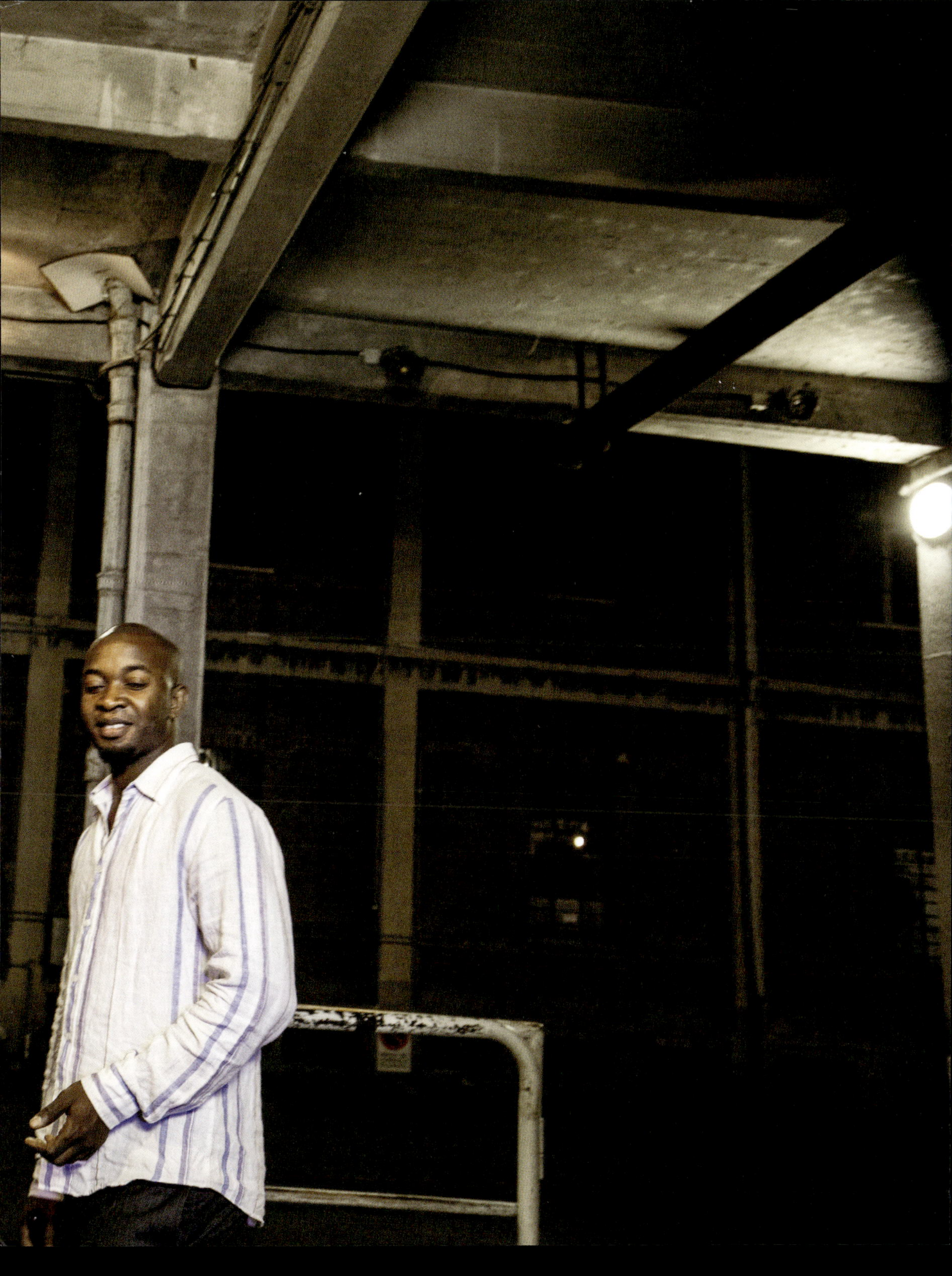

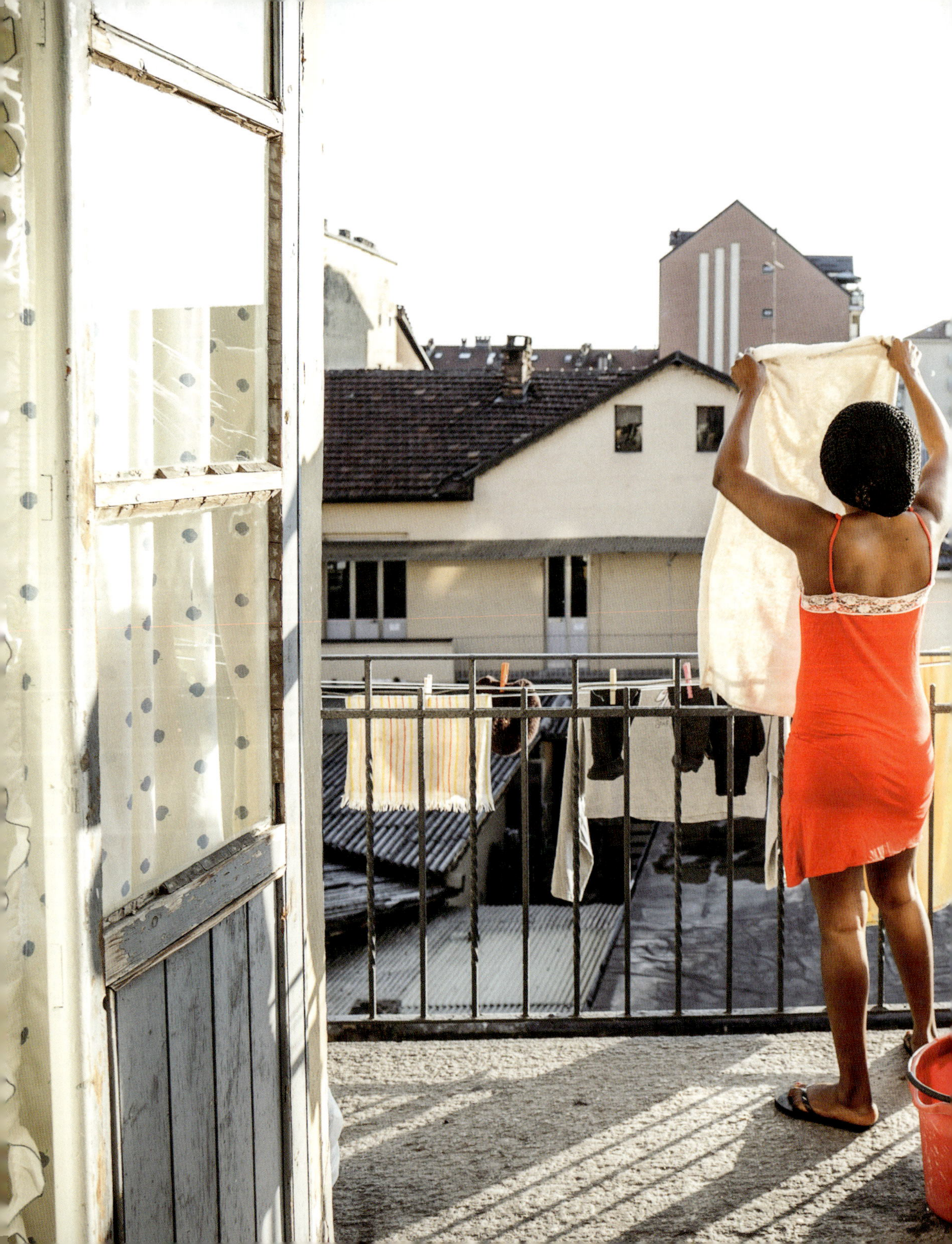

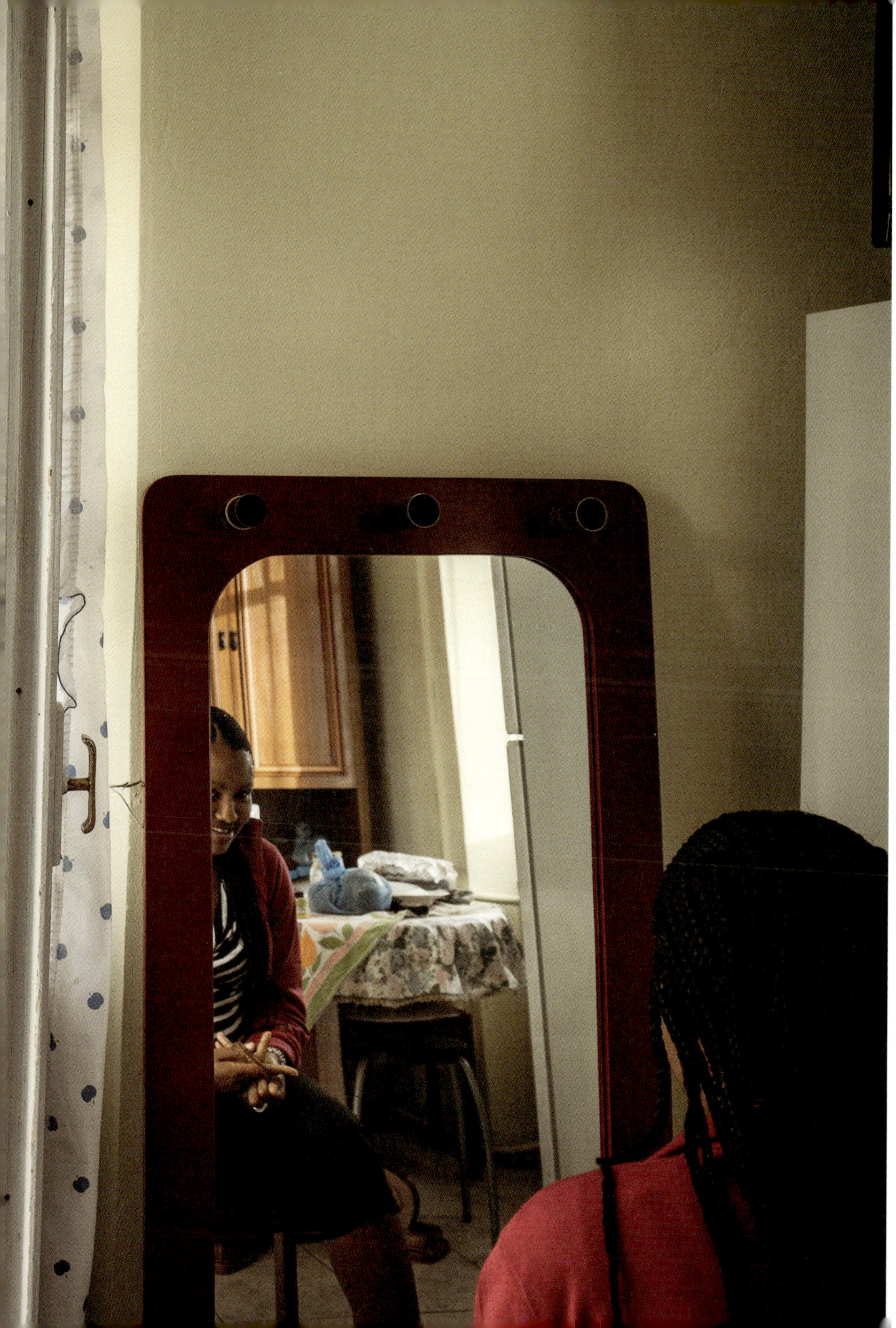

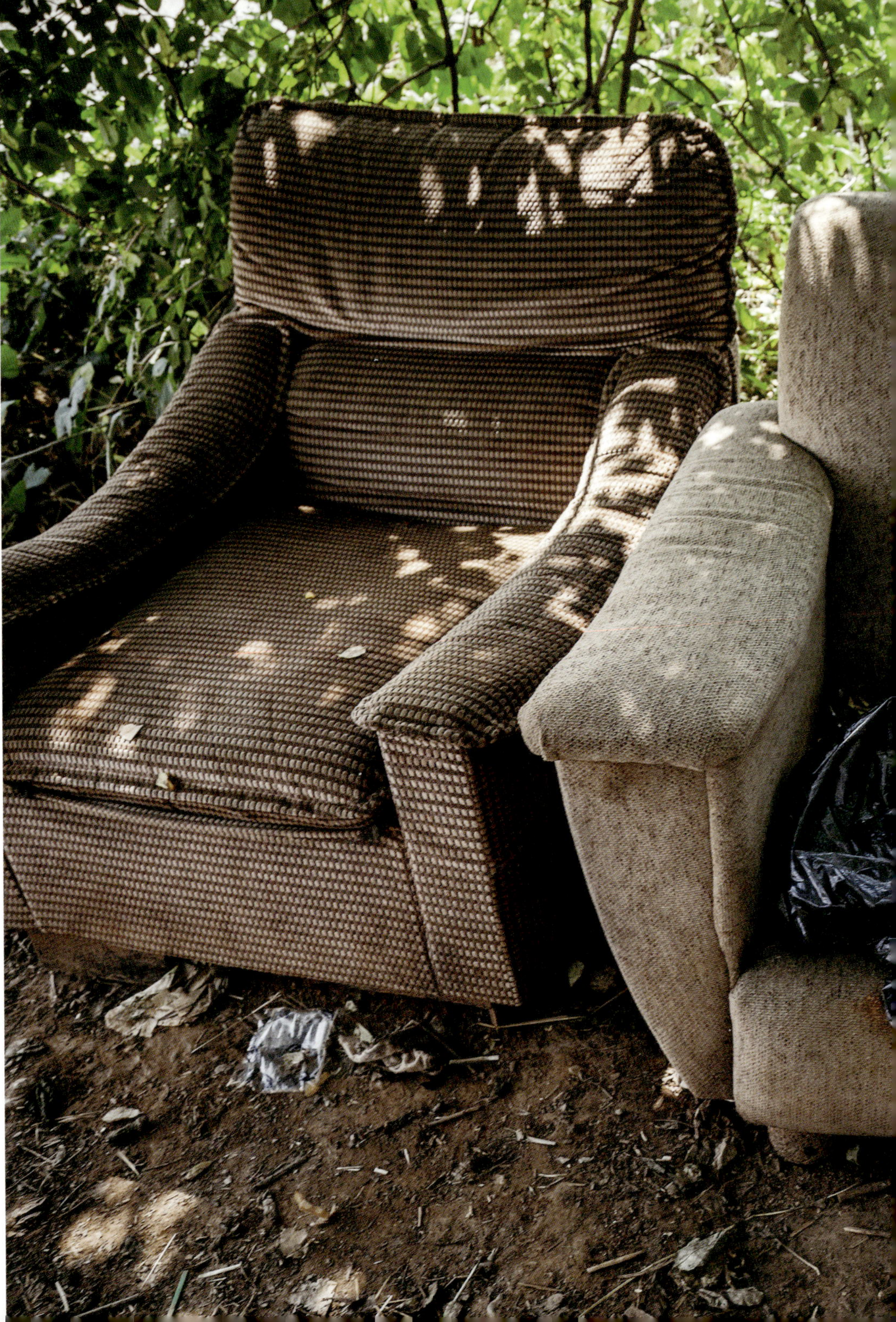

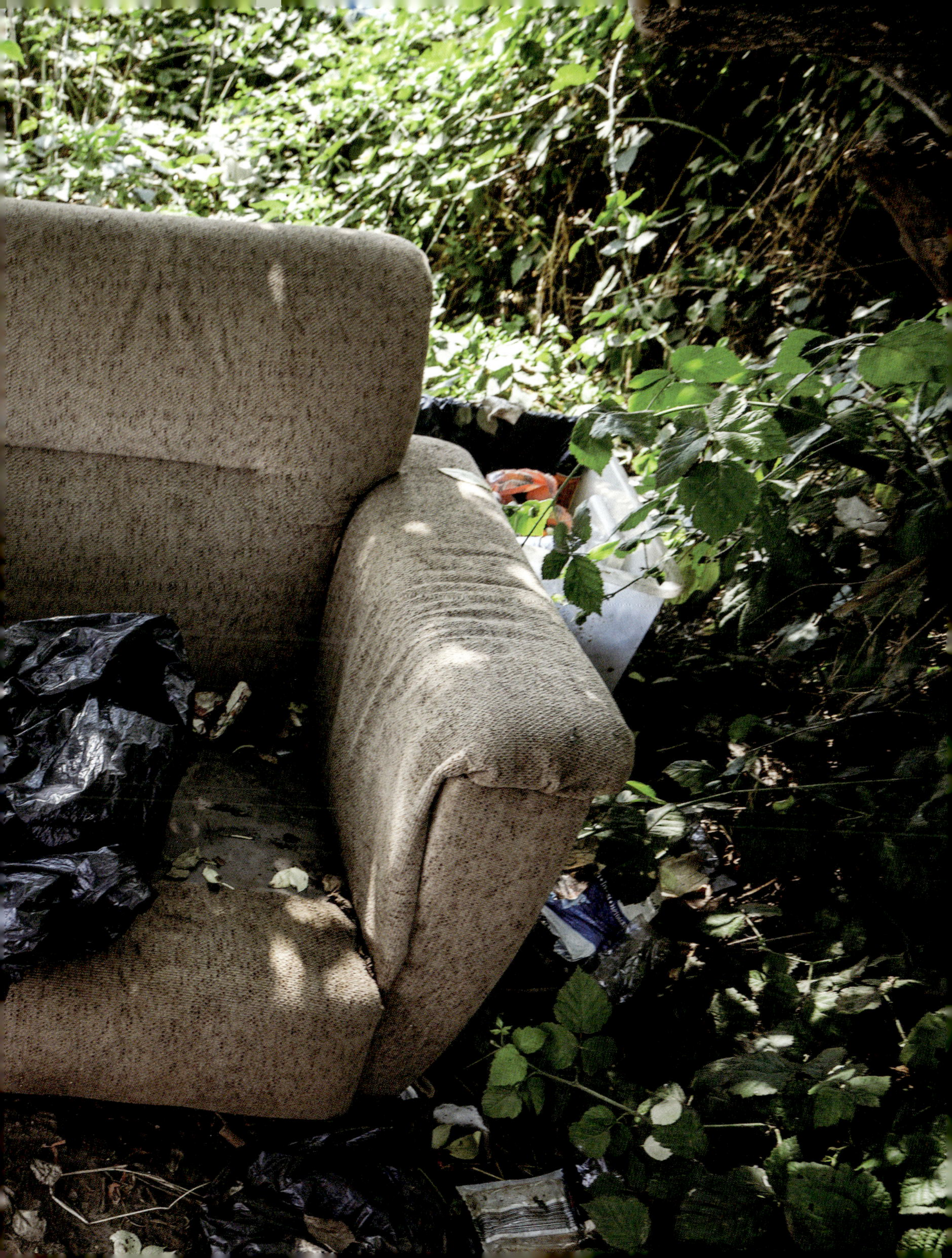

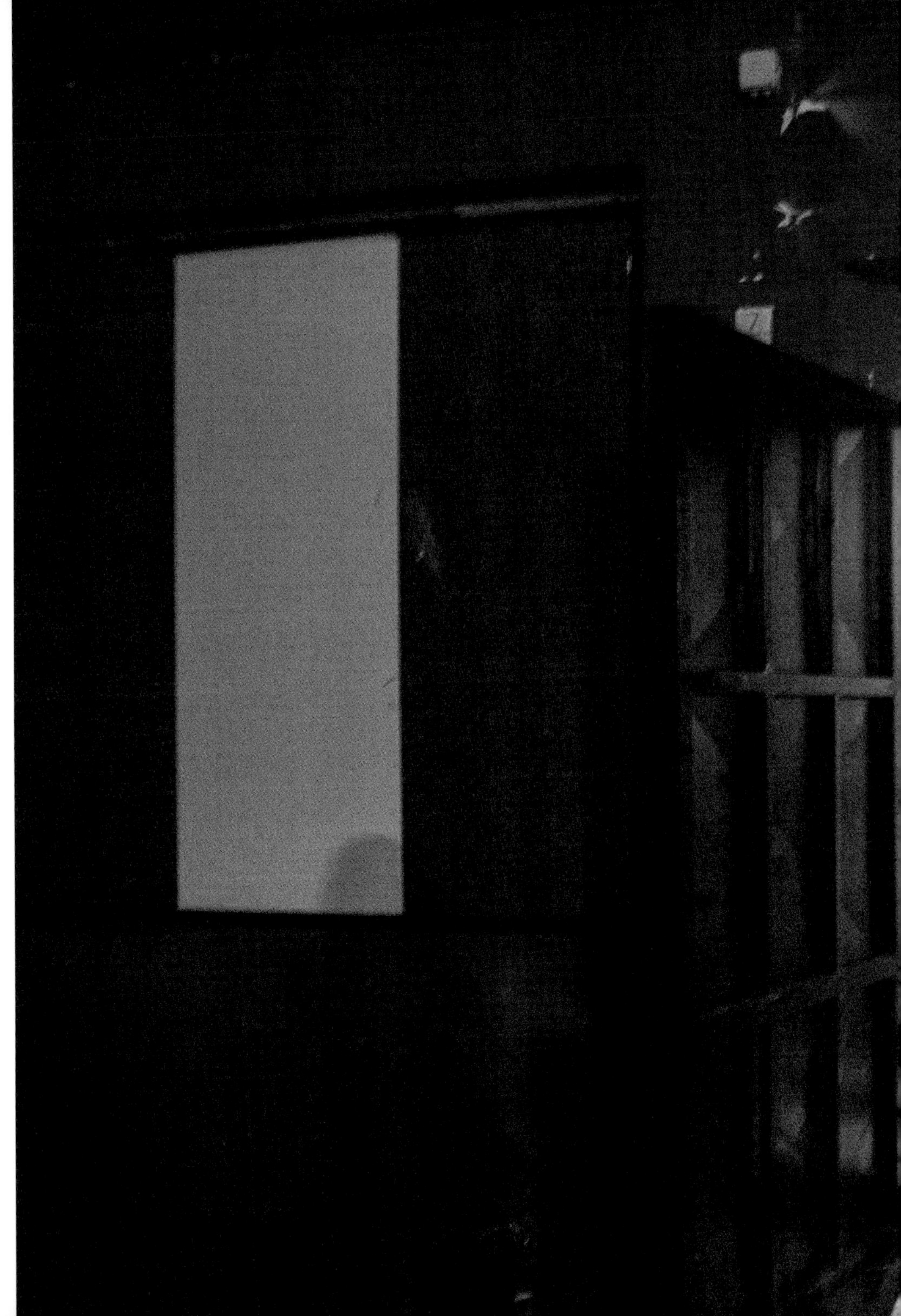

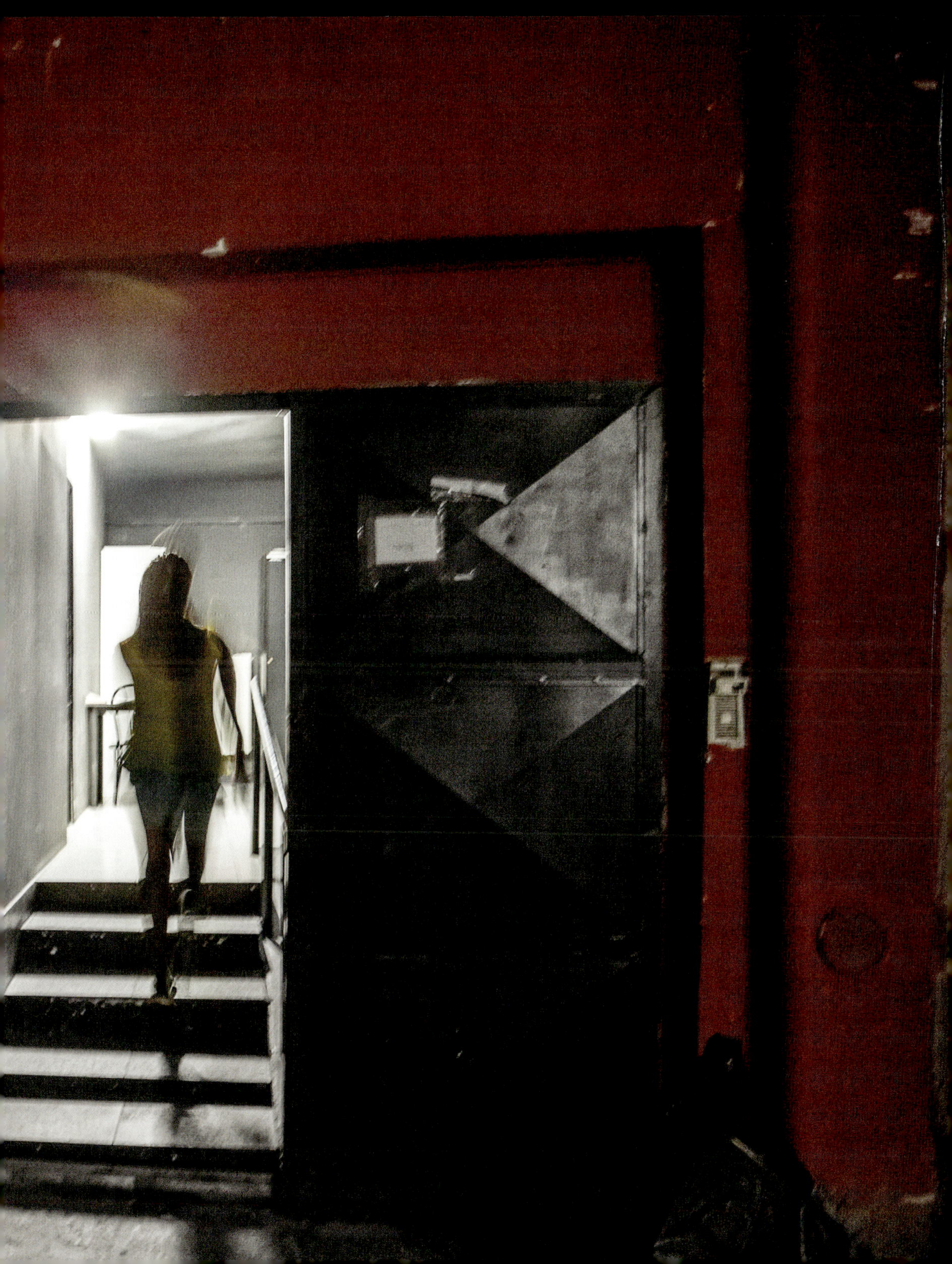

Laura Maragnani, Isoke Aikpitanyi
The Girls from Benin City

Melampo Editore, Milano, 2012

Part one

1.
A week had gone by and Judith said: you can't stay here with no money
and no job. You've got to pay for your food, pay some rent. You've got to
work. And for anybody without papers, there's only one kind of work.

4.
[...] That's how it works in Europe.
If you're not too squeamish you make a lot of money; and then you do
what the other girls did.
So I asked him: What did the other girls do?
It was one of the few things I actually said to him all evening.
He started laughing. They make money, he said. They buy a girl and
they bring her to Europe and she works and earns for them instead of
them having to do it. Wake up, little girl. That's the business we're in.

14.
Judith. My dear friend Judith. It took me a long time, months, years, to
realise that she was my *maman*. My sister, my momma, my madam and
pimp and boss. The woman who had ordered me from the *Italos*, who
had bought and paid for me; and who now expected that I would repay
her what she had spent.

15.
Some girls end up on the street the same night they arrive. And they are
beaten and raped and half-killed if they dare to say no.
That wasn't my case.
And in the end I don't know which is worse.
I was left to agonise in uncertainty for days.

20.
[...] They'd beaten Itohan to death.
Itohan didn't want to be a prostitute anymore.
She'd said she wasn't paying off her debt and she never would.
She was twenty years old.
They found her body months later on the outskirts of Turin, in the
abandoned warehouse of a factory that had been closed for years.
A pensioner's dog found it during their evening walk. It had been
there a long time. Putrefied. All eaten by rats.

21.
So Susan spent the evening with me, teaching me how to work on the
street. [...] She also said: I'll give you some advice. Never ever defy them.
And I'll tell you this only once, as a friend: never trust anybody, not even
me, just like I don't trust anyone, not even you. Here you've got to survive. And if I have to betray you to survive, I'll betray you; if I have to rob
you, I'll rob you; if I have to hurt you, I'll do it. Do you understand?
Yes.

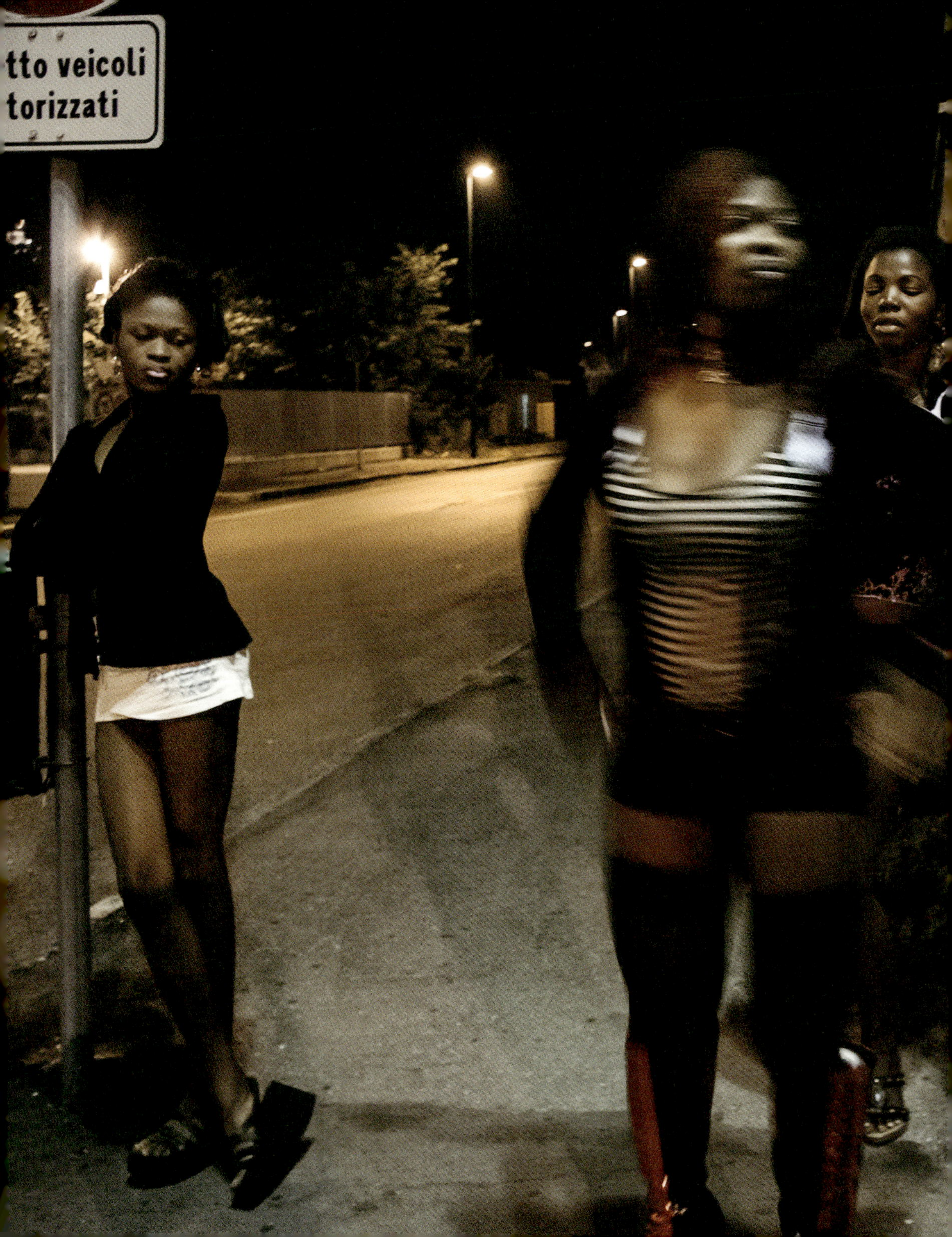

tto veicoli
torizzati

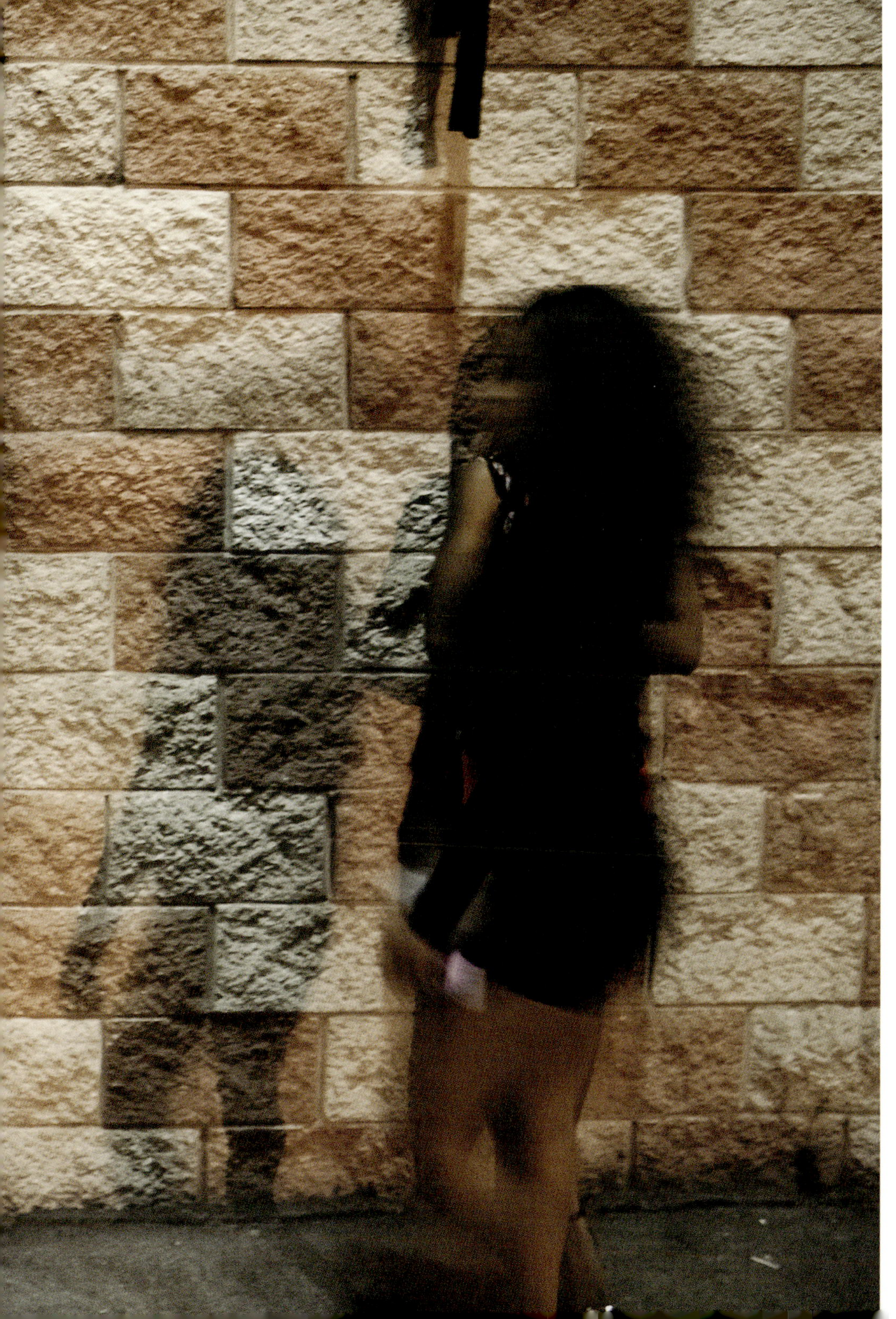

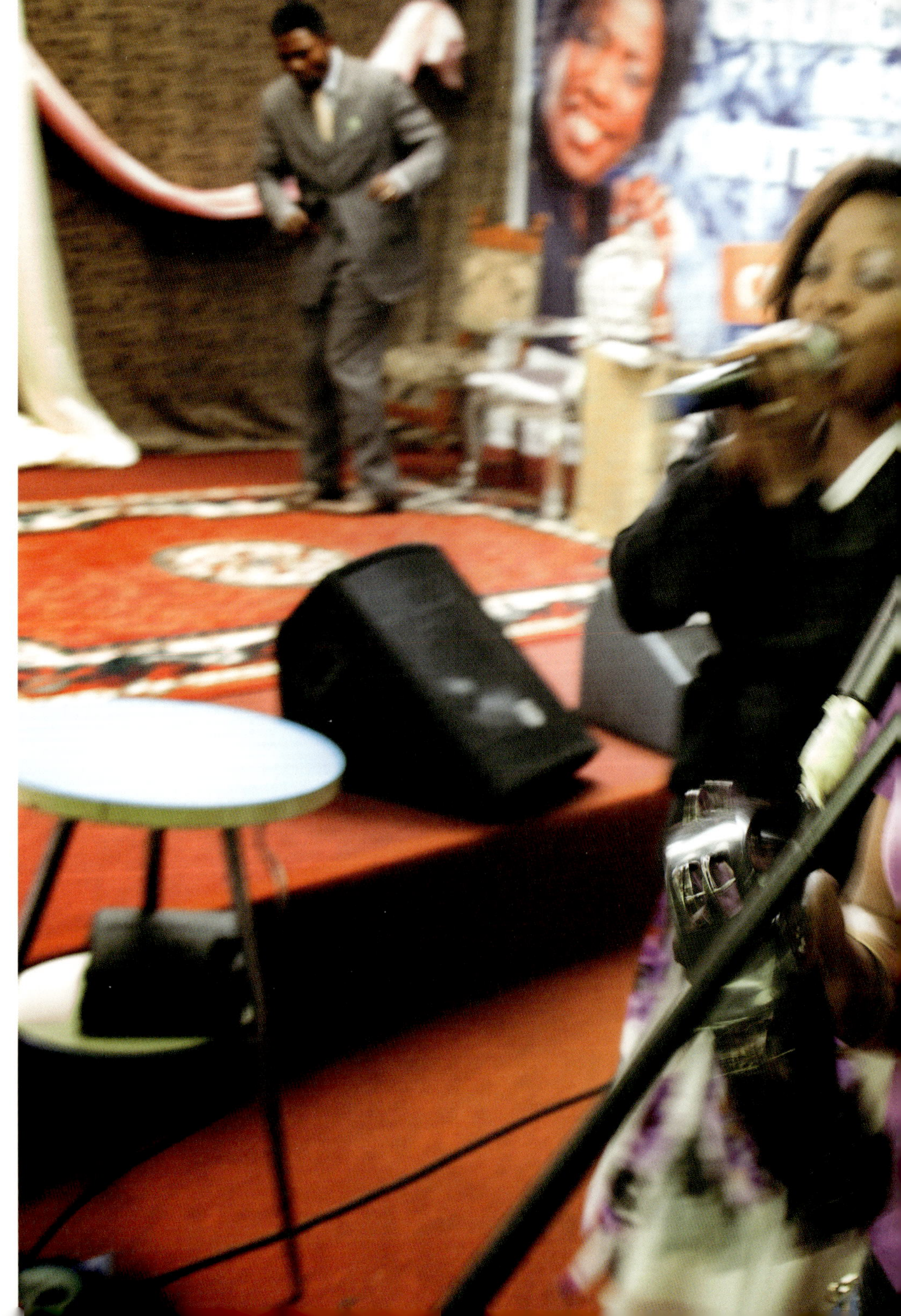

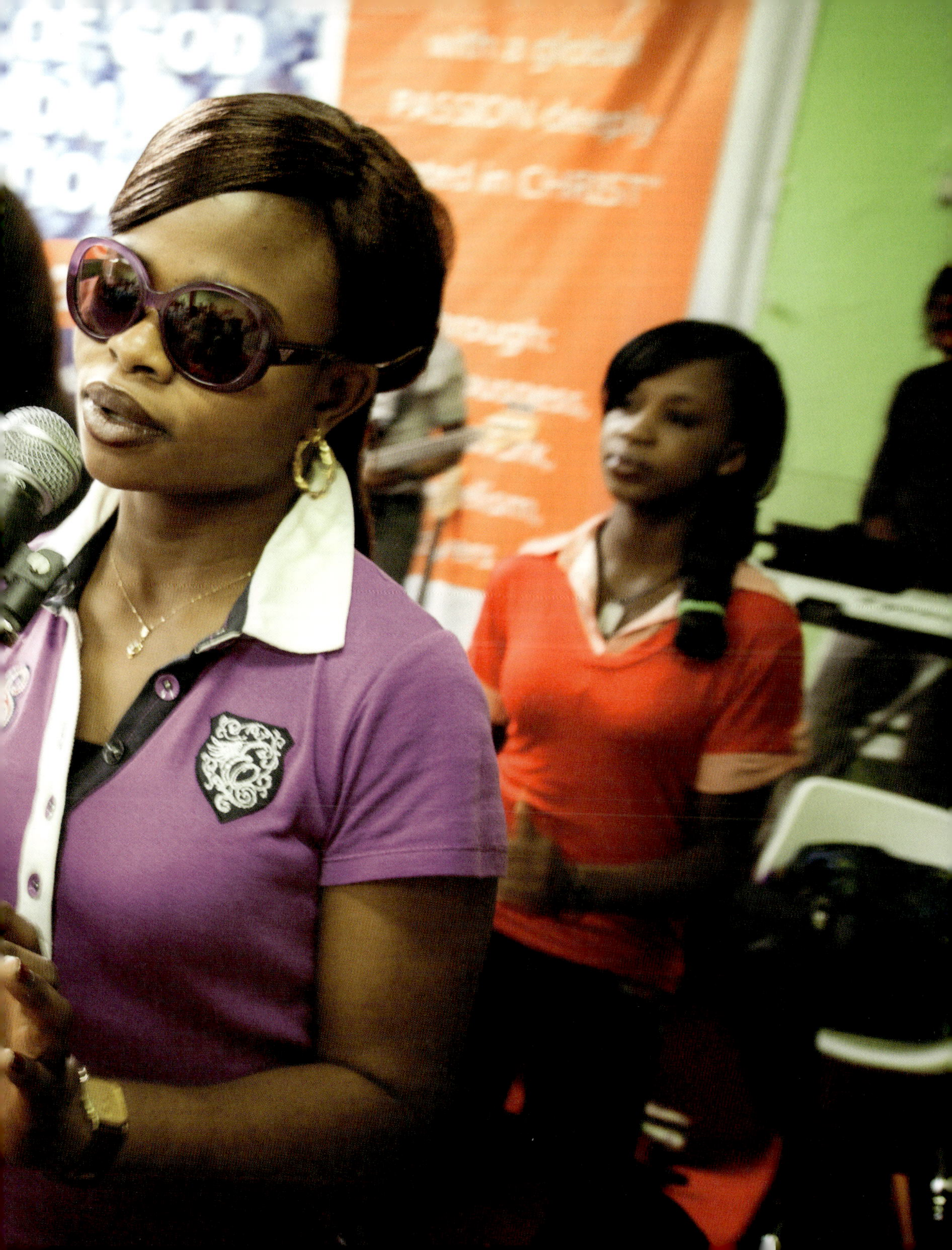
OF GOD
with a global
PASSION for
...ed in CHRIST

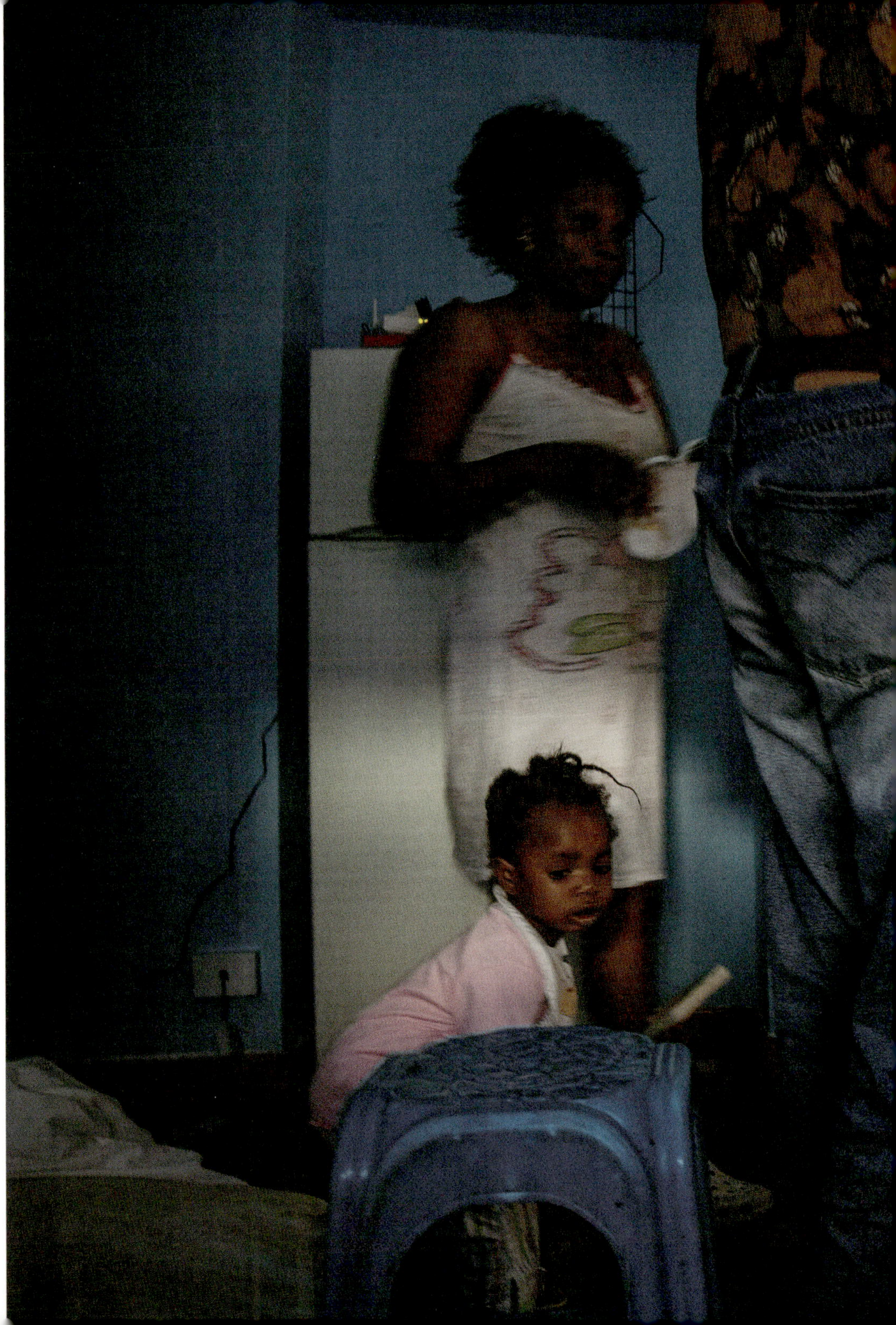

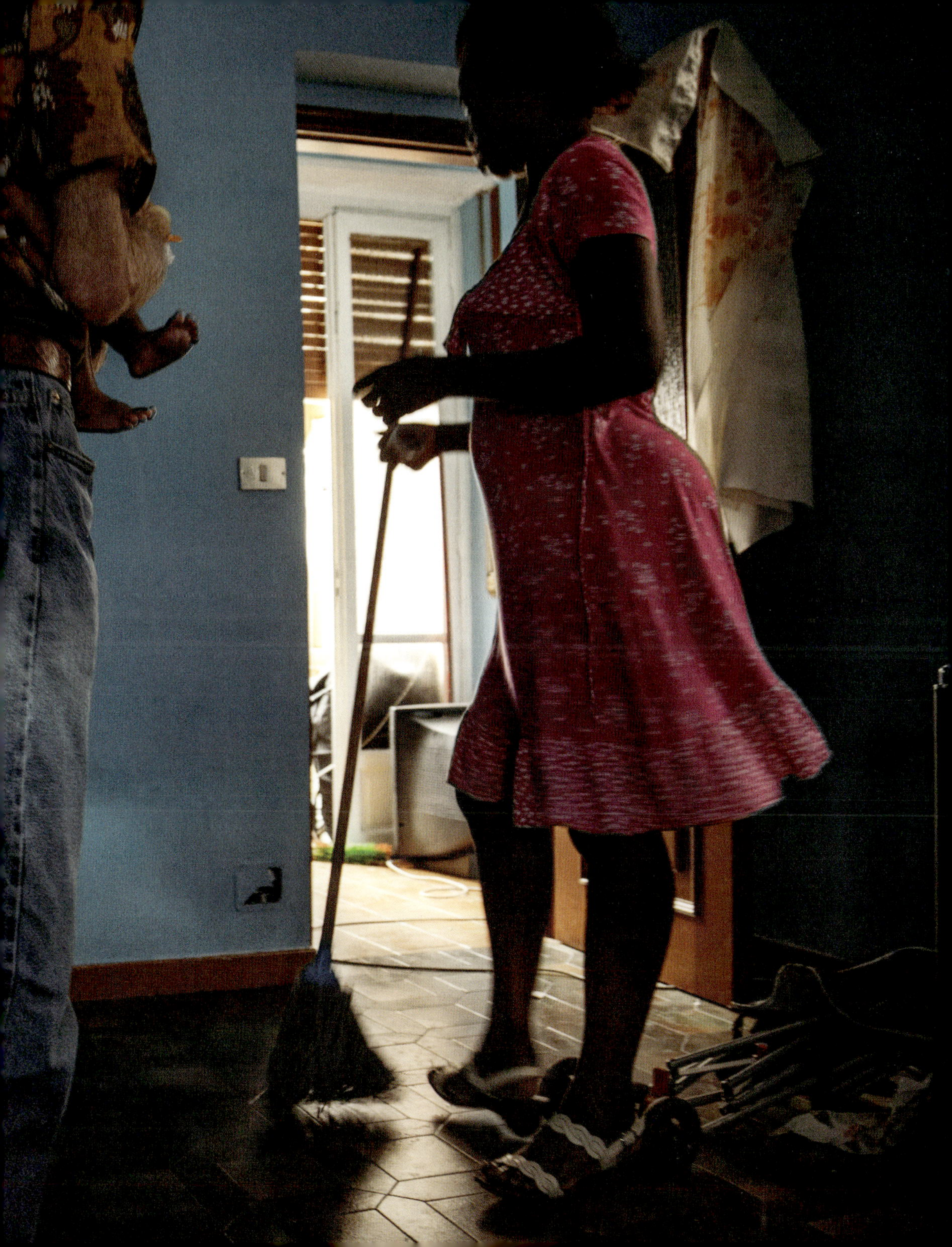

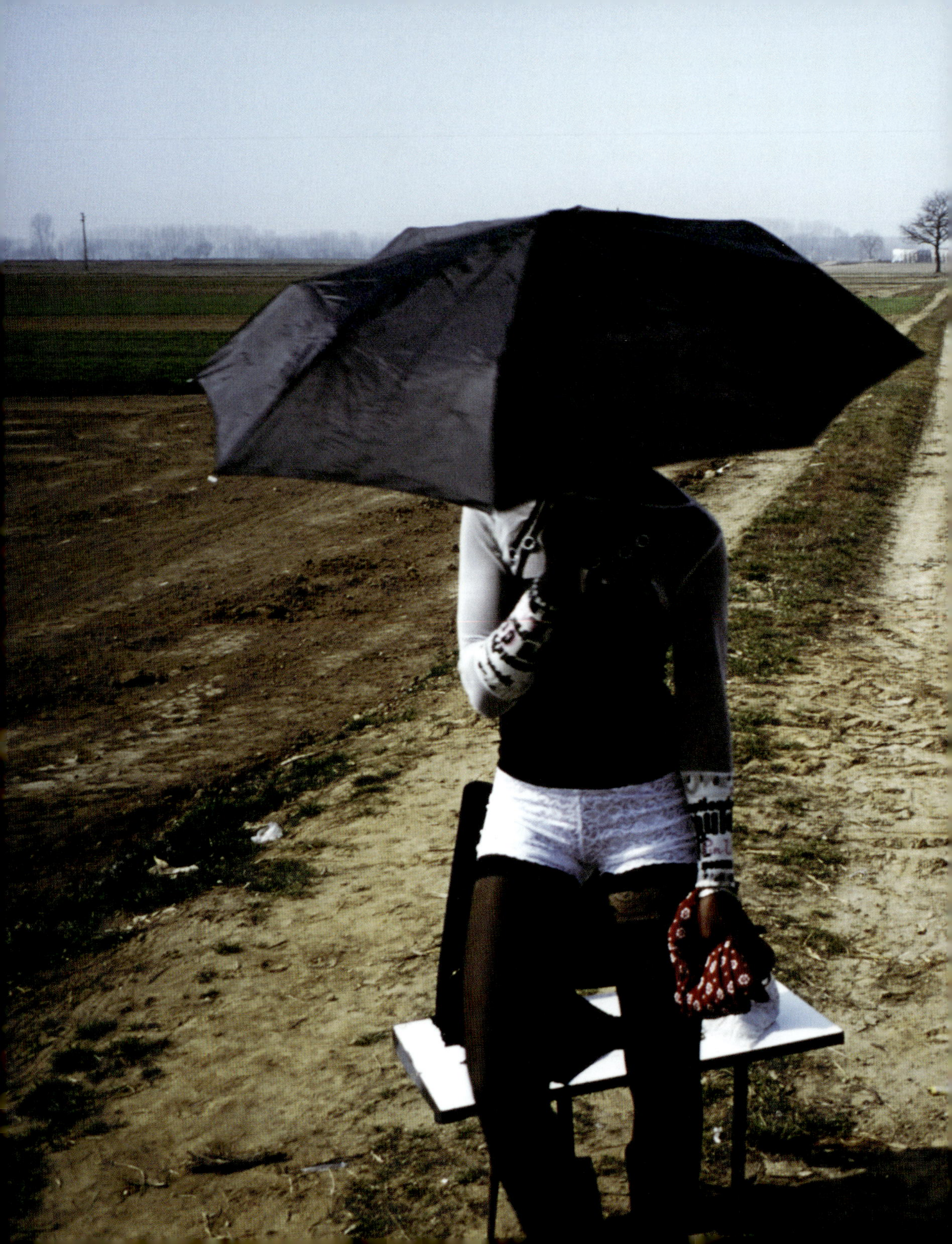

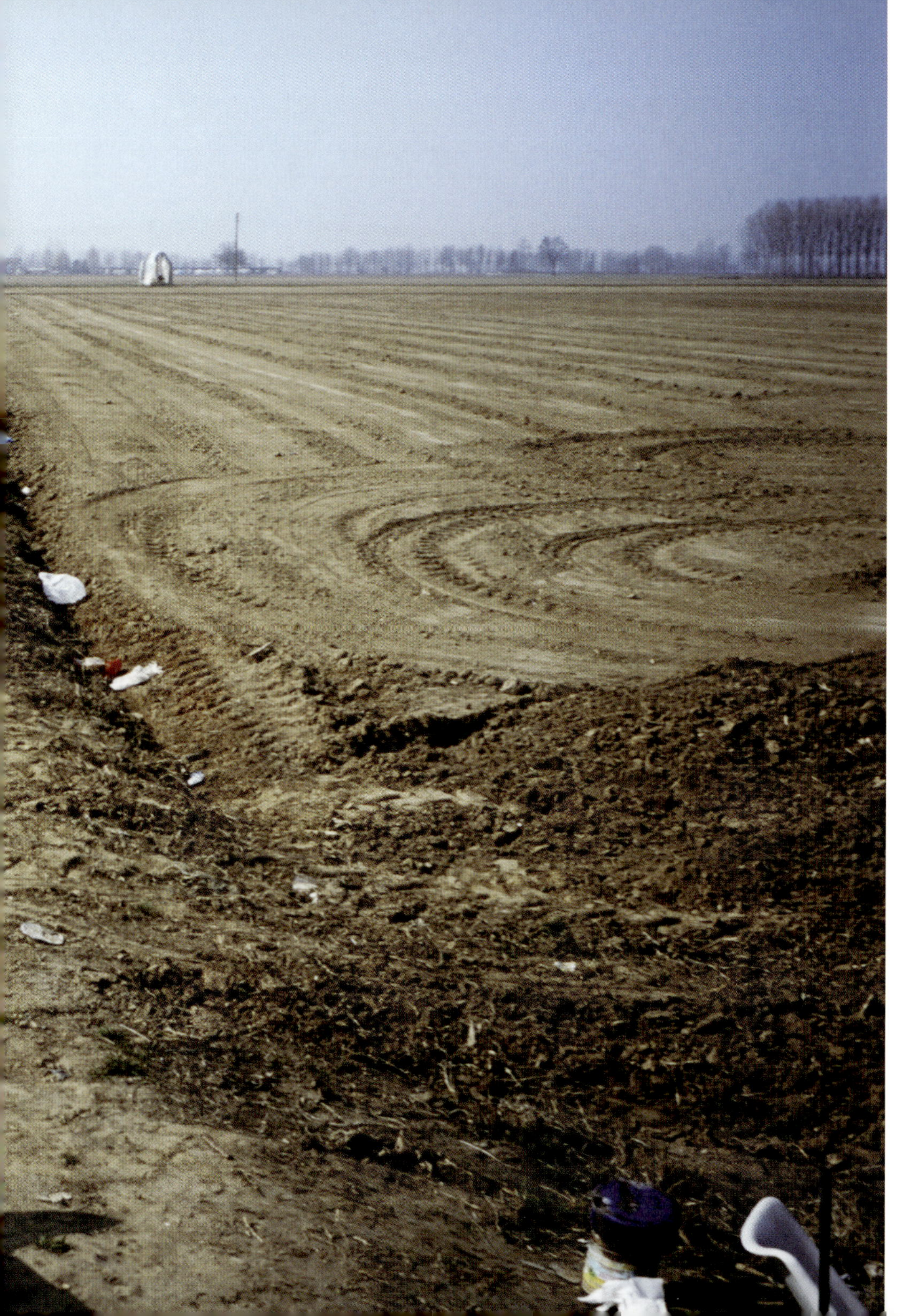

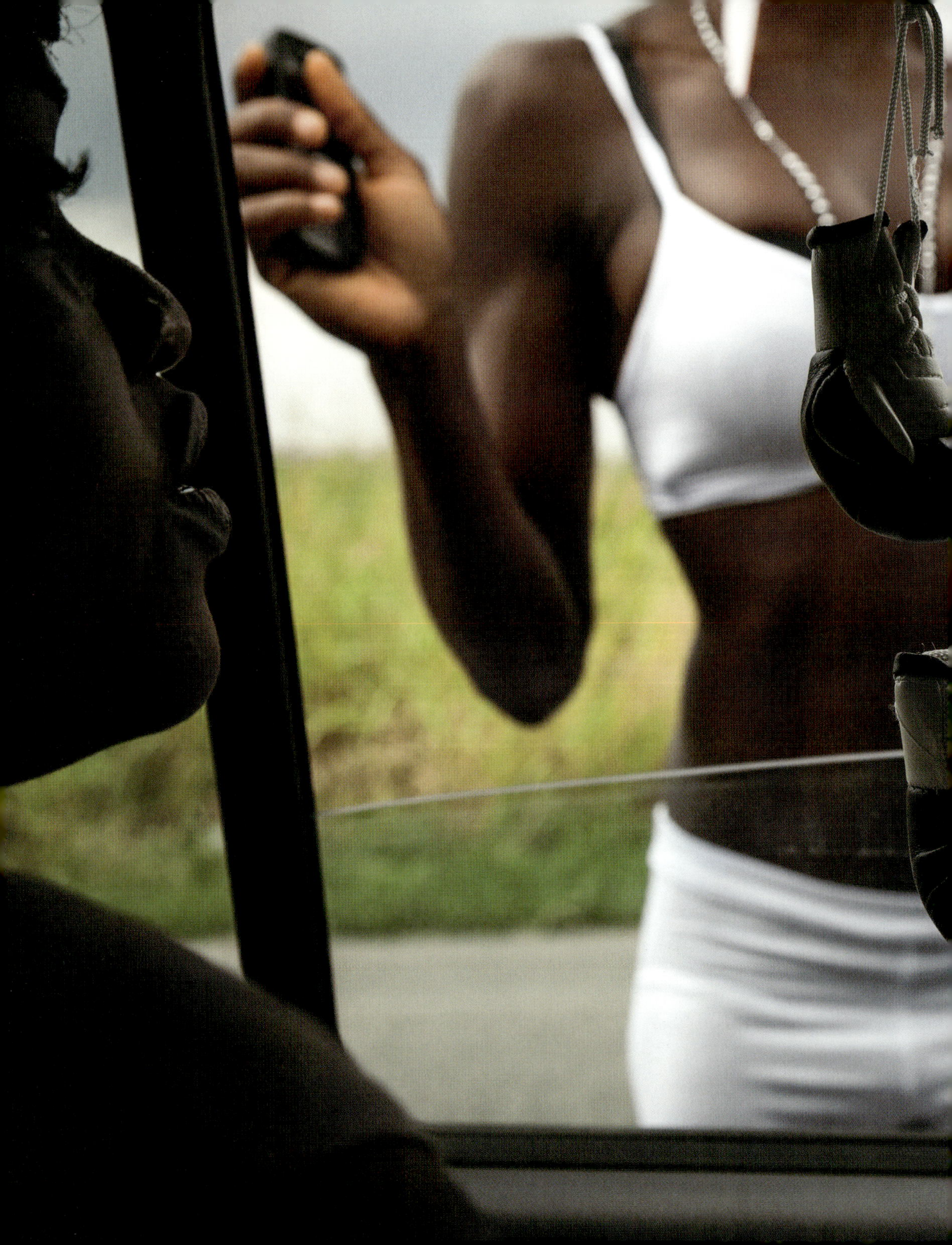

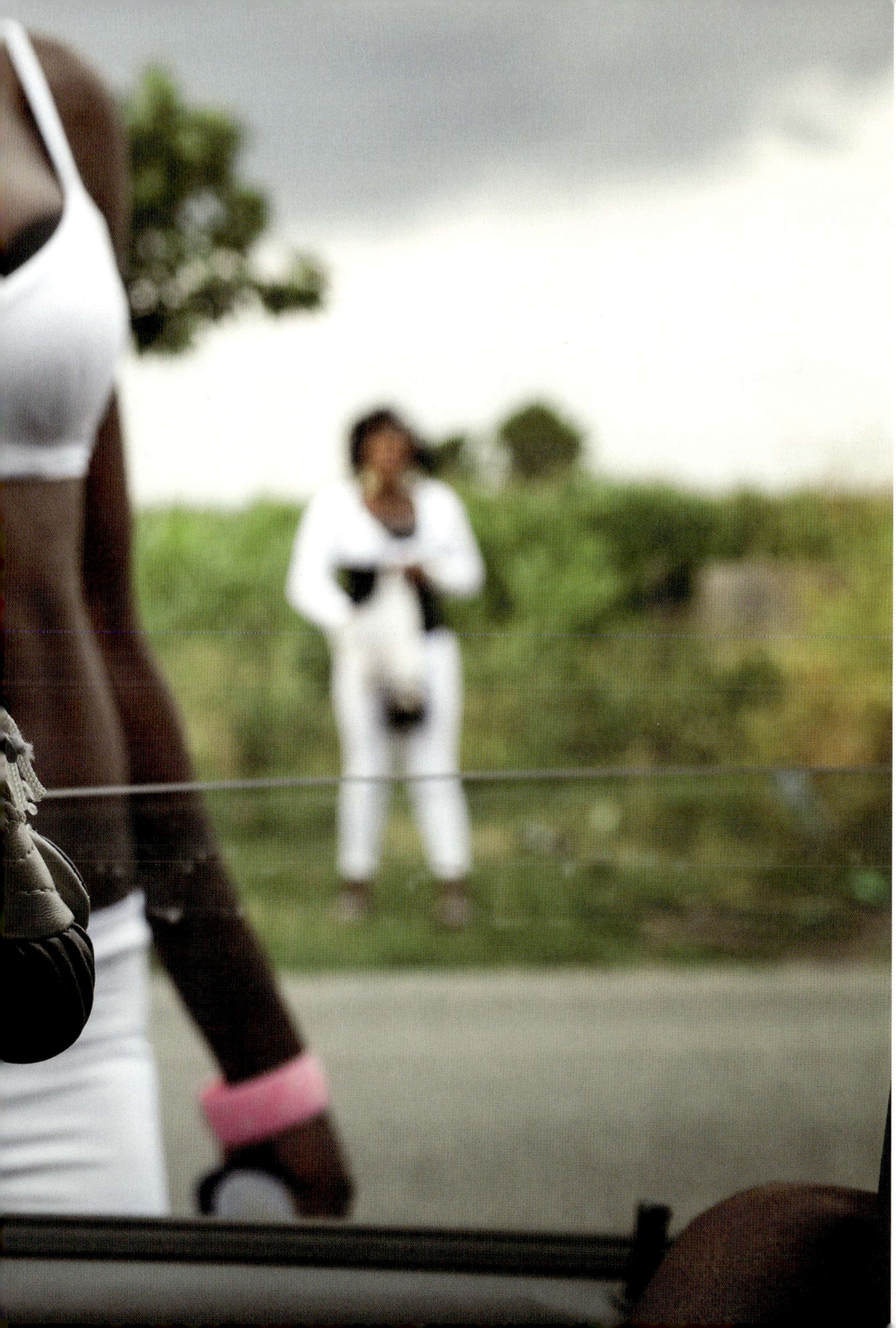

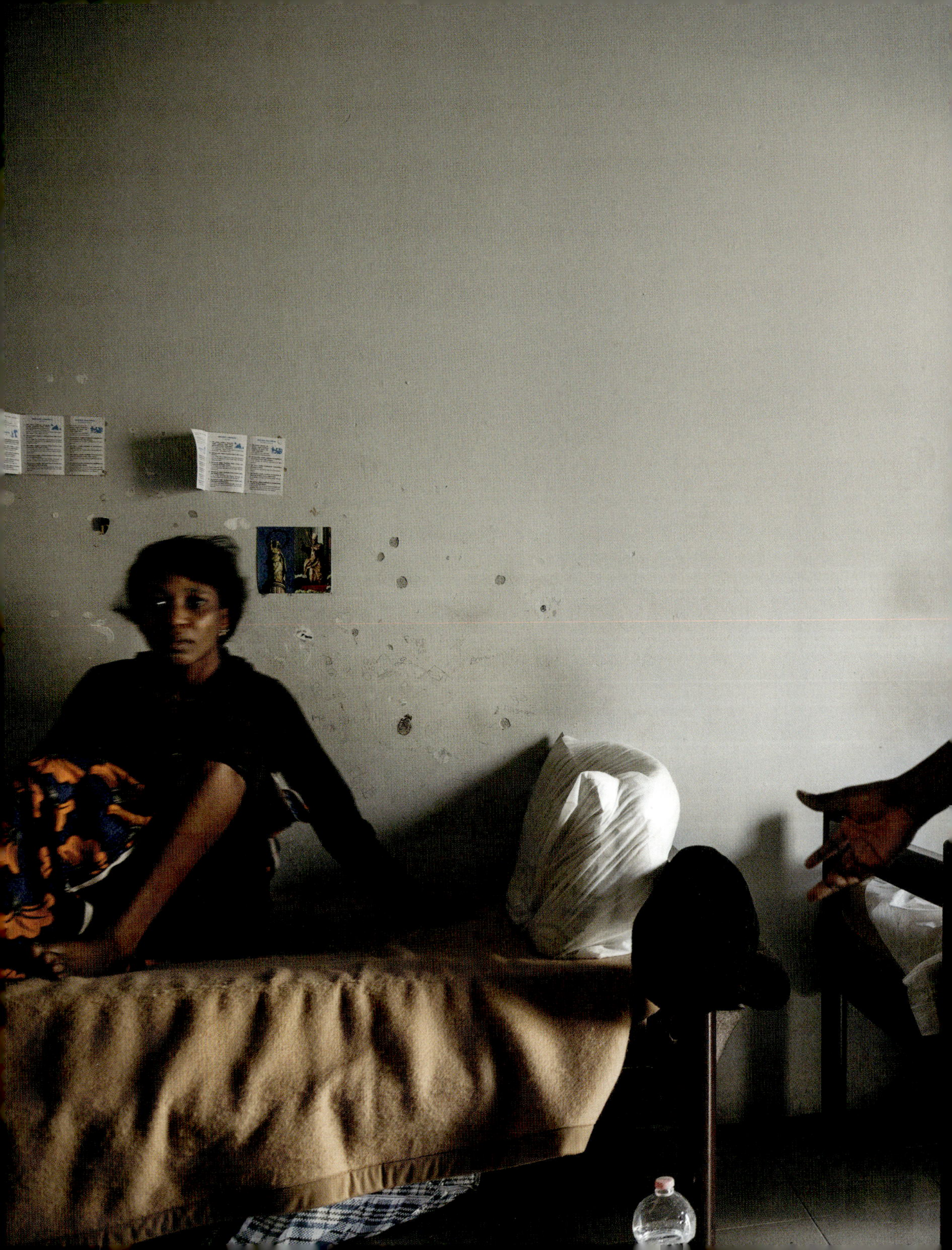

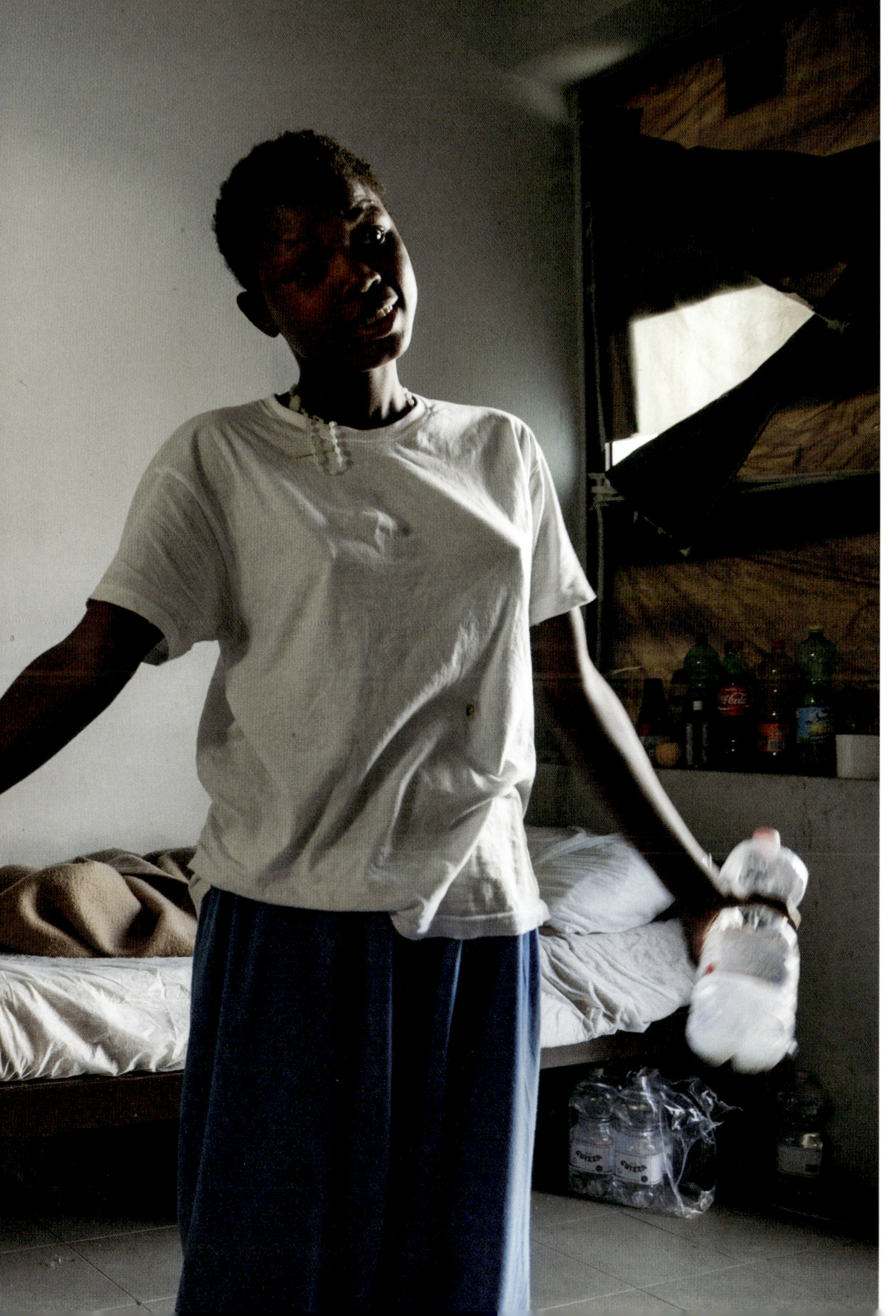

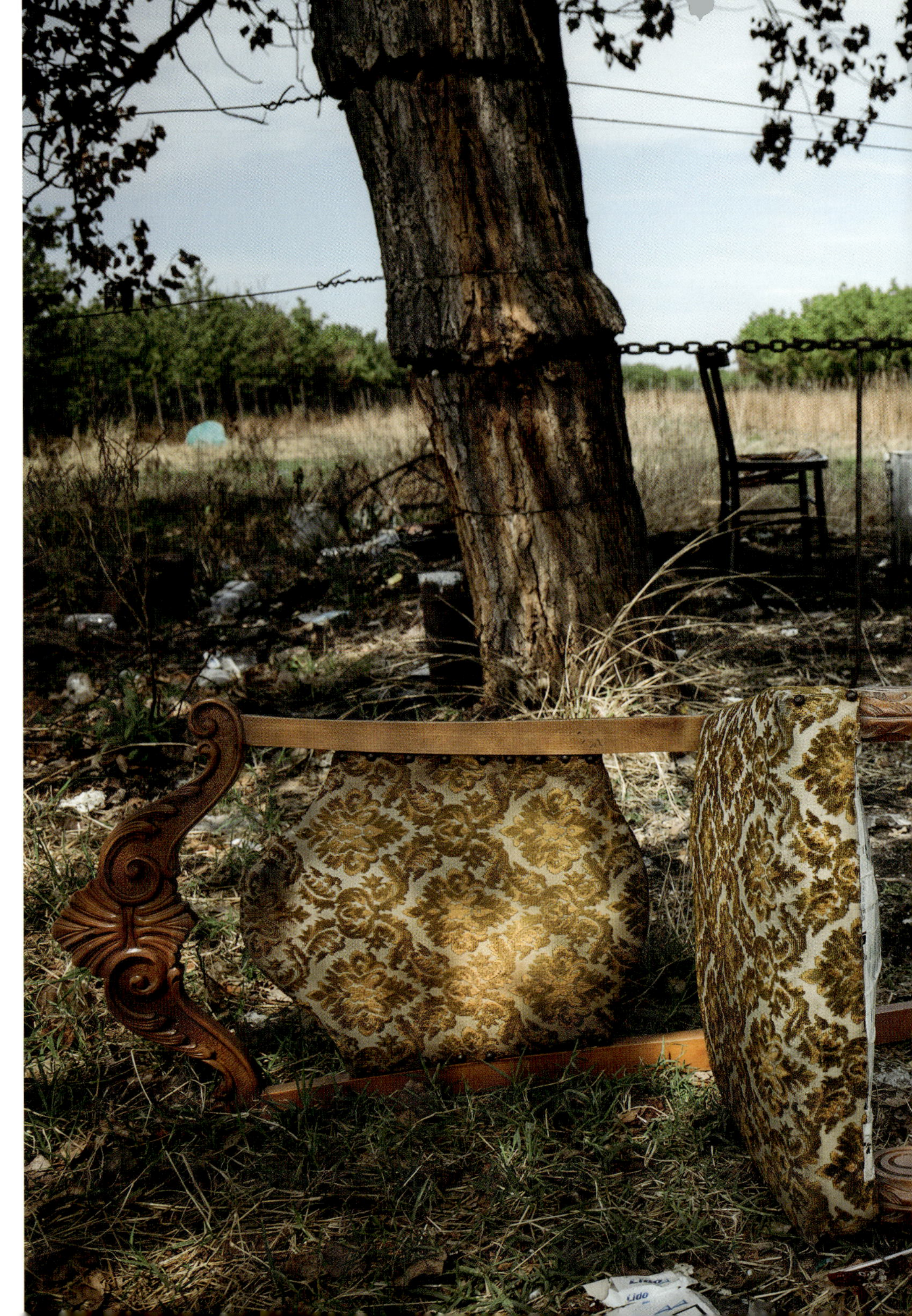

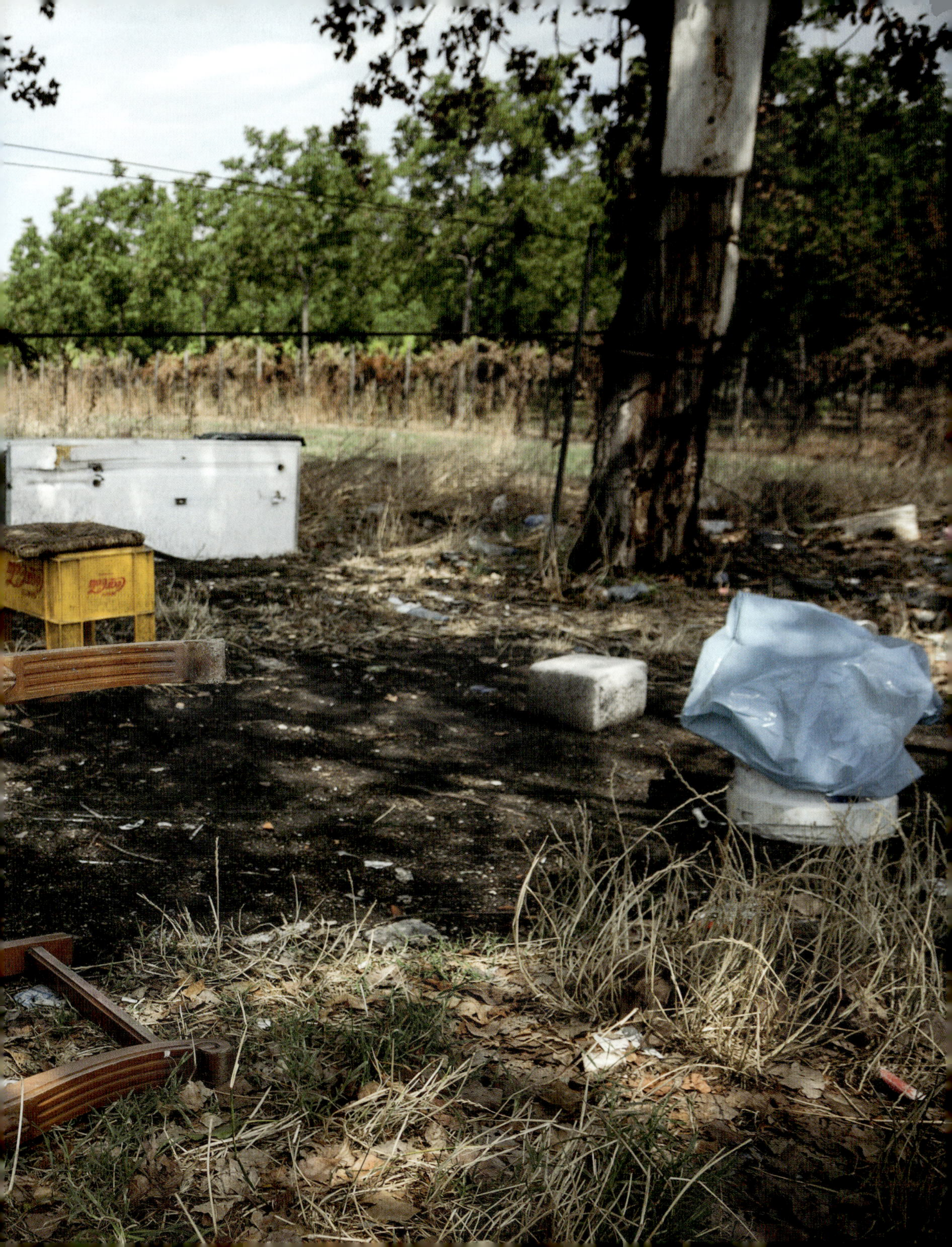

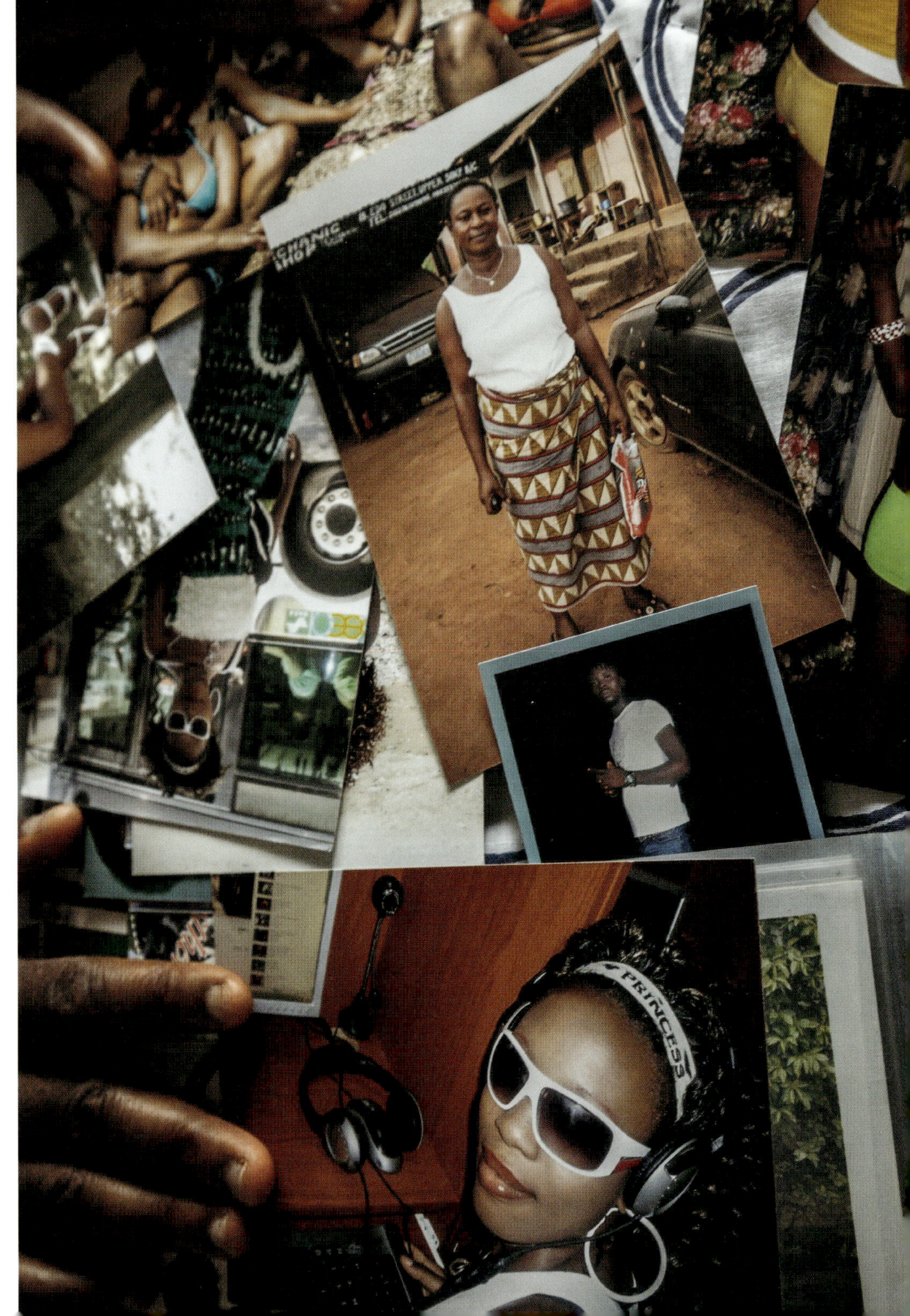

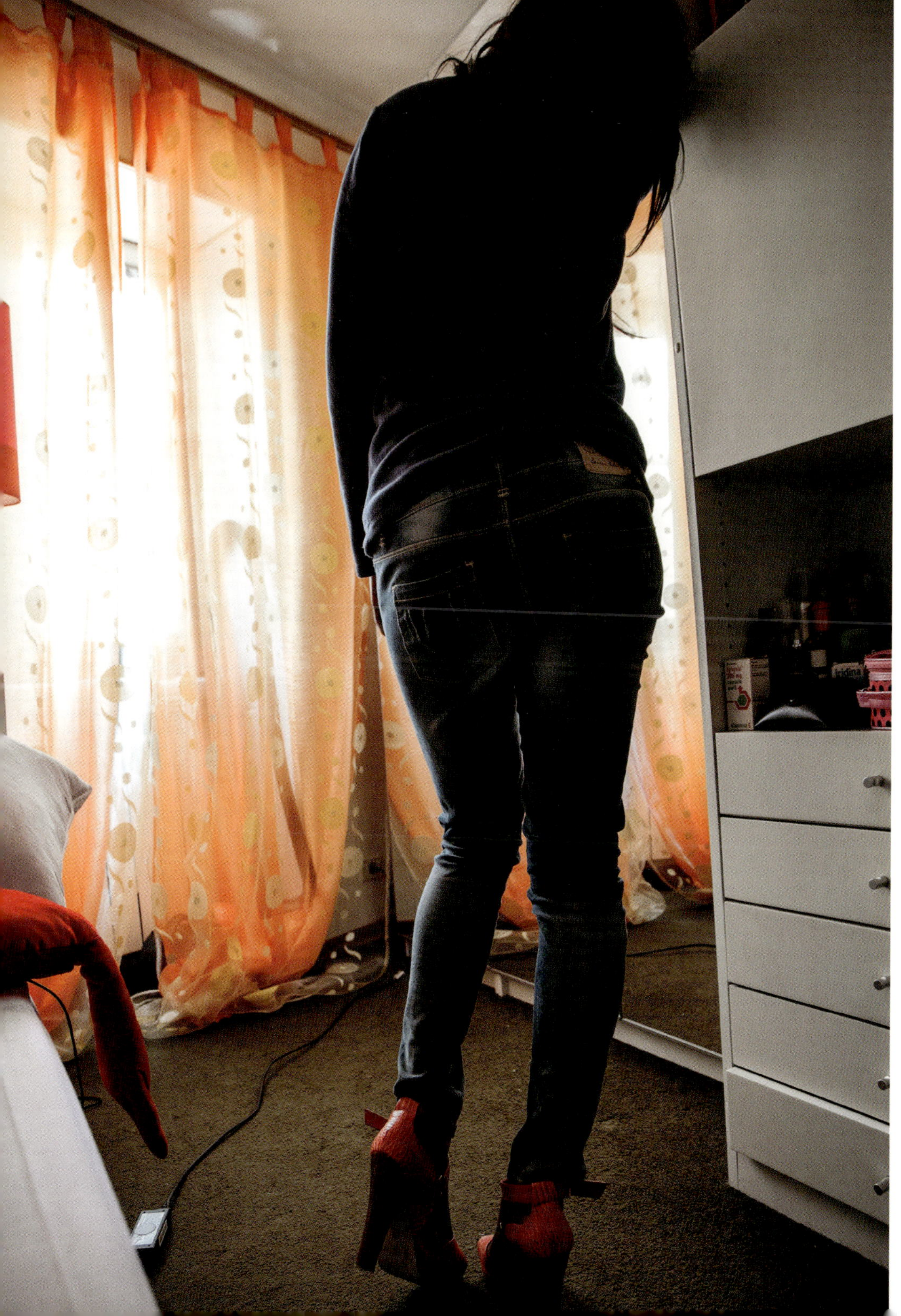

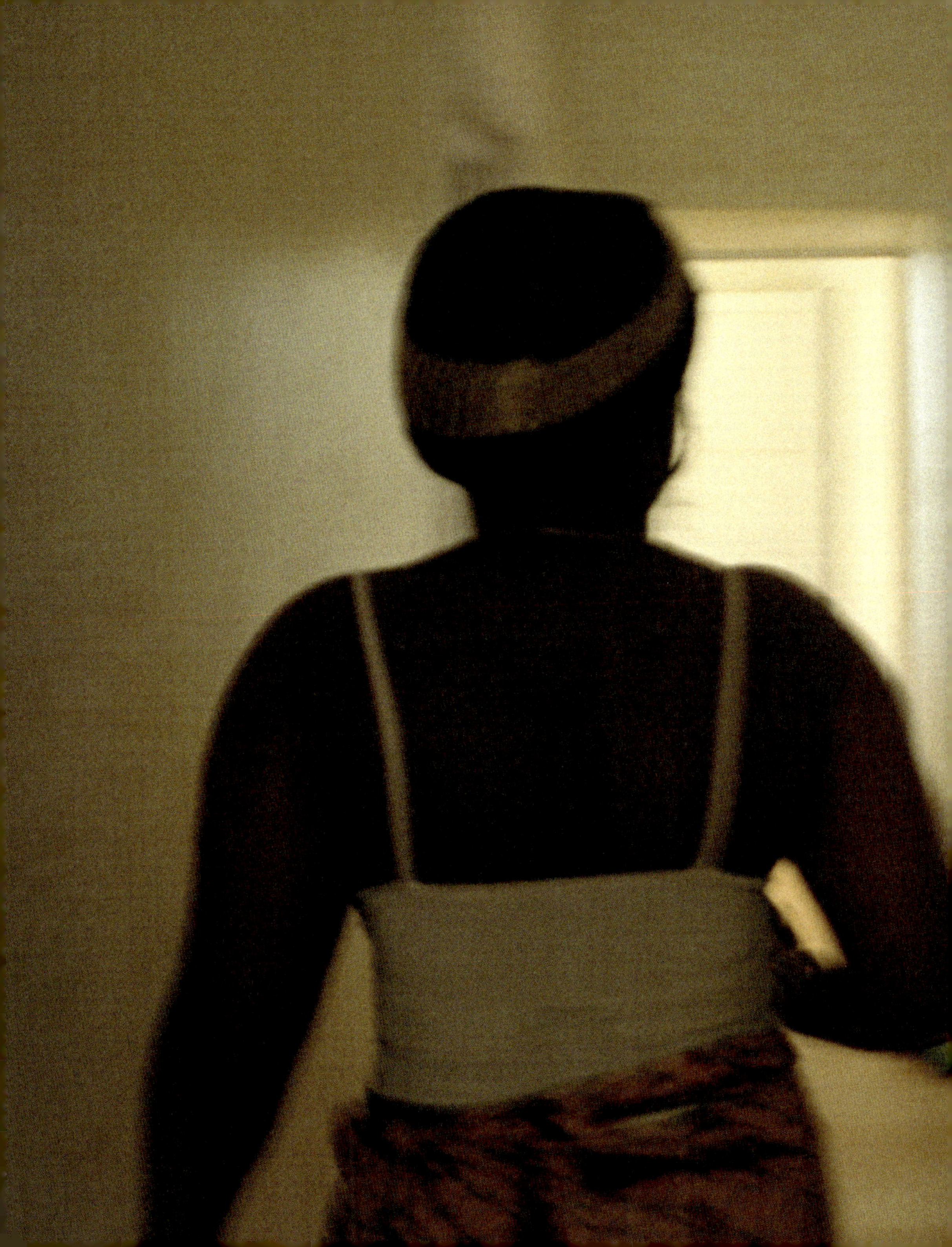

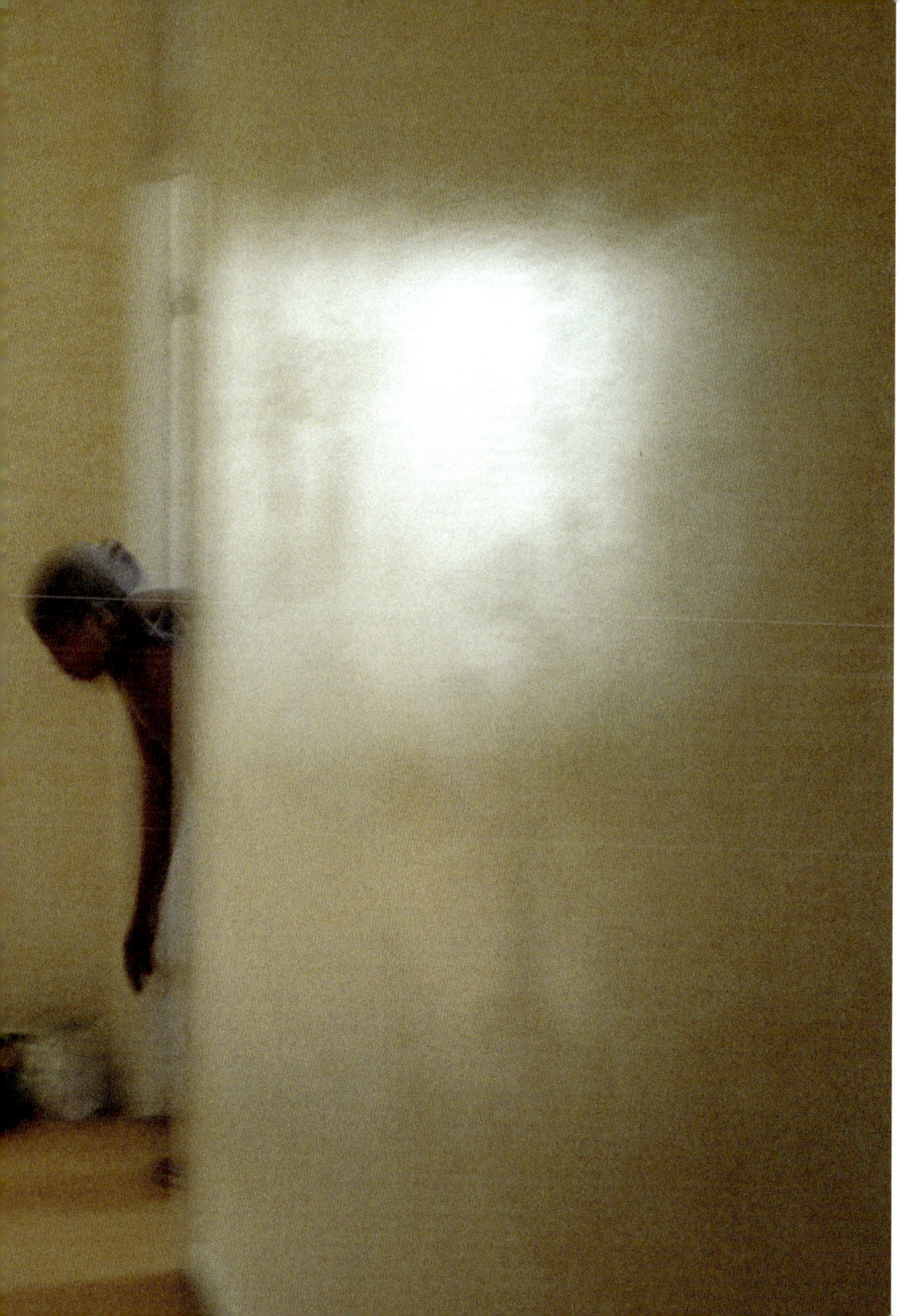

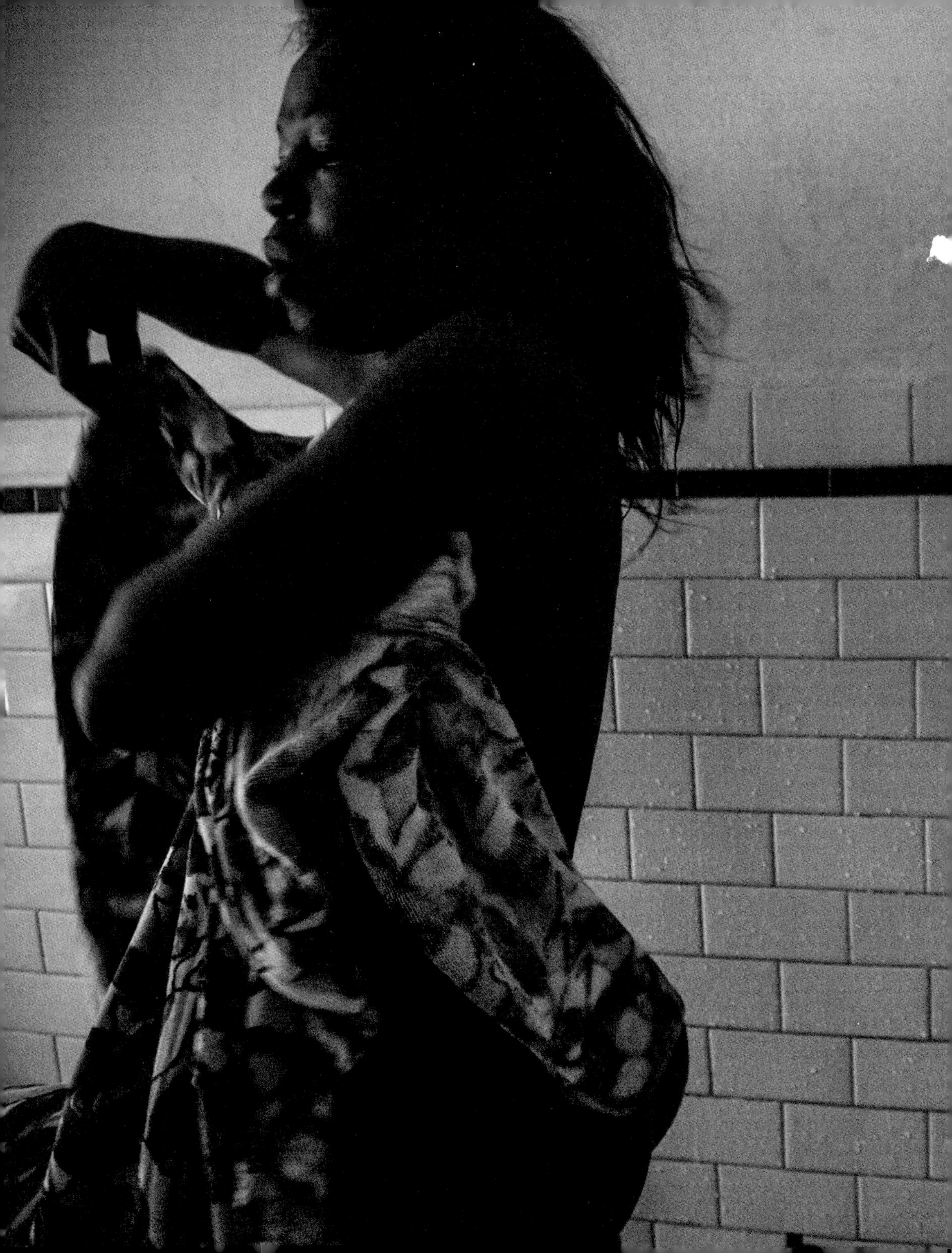

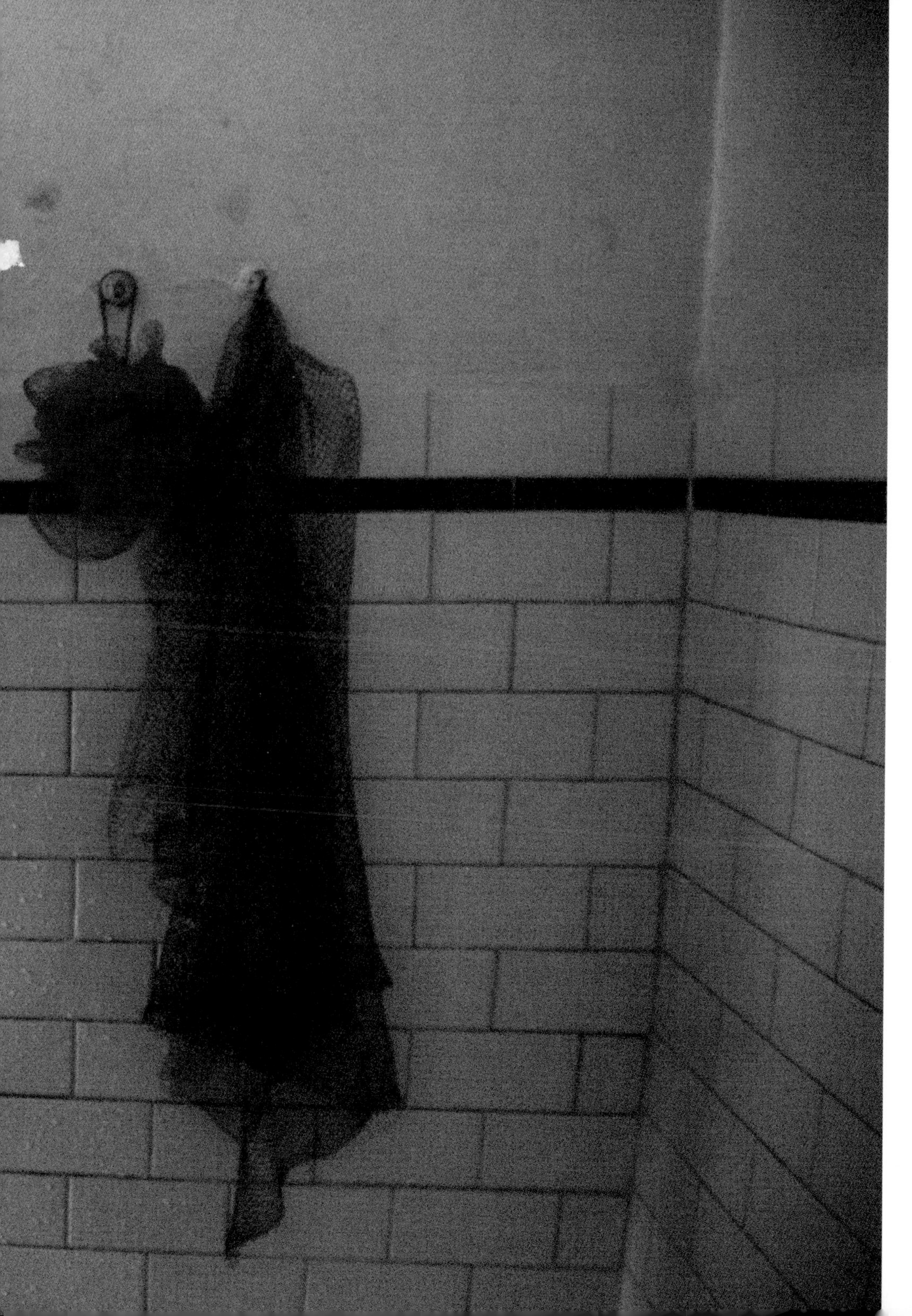

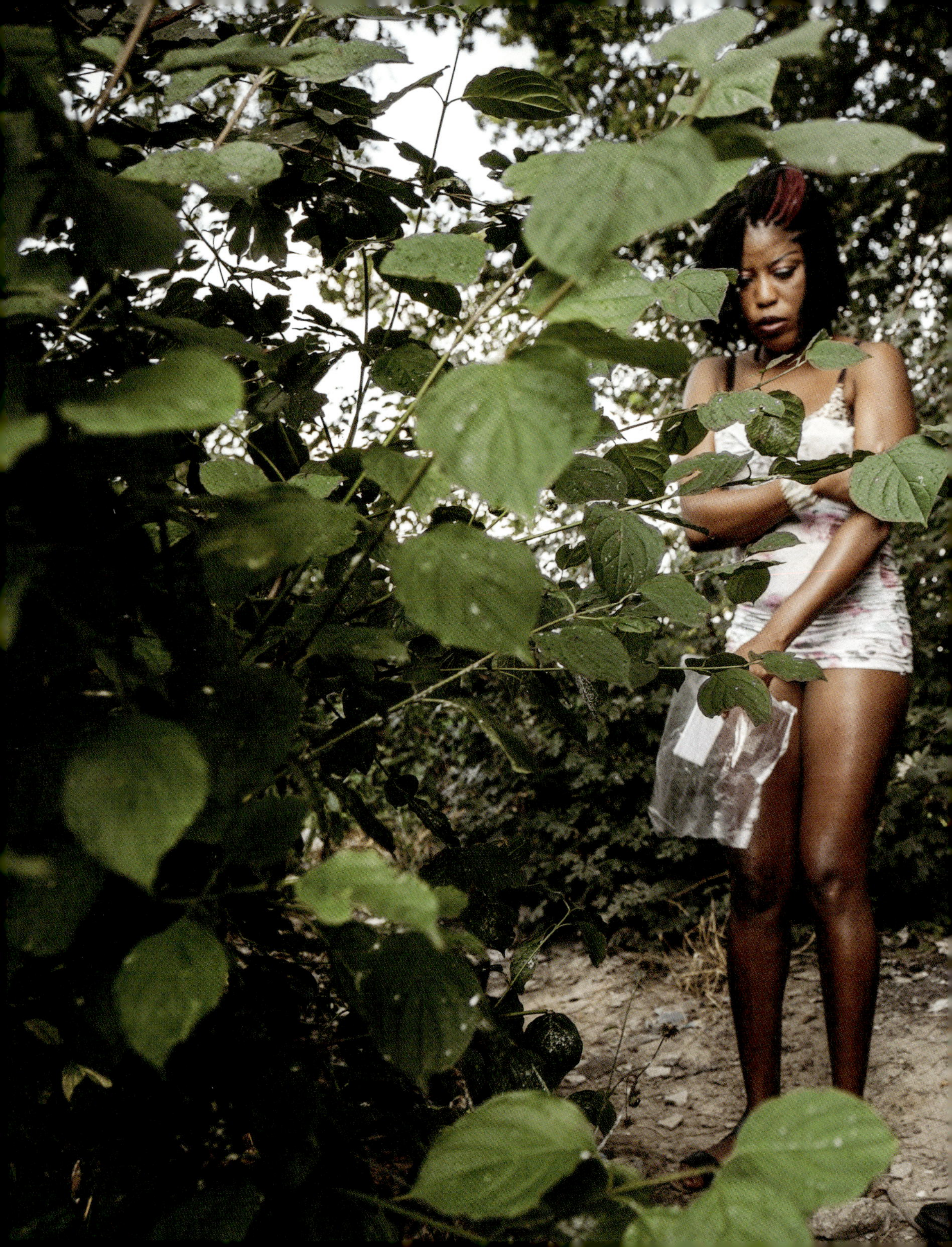

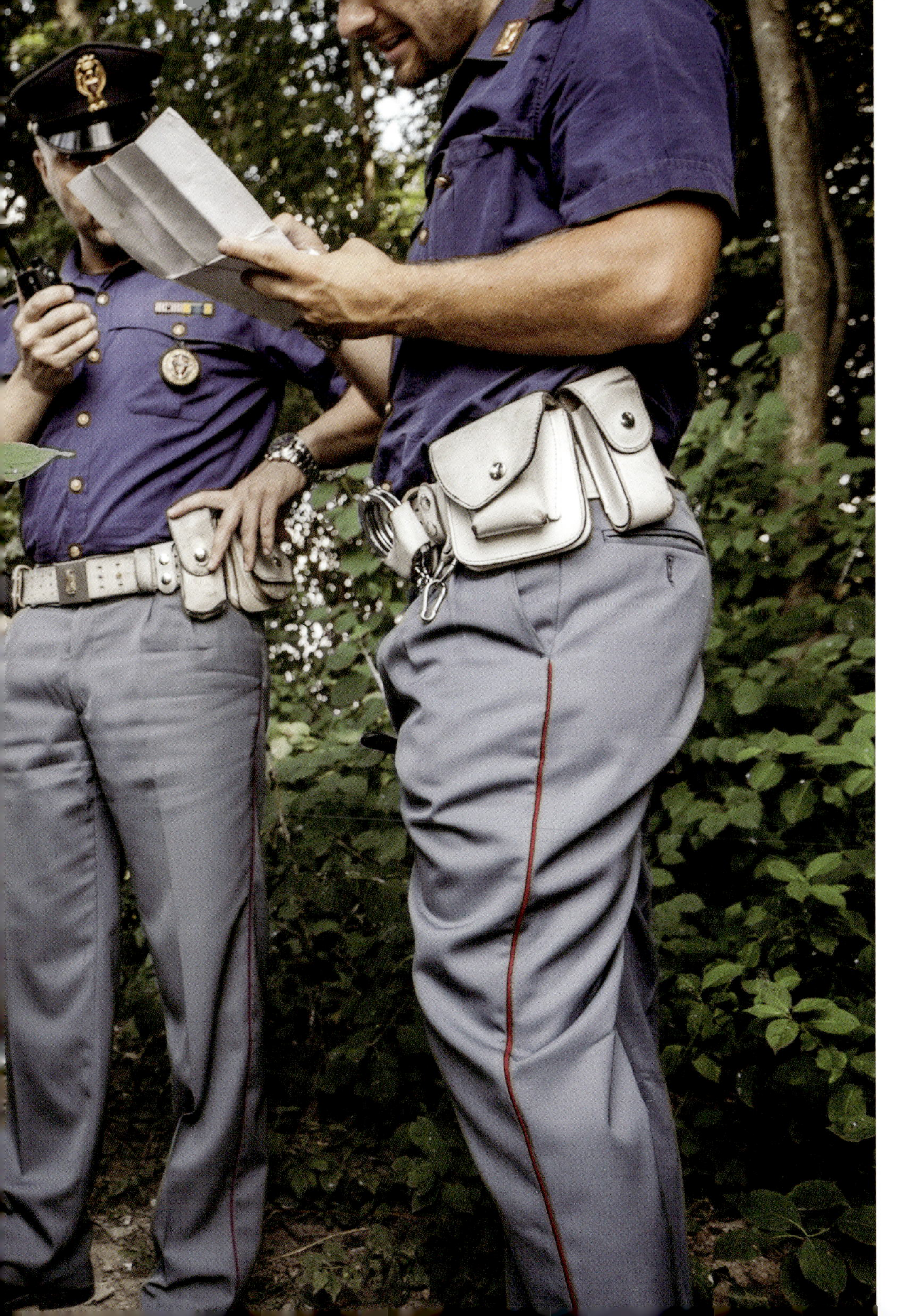

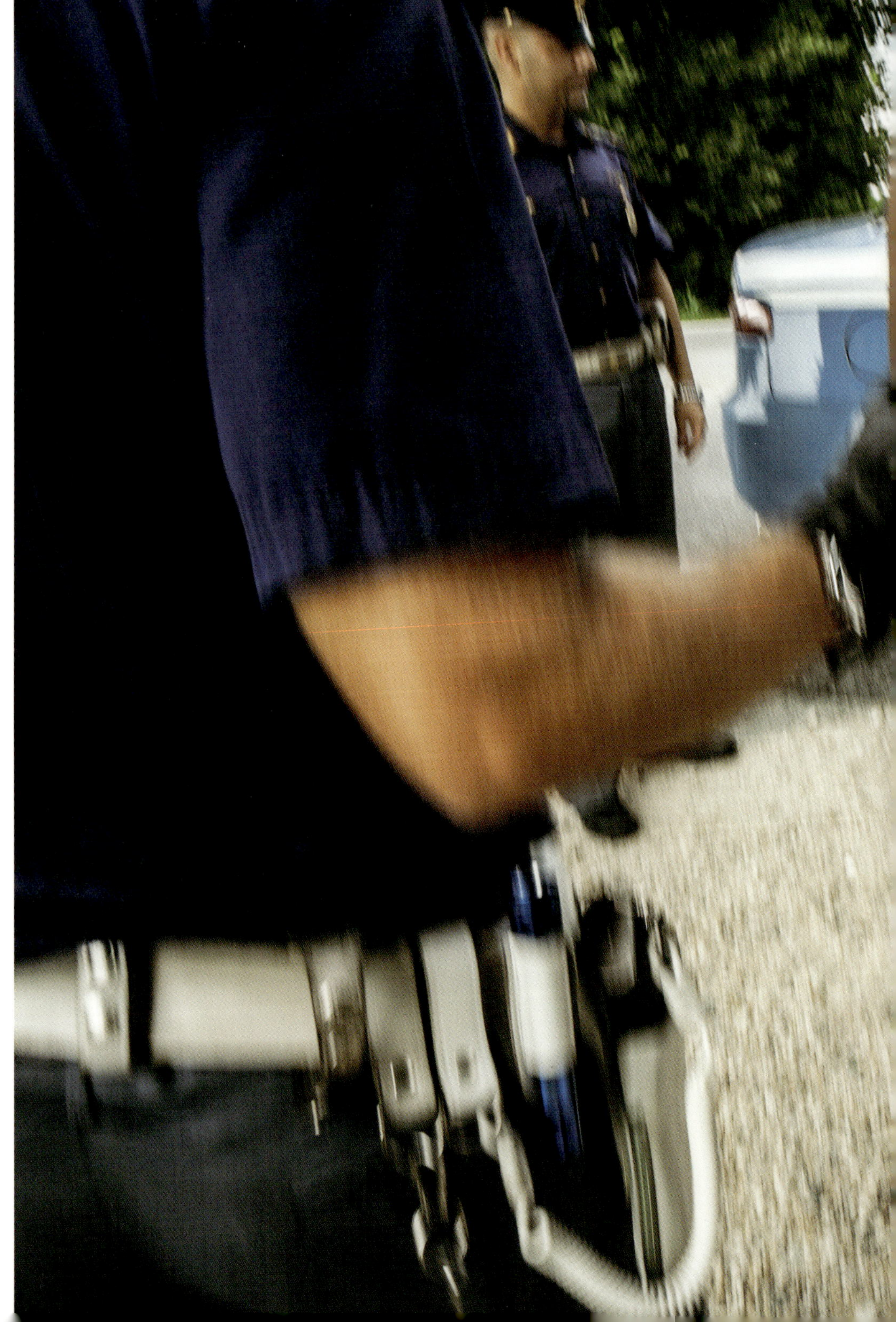

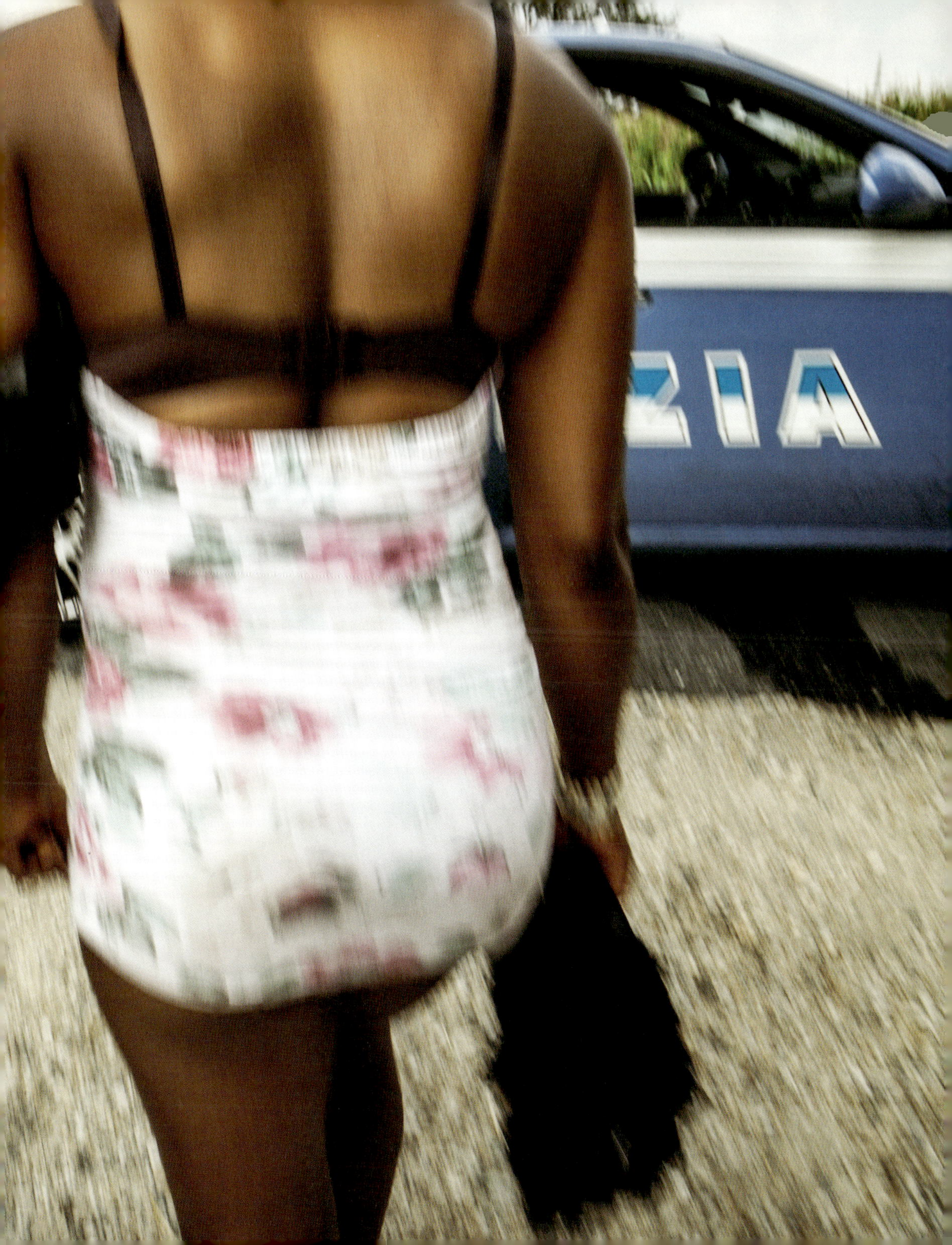

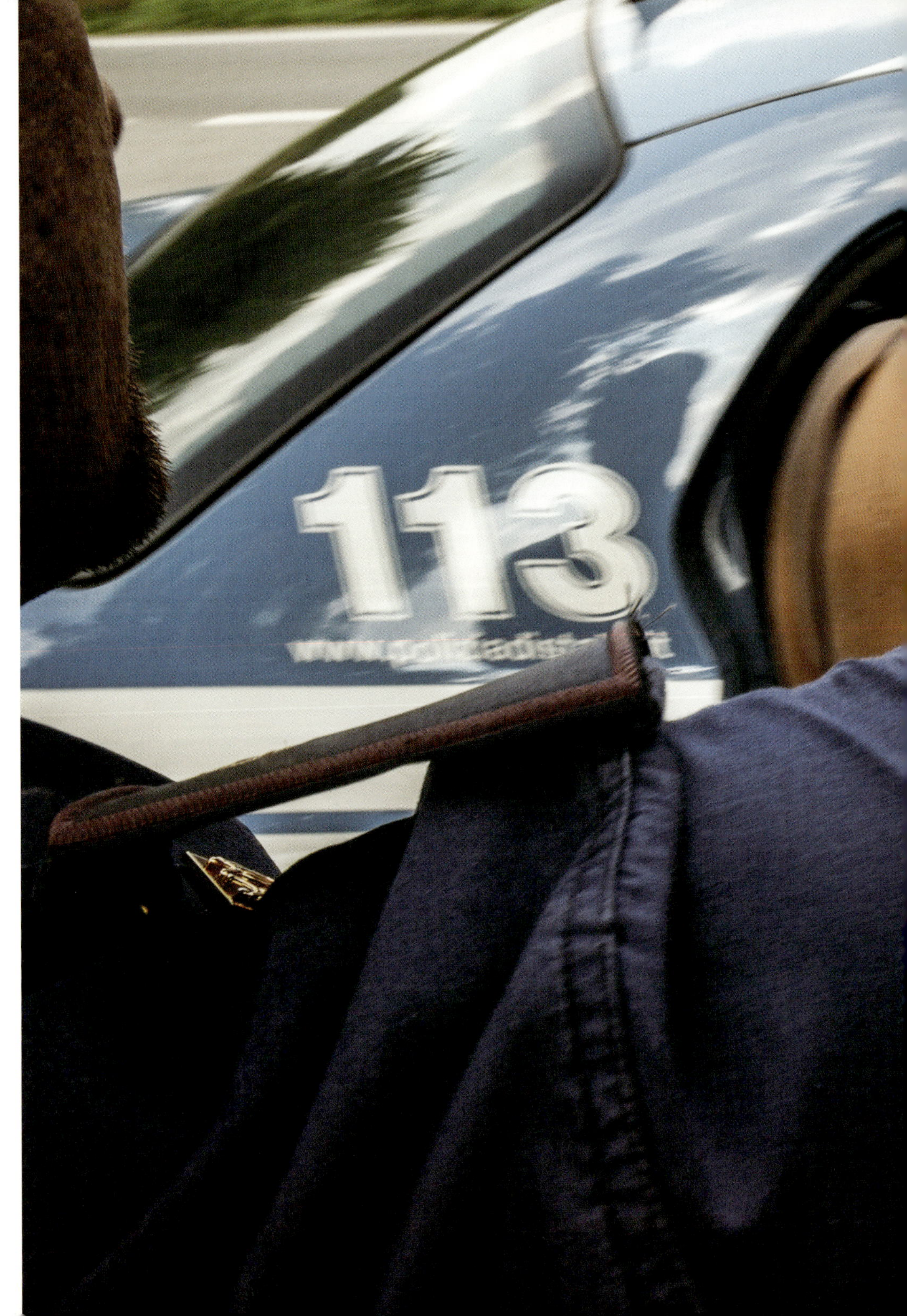

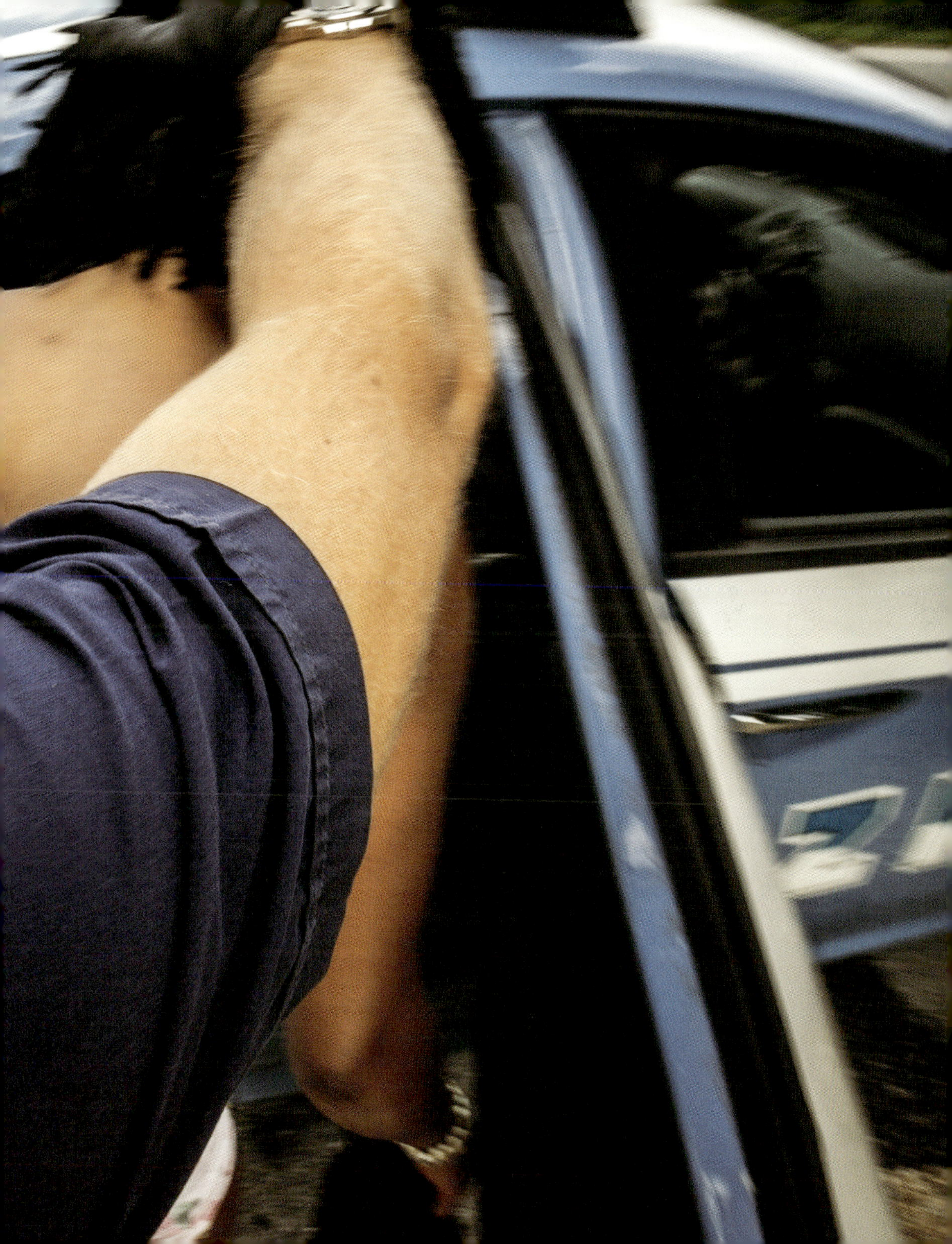

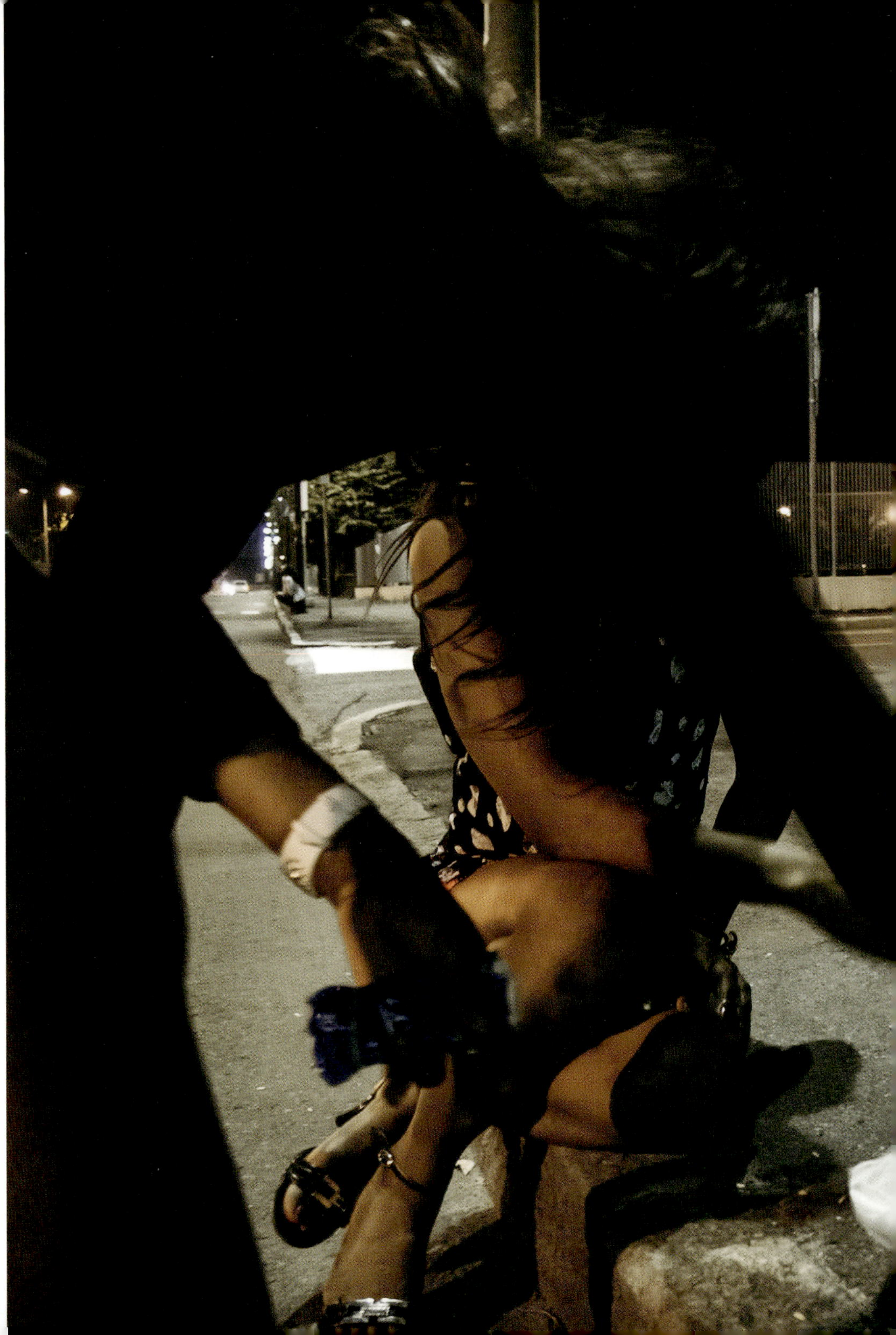

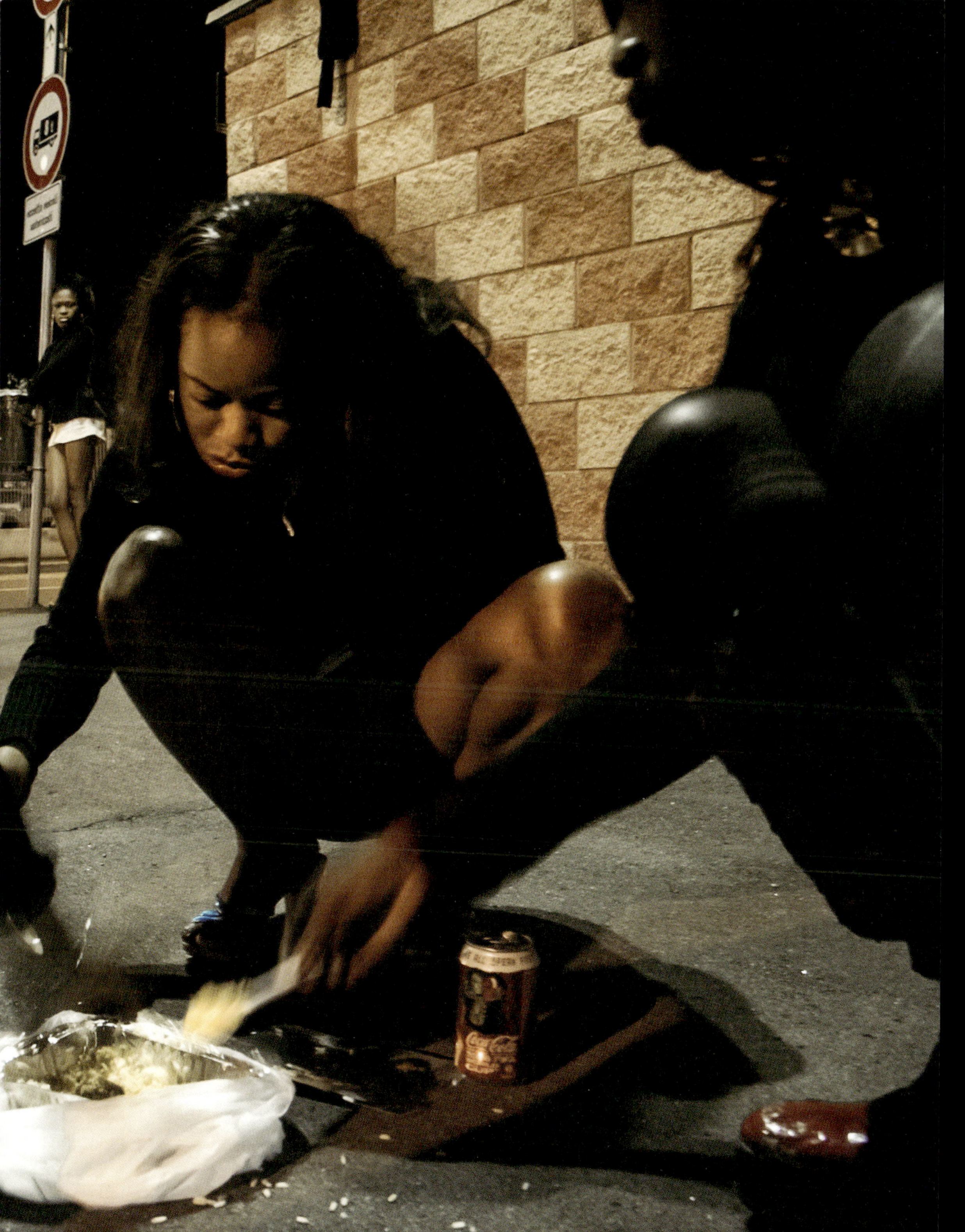

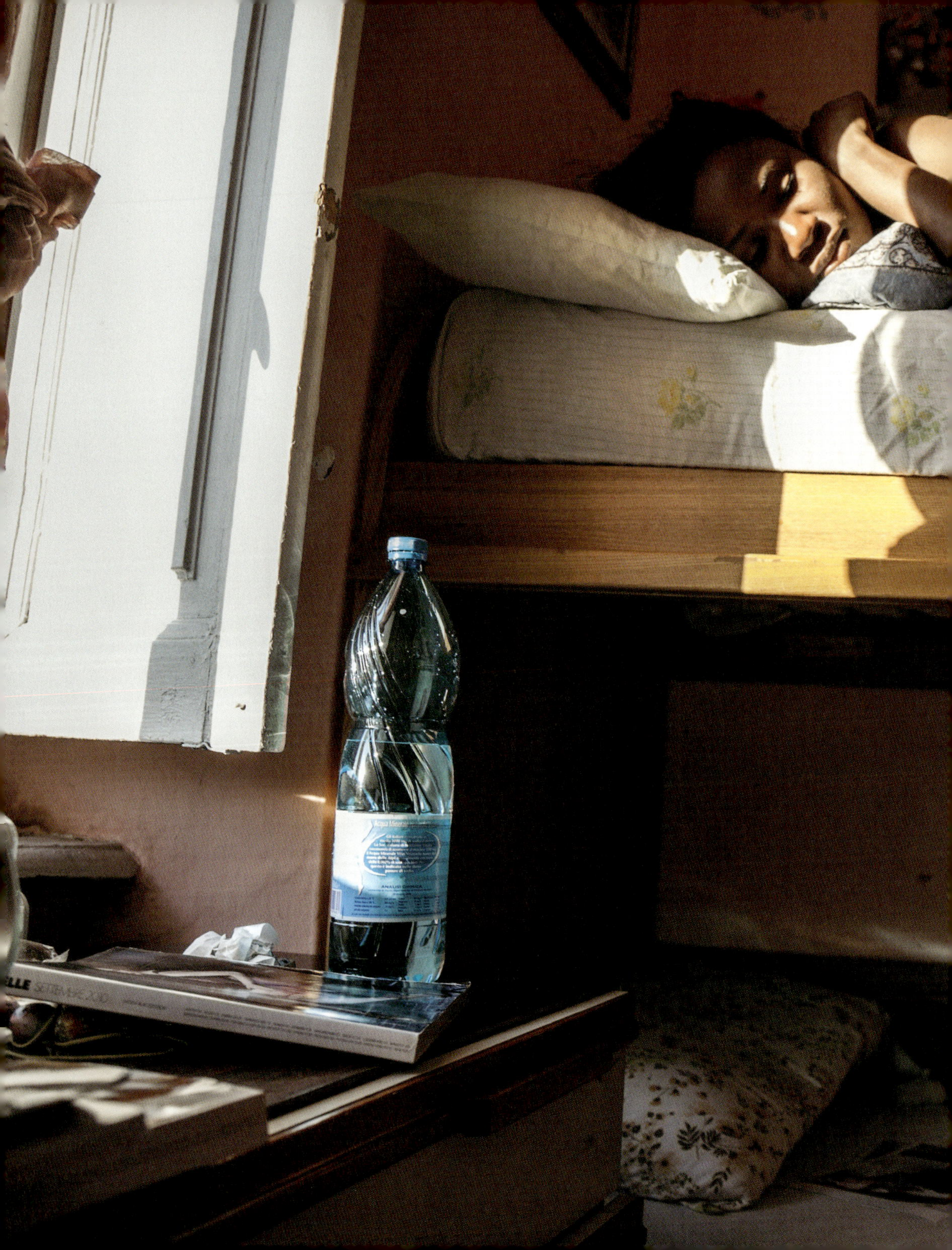

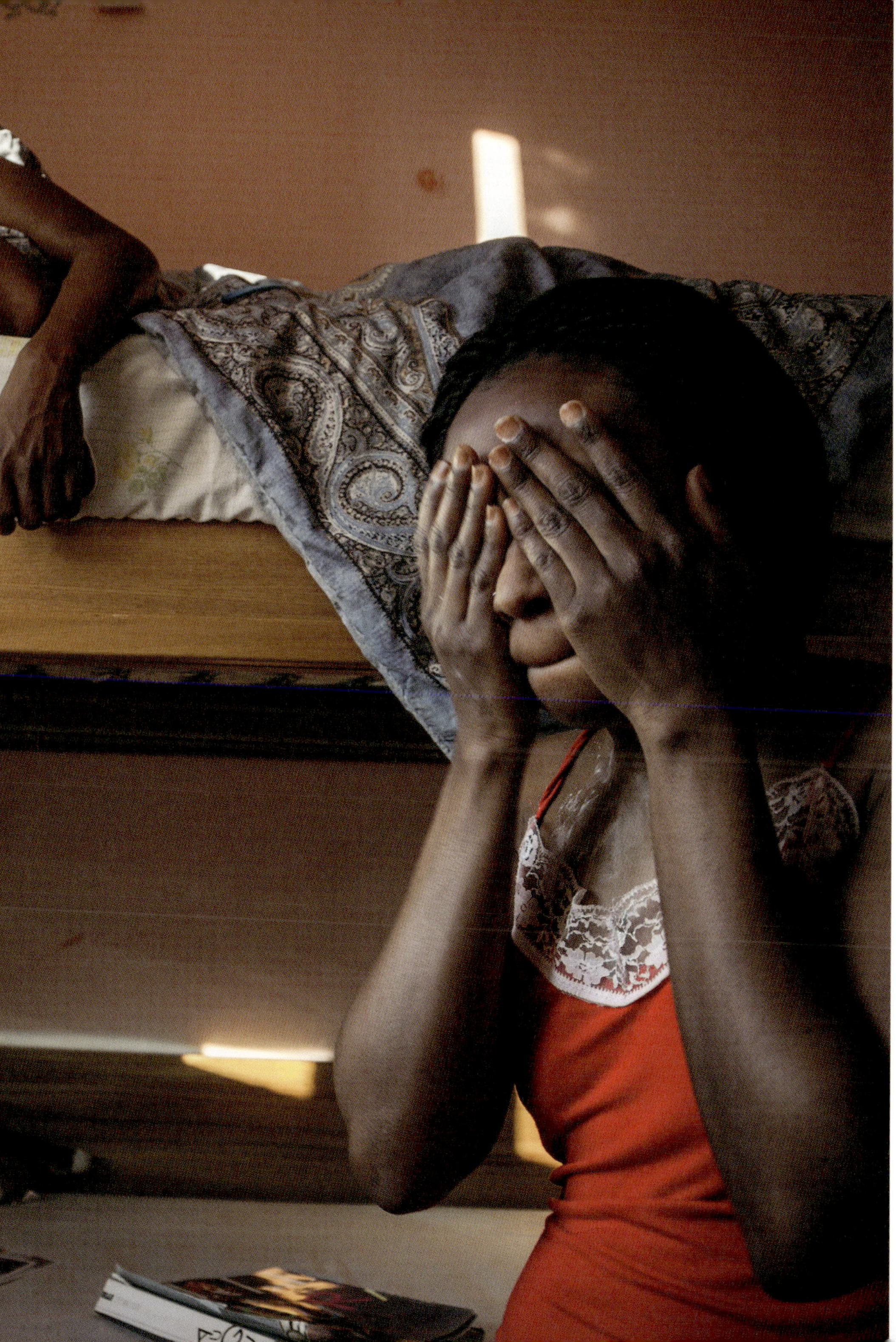

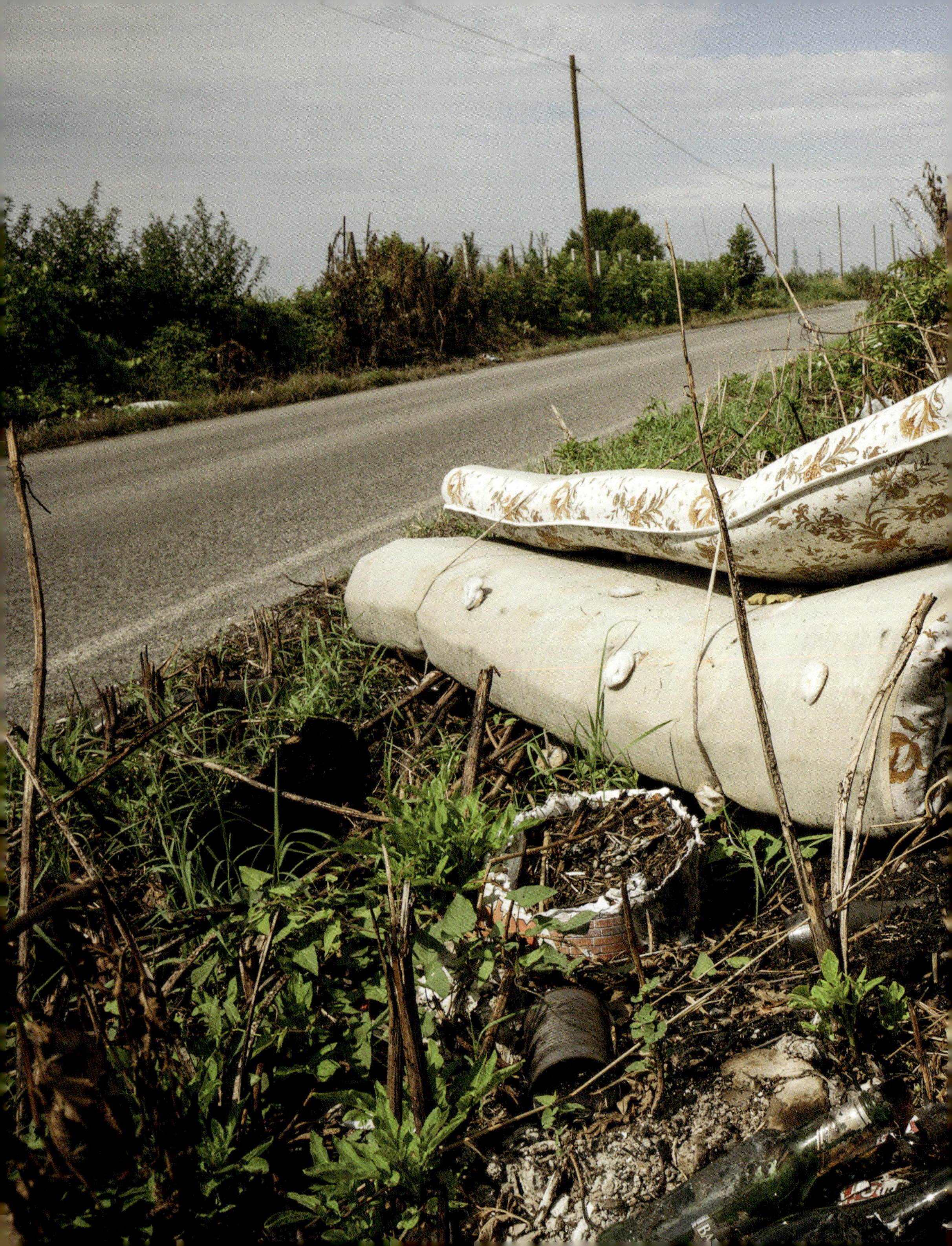

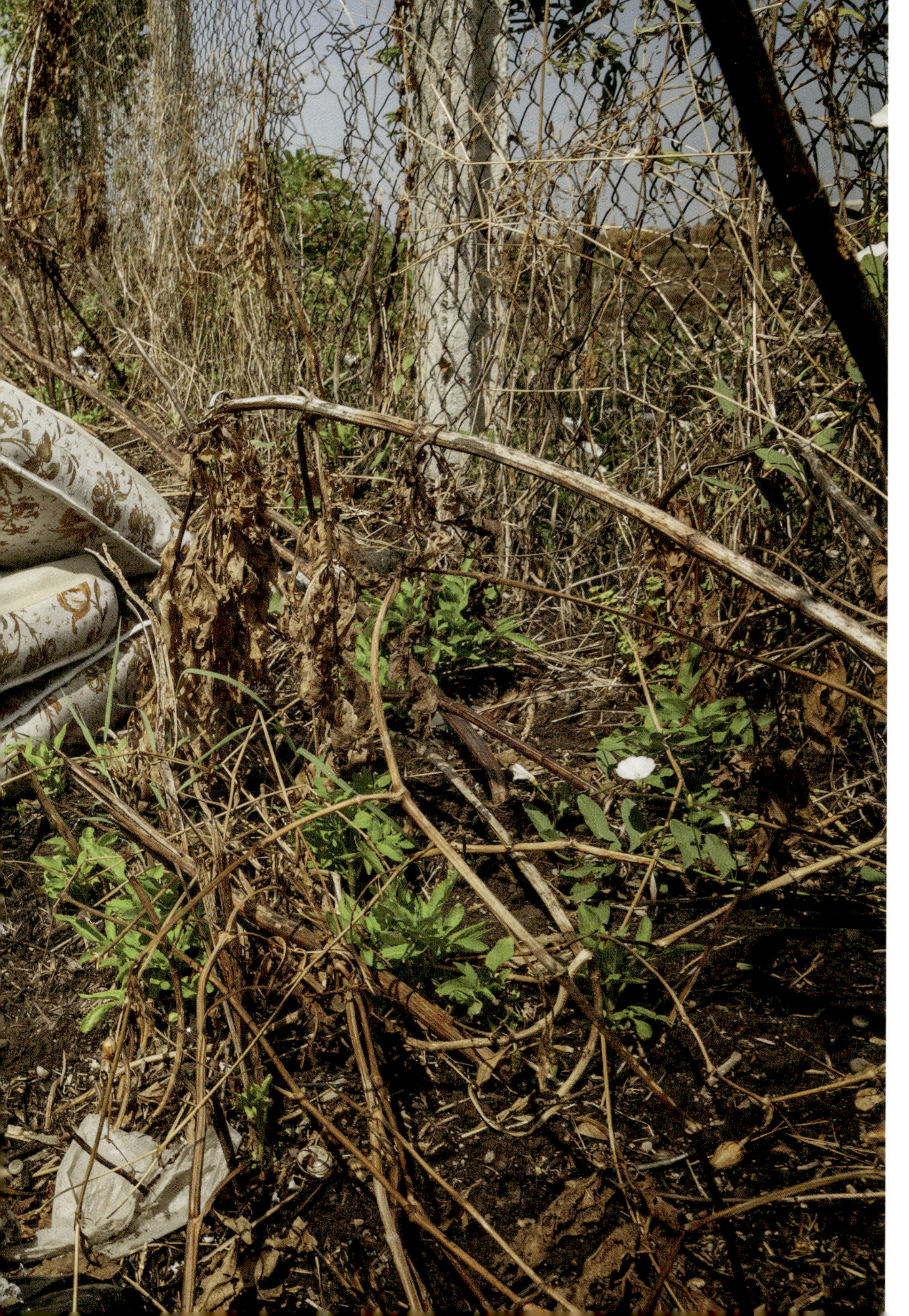

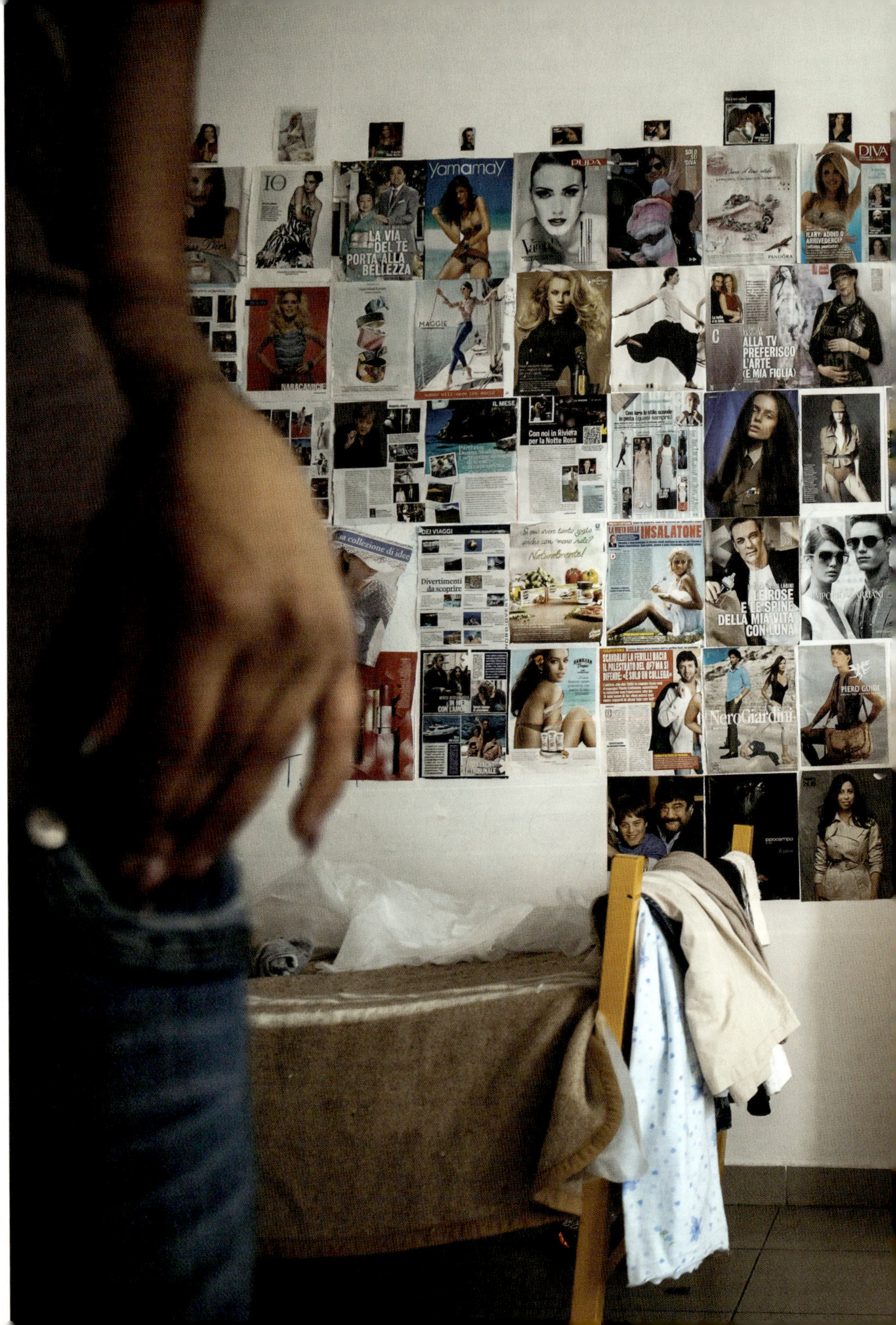
IO
Yamamay
PUPA
DIVA
LA VIA DEL TE PORTA ALLA BELLEZZA
PANDORA
ILARY: ADDIO O ARRIVEDERCI?
NARACAMICIE
MAGGIE
ALLA TV PREFERISCO L'ARTE (E MIA FIGLIA)
IL MESE
Con noi in Riviera per la Notte Rosa
DEI VIAGGI
Divertimenti da scoprire
Si può avere tanto gusto anche con meno sale?
Naturalmente!
INSALATONE
LE ROSE E LE SPINE DELLA MIA VITA CON LUNA
EMPORIO ARMANI
SCANDALO! LA FERILLI BACIA IL PALESTRATO DEL GF7 MA SI DIFENDE: «È SOLO UN COLLEGA»
NeroGiardini
PIERO GUIDI

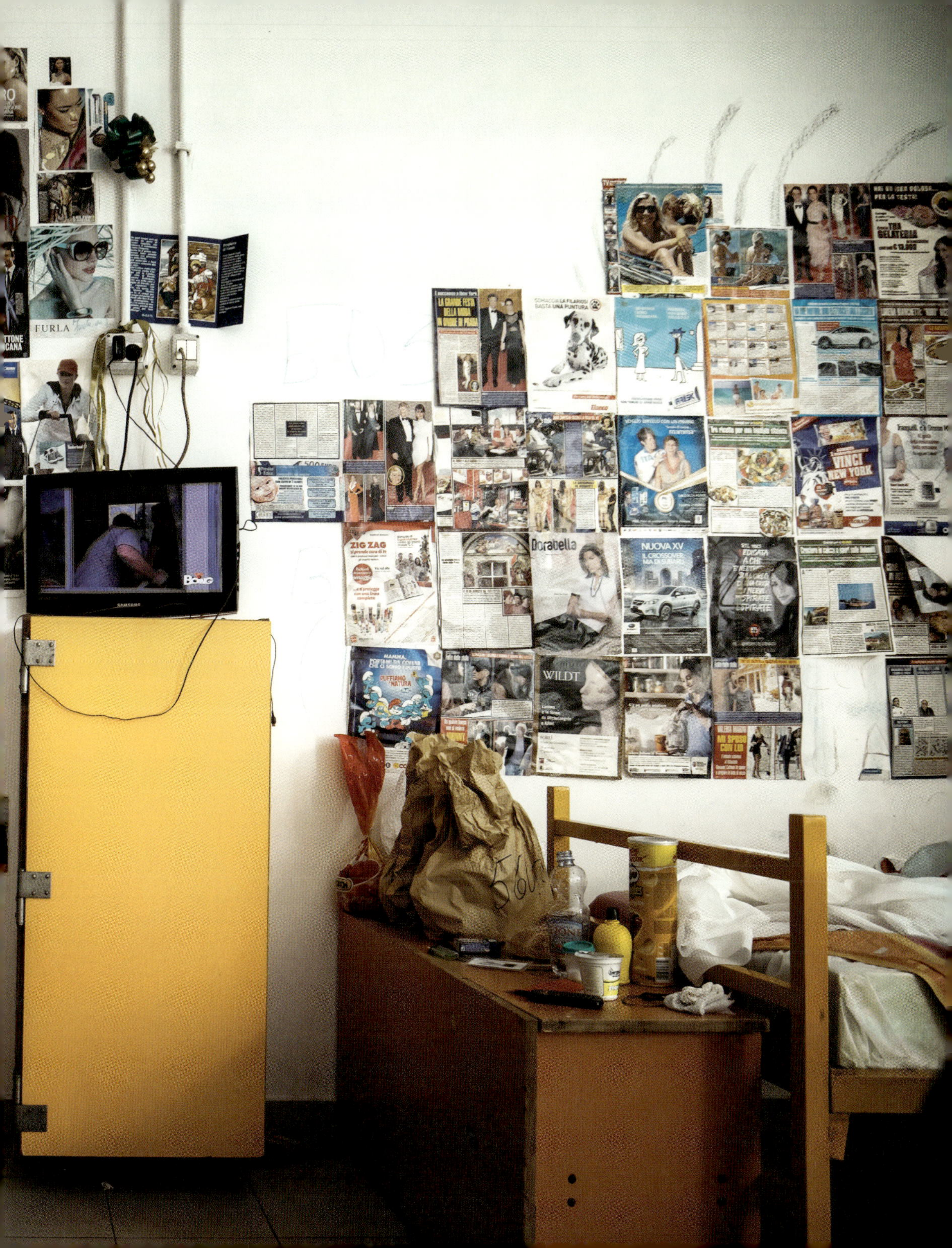

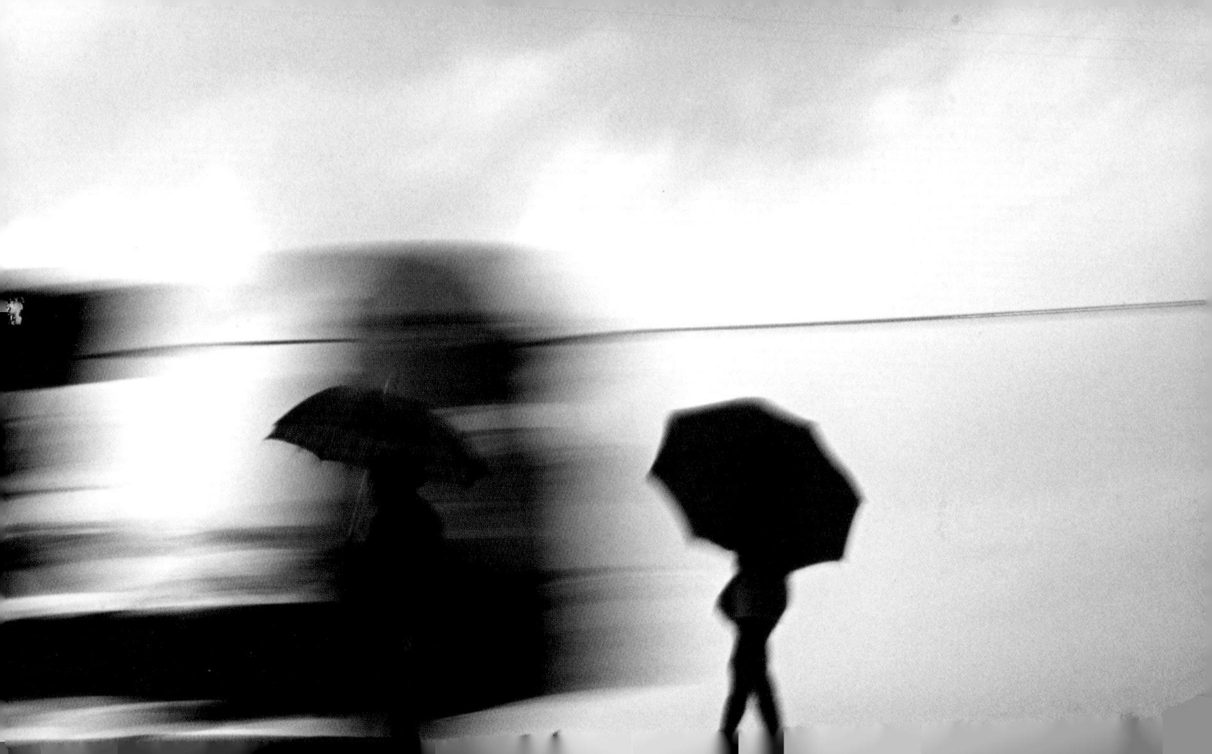

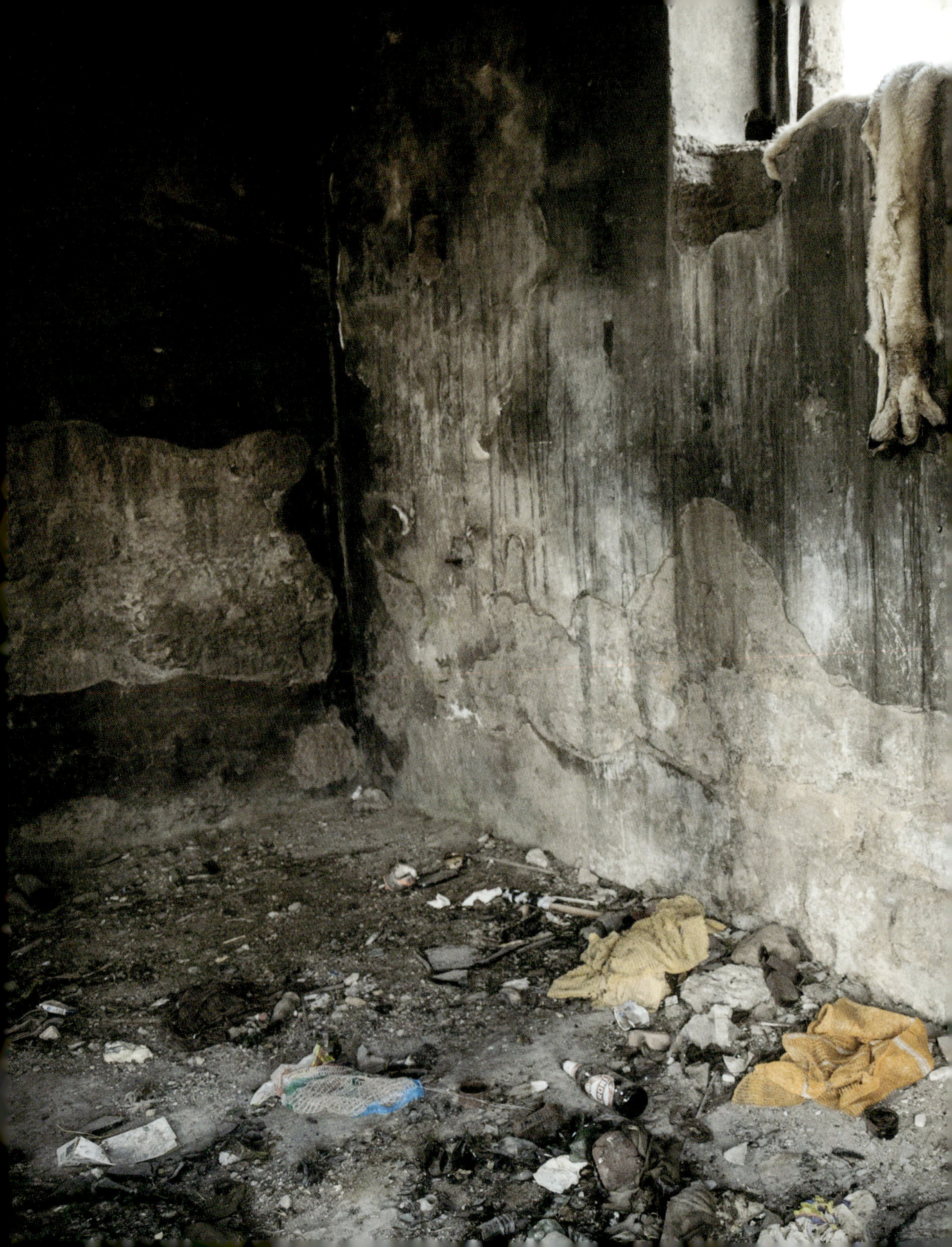

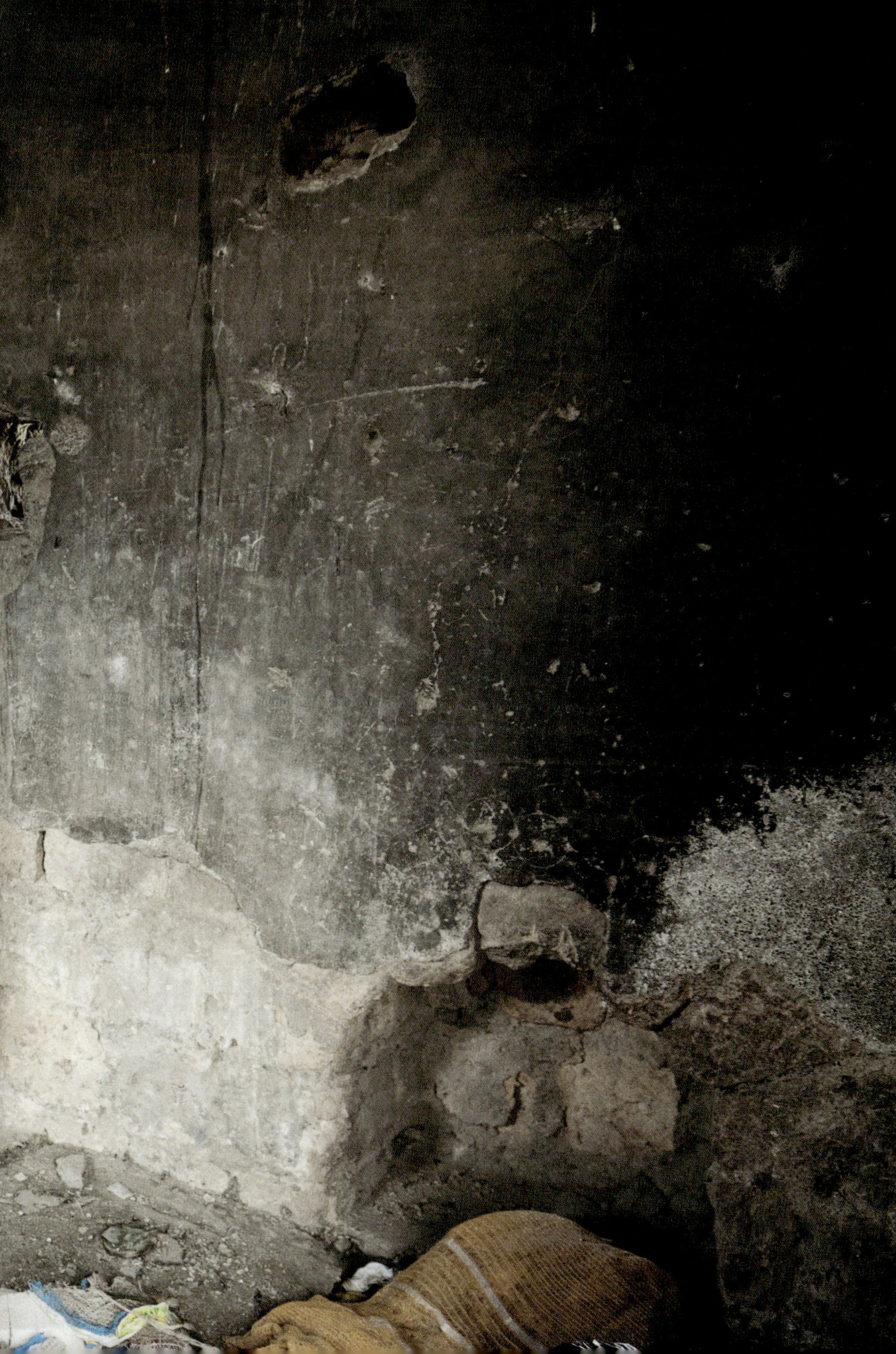

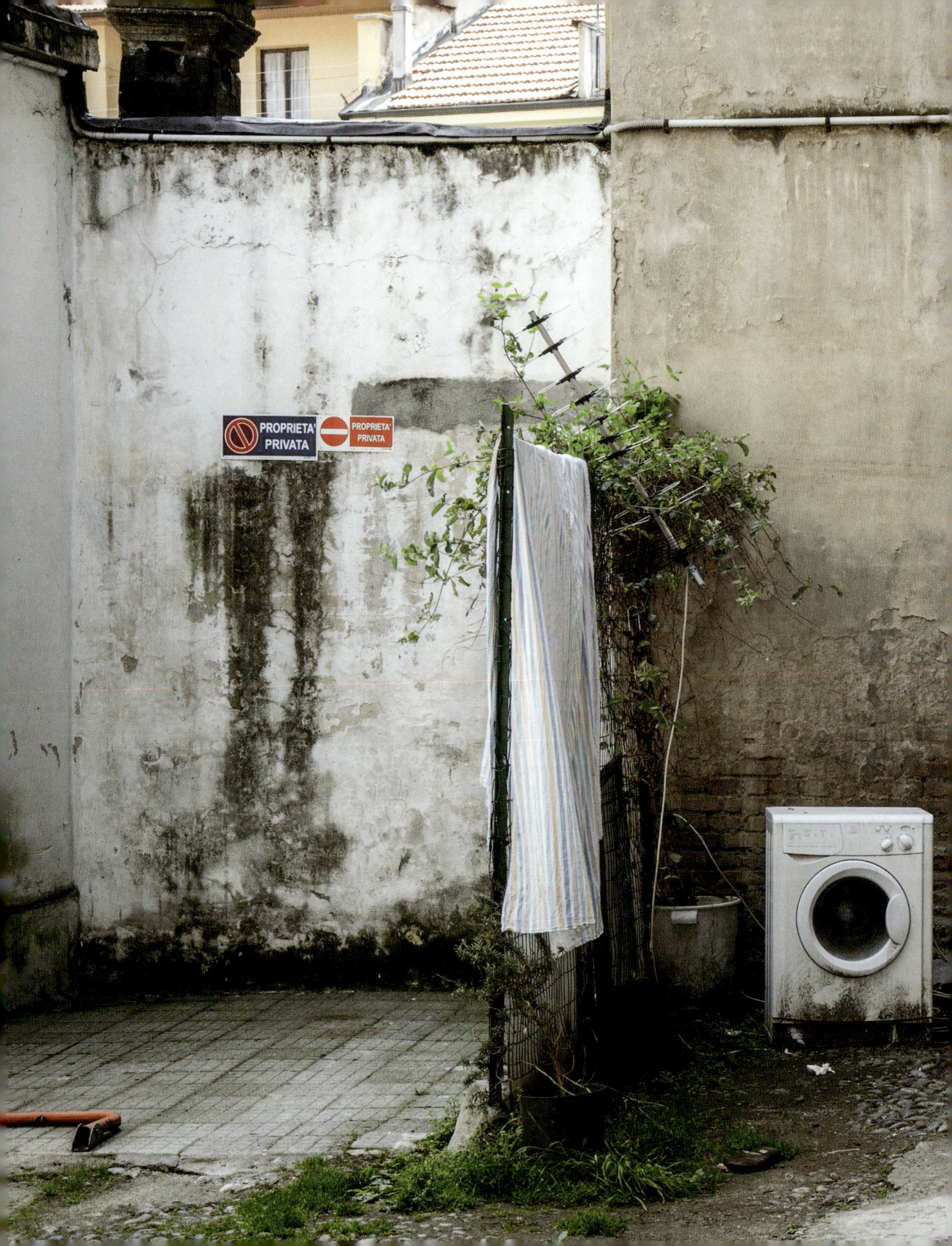
PROPRIETA'
PRIVATA
PROPRIETA'
PRIVATA

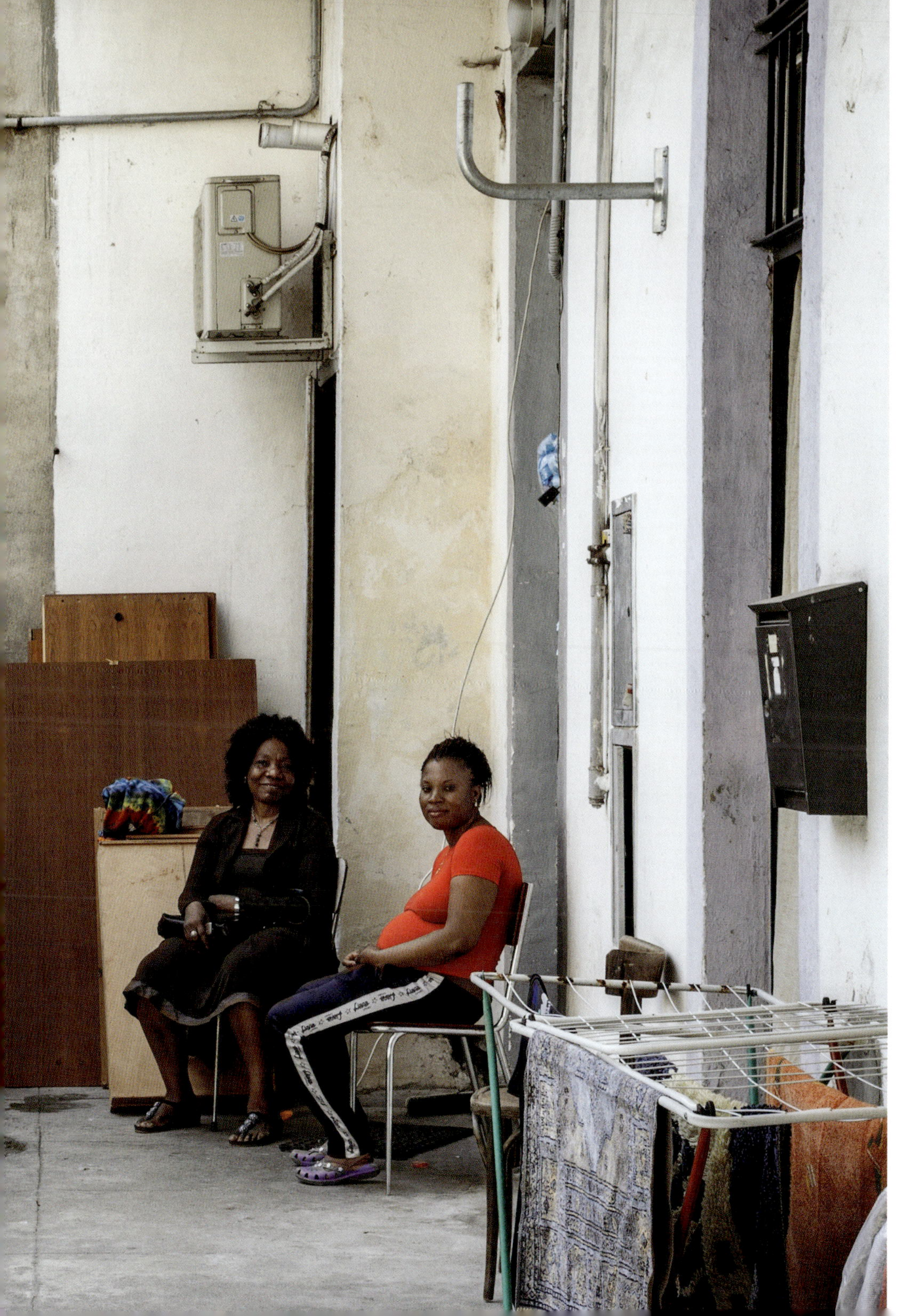

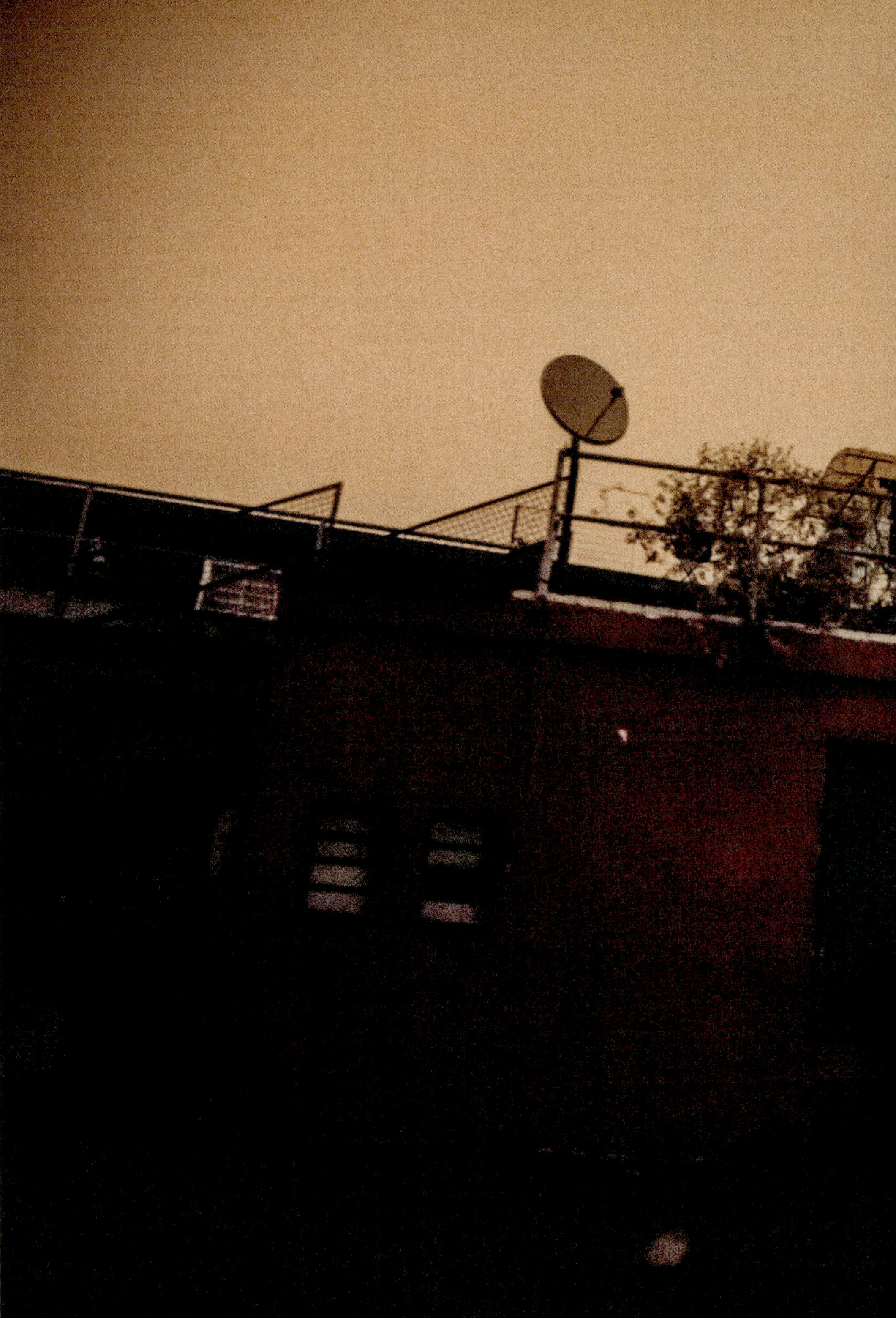

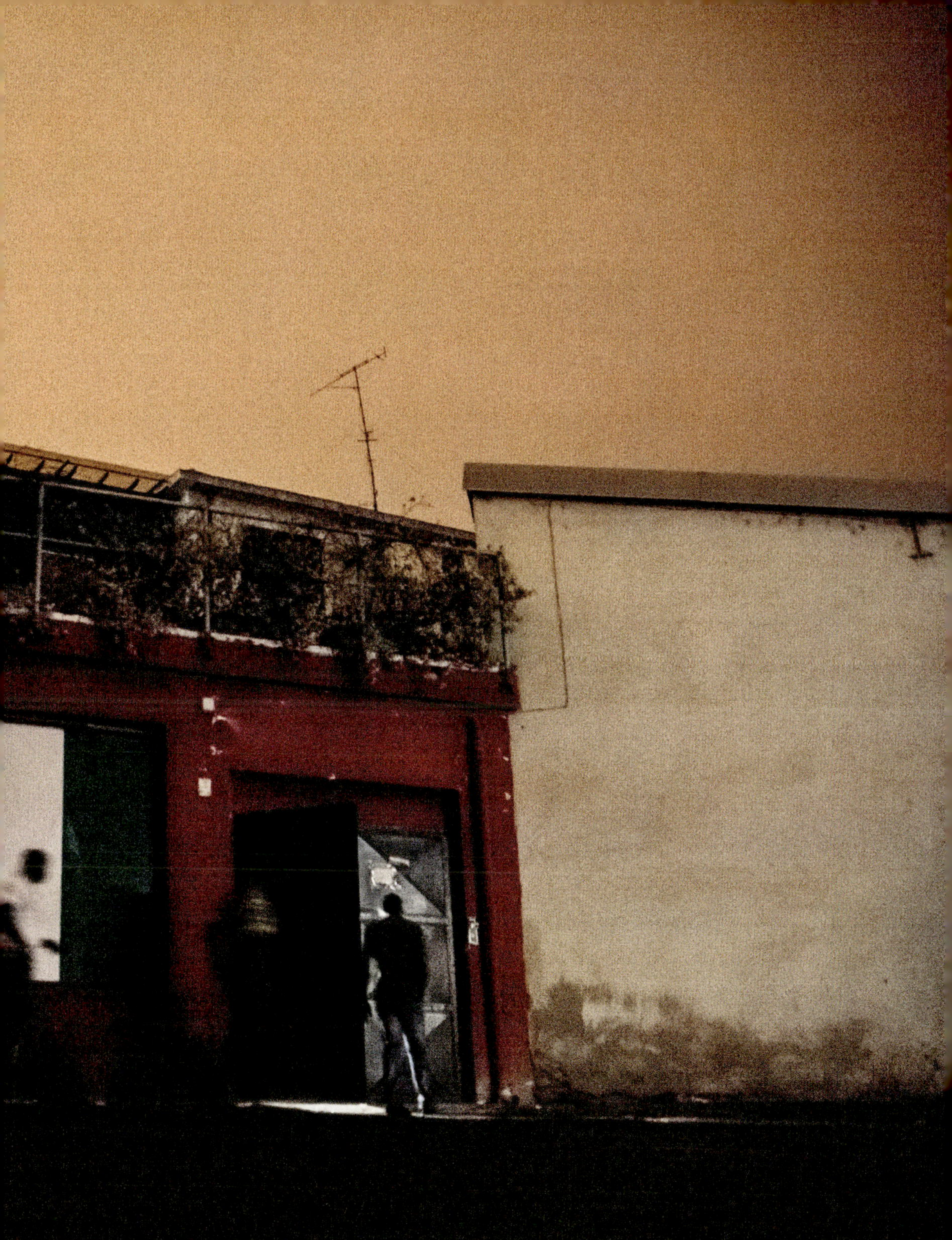

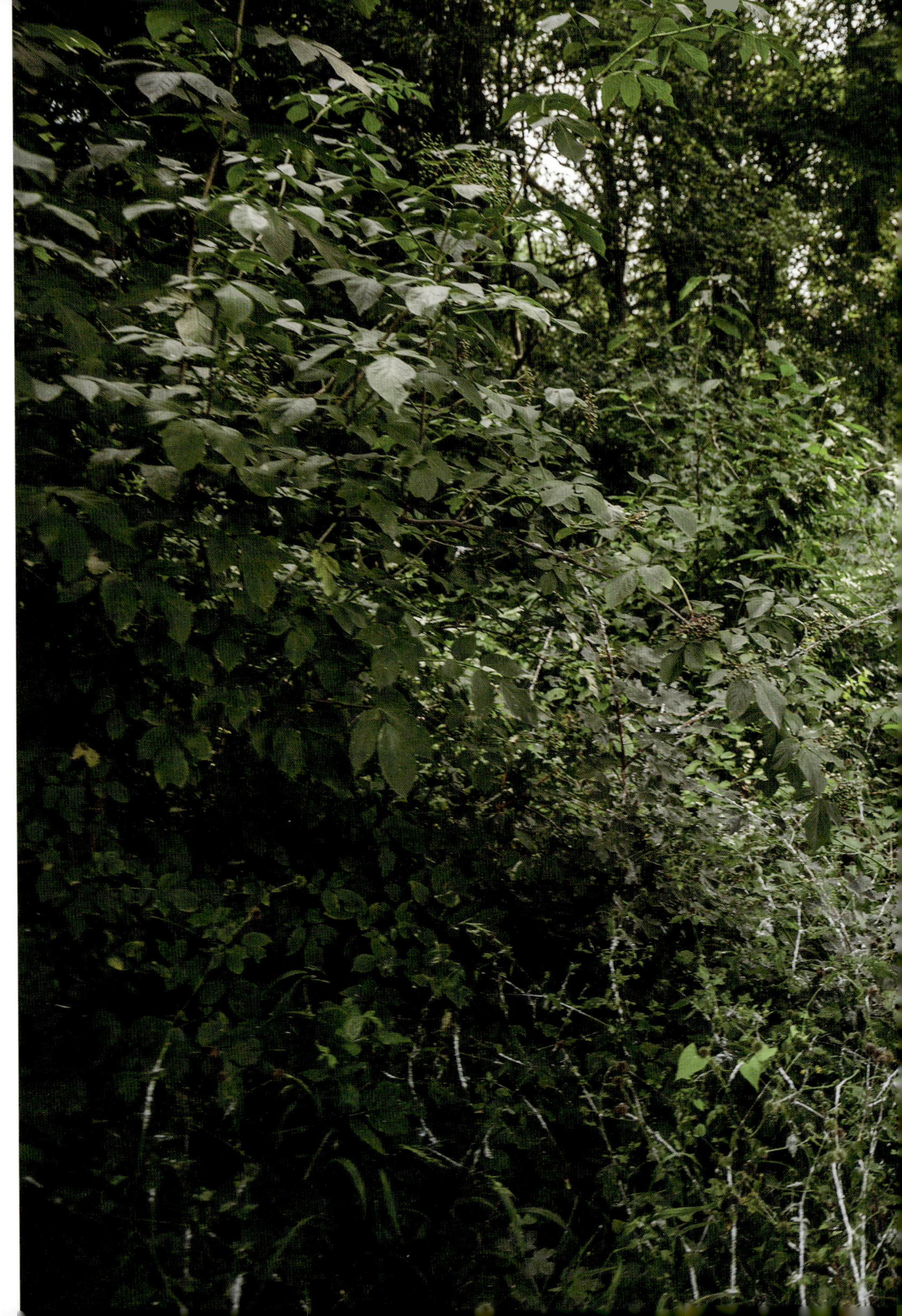

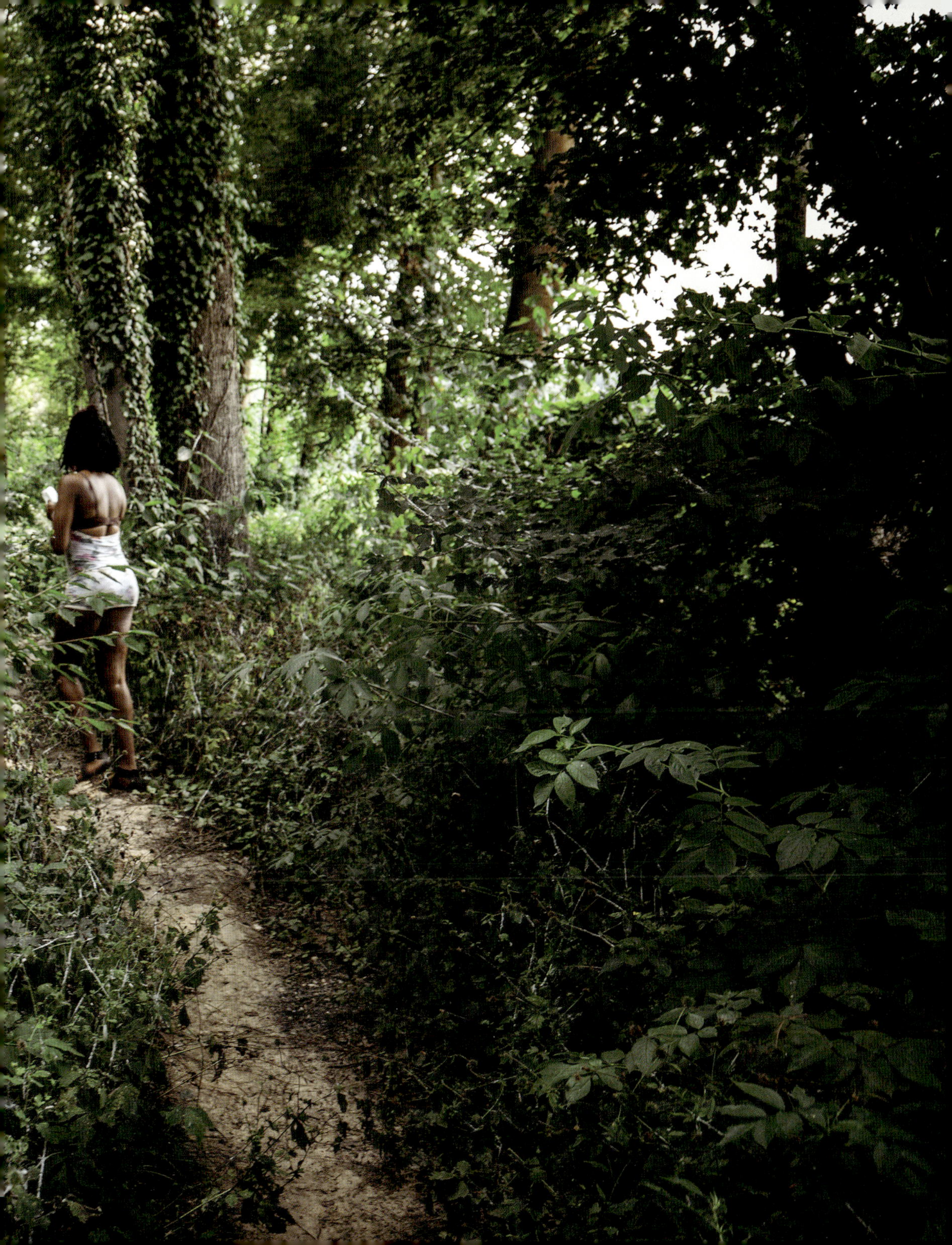

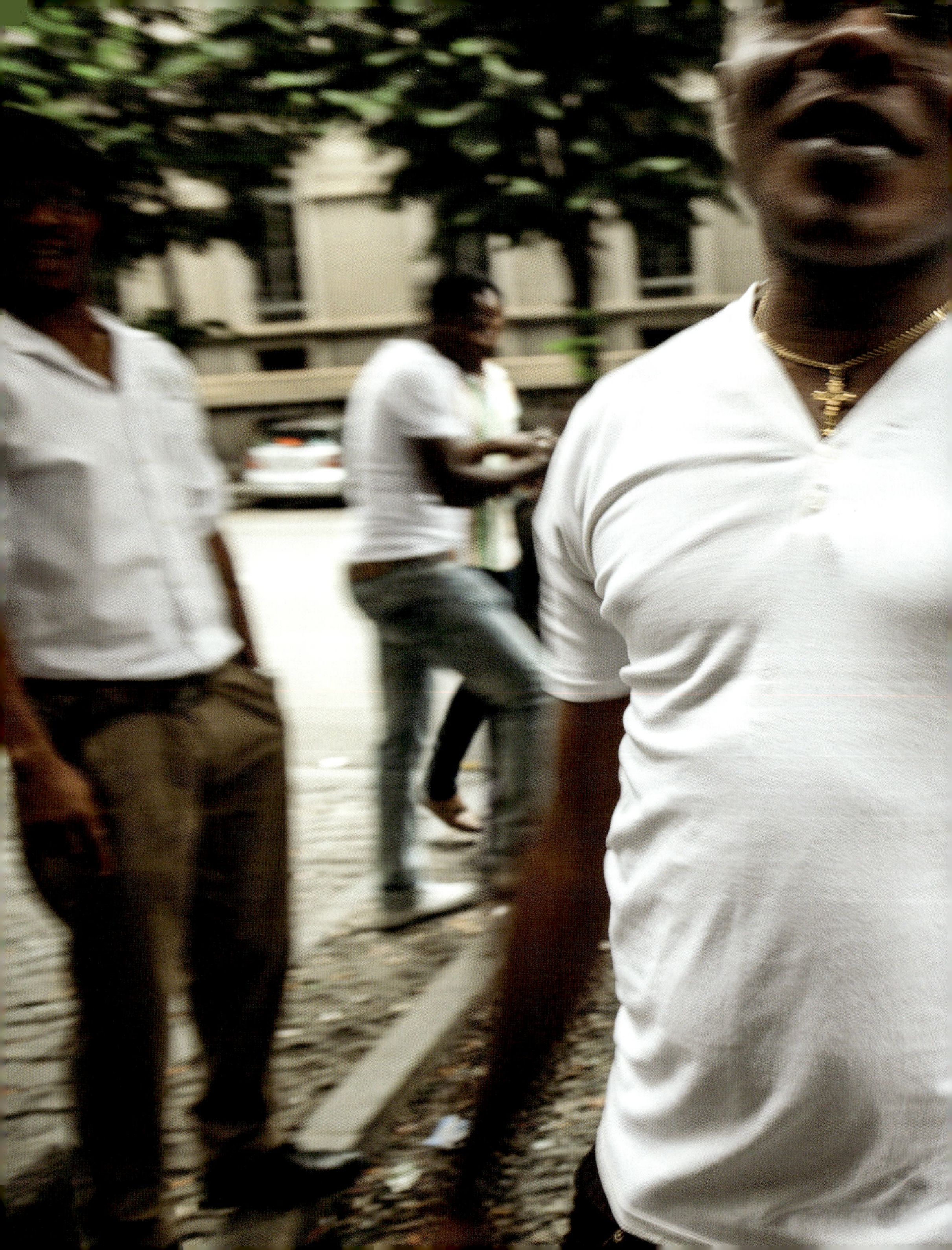

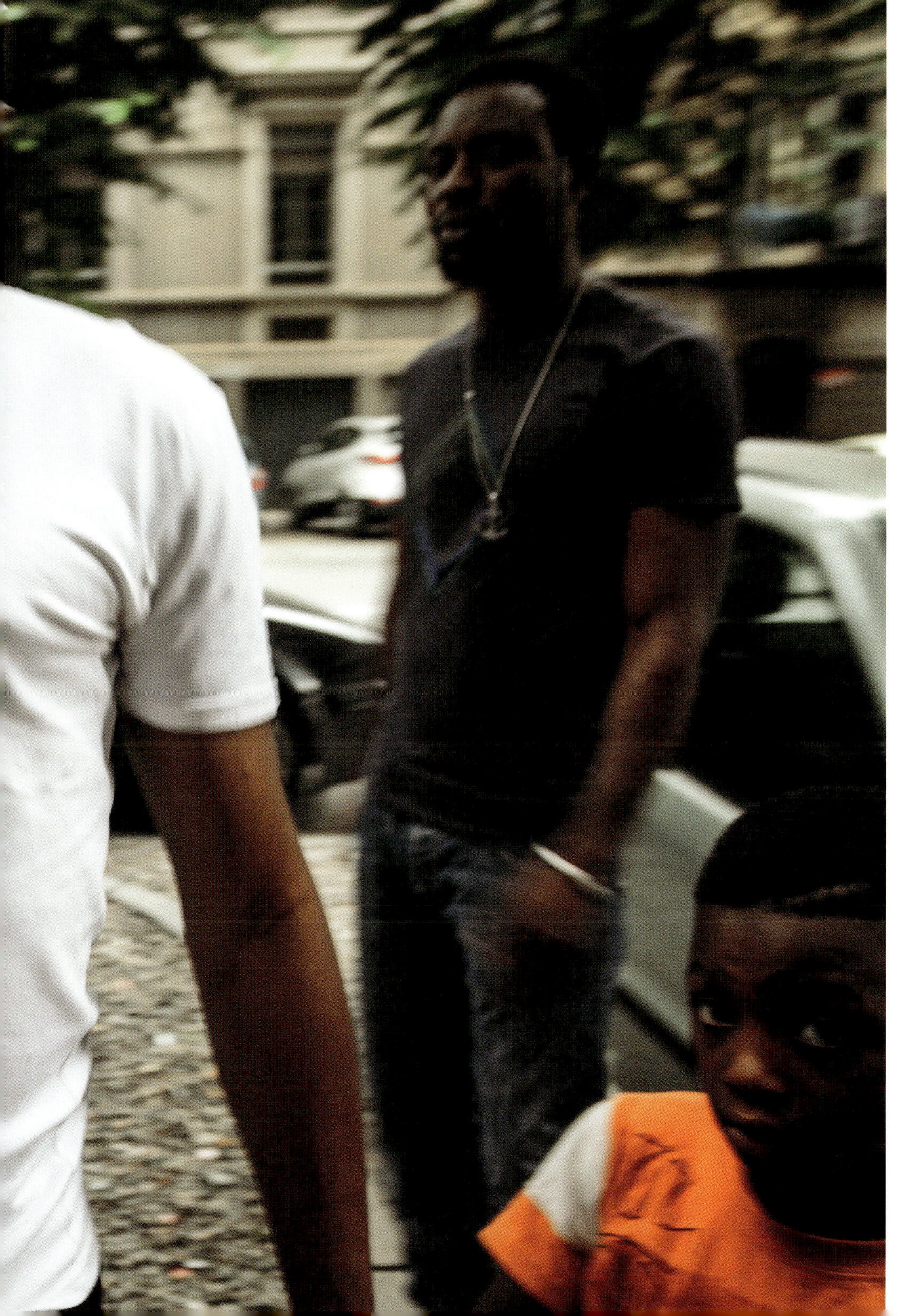

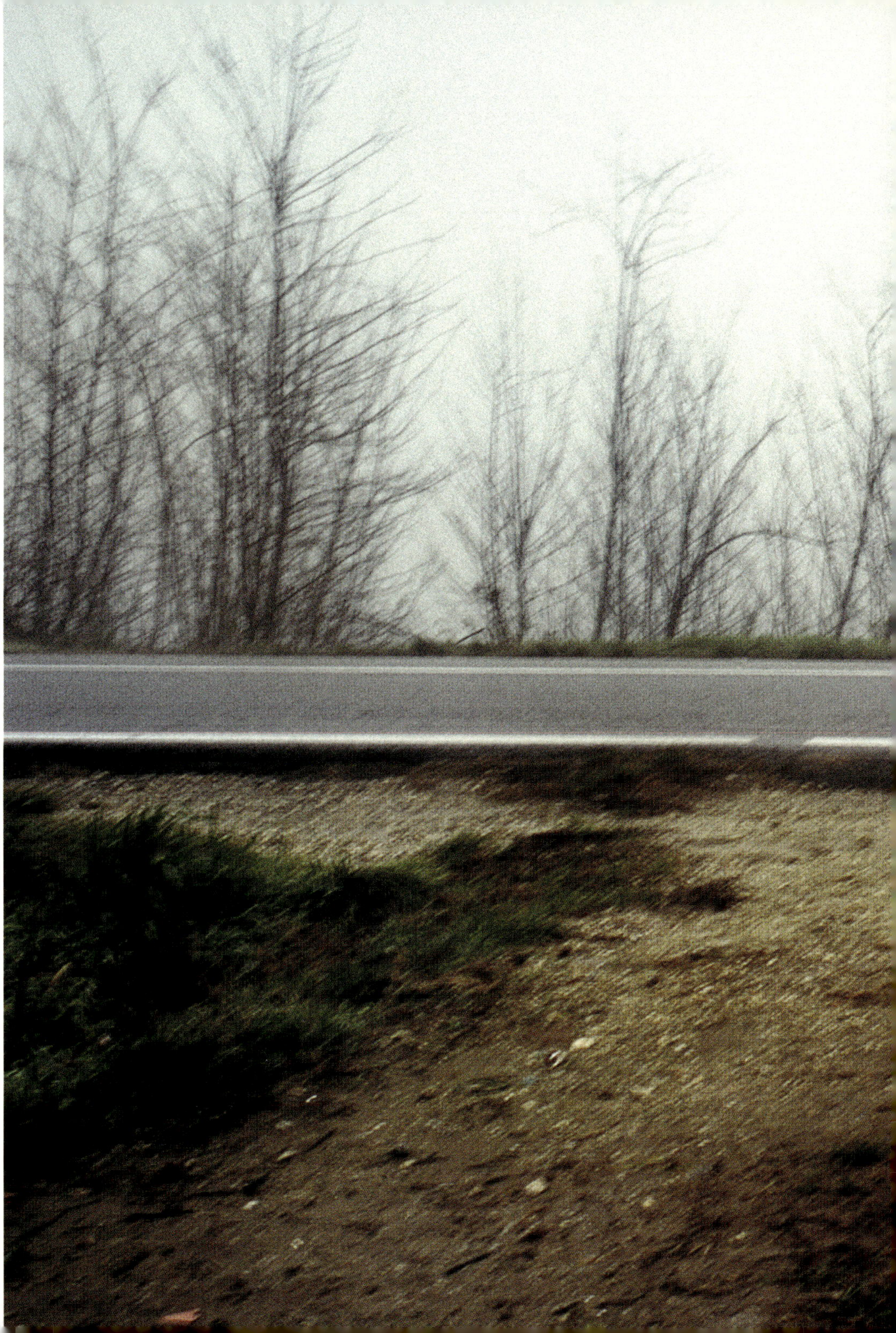

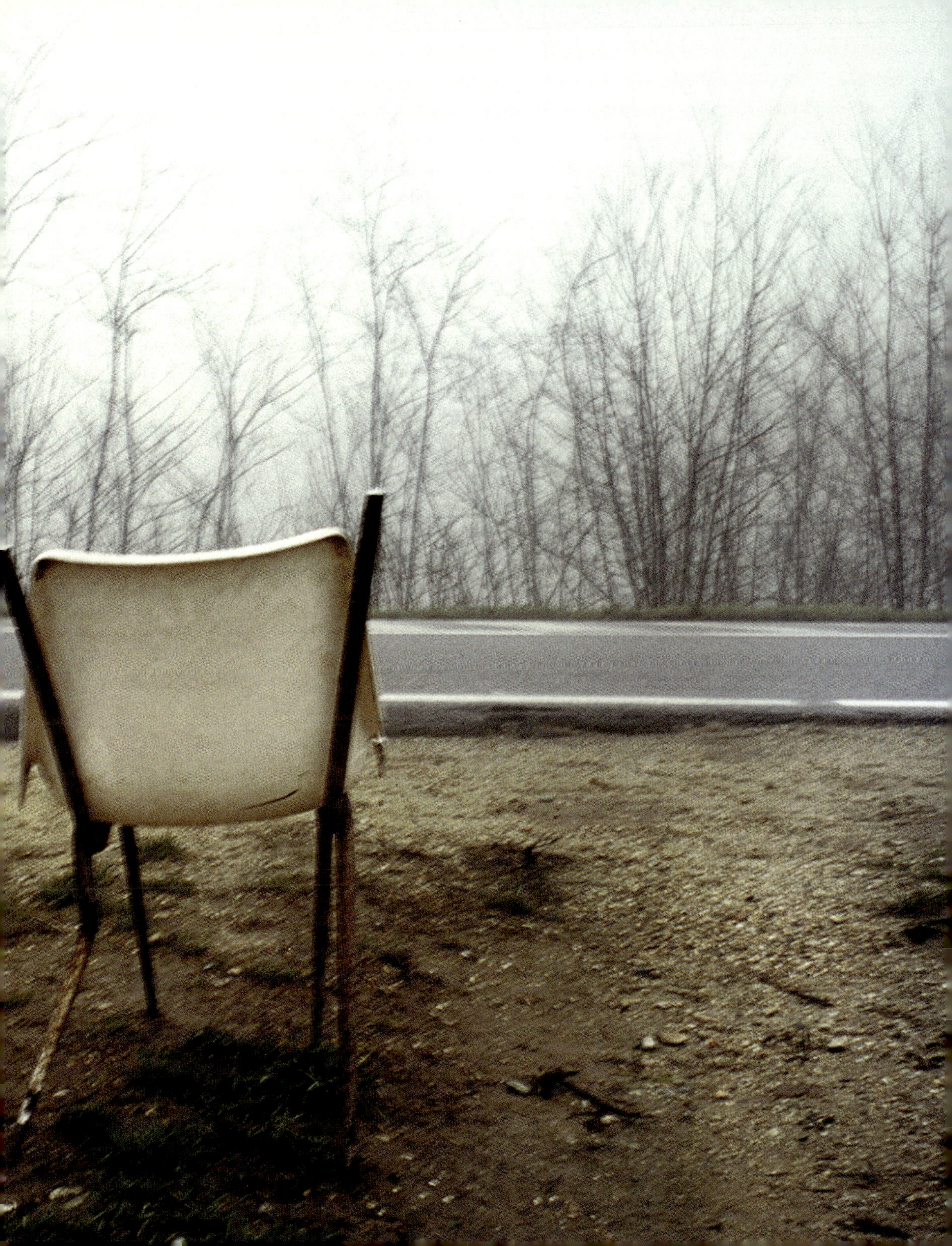

Part two

1.

On the outside I'm calm and composed and strong and I try to make
everything alright.
Inside nothing is alright, not even for me.
Inside, well, I'm full of anger.
And shame.
And guilt.
Because I am here and I'm alive.
Itohan and Izogìe and a thousand others are not.
[...] I'm no better than the others who are dead. Survival, in itself, is not
an absolute value.
[...] Listen: the girls from Benin City pay an incredibly high price to
survive, a higher price than the street and the beatings, the humiliation
and the solitude and the sense of shame: they are alive because they
have accepted the unacceptable. When they were told to shut up, they
kept silent, when they had to lie, they lied. They watched their girl-
friends bleed to death and they didn't go to the police, out of fear or out
of cowardice. They thought only of themselves, every last one of them;
and to save themselves they stole and they cheated and betrayed and
did things they never, ever would have thought themselves capable of.

2.

The only problem is where to begin.
From Osas, then. From Osas and her journey.
[...] She was eighteen or nineteen years old when she left. The journey
took two years. Two interminable years in the desert and the forests. [...]
Thirty of them left by ship from Lagos. They arrived in Morocco. There
the guides stuck them in an apartment to wait for another ship that
would take them to Italy.
Says Osas: we hardly ever slept, there were shifts for lying down on the
beds, an hour's sleep then it was back on your feet so that somebody
who was standing could lie down and sleep for an hour. This went on all
day long. They lived in the forest for months.
[...] When it rained they'd shelter by holding a sheet of plastic over their
heads, standing with their arms above their heads, and sometimes

they'd spend the whole night with their arms up; the whole night, with
the rain coming down around them. One morning one of the girls in
the middle was dead. Her arms were still up. She'd died standing next to
Osas and she hadn't fallen to the ground because everyone was
squashed together so tight trying to keep the rain off.
No-one had noticed.

[...] Then one day they left the forest and headed towards the desert. We
crossed the desert on foot, says Osas. [...] Sometimes the guides got hold
of a truck to carry them part of the way.
The trucks were always full to bursting point. Osas says that one time
when there was no more space they simply threw the extras over the
side and left them there in the middle of the desert, with no water, with
nothing. [...] And you leave them behind and head off along this road
through the desert and you see the white, white bones of people along
the sides of the track. You see bodies dried out by the sun.
Osas says: the only thought in your head is: I've got to keep going, I've
got to endure.
[...] But if you don't understand the anger and the fear and the anguish
of the journey you can't understand what it means to arrive. And if you
don't understand that, then you can't understand what the lives of us
girls who set out from Benin City are like, either.

3.
[...] Only when it became apparent that the girls were a profitable business did the whole mafia thing begin, the meticulous organisation, the
journeys planned very carefully so the merchandise arrives in the best
possible condition. That was when they began to involve the families in
the contracts, so they could exercise control at the point of origin.

4.
[...] The organisation goes to raise hell at your parents' place. [...] They
say: the girl must keep her side of the bargain or else you're in very deep
trouble, all of you.
It's a threat that always works, especially when it was the parents themselves who took the girls to the *Italos*, as in the last two or three years.
Little girls, thirteen and fourteen years old. [...]

So there's always somebody at the village festivals and the weddings
and the funerals filming girls, and then the mamans watch the films:
that one's too short, that one's too flat, that one's too old, that one, yeah,
just right. That little one there. She's the one I want.
And when the choice has been made, the sponsor goes to the family,
takes them gifts. [...] And the family almost always says yes. In fact, it's
the mothers and the fathers who take the initiative now, who take
their daughters to these people. They know that in that house over
there live the parents of a woman who takes girls to Europe, they've
seen the family buy themselves a car, buy themselves a house. So they
say: me too.
I think they know exactly what's going on.
These days, oh yes, they know.

5.
At a certain point you just have to resign yourself. You say: if I refuse,
they'll kill me, who knows what'll happen to me. And then you start
doing the sums. How much is the debt, how long will it take me to pay
it off, how can I pay it off as fast as possible? The debt is usually some-
where between thirty and sixty thousand euros.
[...] You pay to eat.
You pay for the revolting clothes you have to wear on the street.
You pay for heating separately, when it exists.
You pay for the electricity.
You pay rent on your piece of the pavement.
They practically make you pay for the air you breathe.
[...] When the *Italos* contact you they say ah, in a year you'll earn a hundred million naira. A crazy figure. They say: in a year or even in six
months, if you're quick, you can pay off the debt, then what you earn is
for you and your family. Right there before your eyes is the example of
the families who already have a girl in Europe. [...] Everybody's dream is
to own a Mercedes, the white one with the long bonnet, that here in
Europe you never see anymore. When money arrives for the family it's
the first thing they buy, if possible with air conditioning and fake leop-
ard-skin seats, and when they drive through the villages, little barefoot-
ed kids run after them.
A hundred million naira in one year.

How much is that in dollars, how much is that in euros?
How many clients.

6.
[...] Don't think the girls are friends, just because they're all in the same
boatful of misery. Forget it. The maman doesn't want any friendships
developing in the house, because that's the beginning of dangerous
solidarity. Of a potential rebellion. In the house you can never talk,
because she has ears everywhere. You can never trust anybody, not even
your roommate, because she may be deliberately inviting confidences
so she can go and inform on you to the maman. That way she gets
better treatment.
[...] The girls from Benin City never eat Italian things, no-one ever
teaches them how to. [...]
So in their little Italian rooms, when they get back from work they
continue to eat exactly the same way they would if they were in Nigeria. They eat rice with chicken and vegetables, fish, meat and tomato
stew, white rice boiled with salt, bran/semolina, peanut butter/sauce.
All cooked exactly the way they're cooked in Africa. And so there's a
market which brings these things into Italy, a market run by the
Chinese, who bring the products in via London. Of course they charge
incredibly high prices.
[...] They're living in Europe but it's as if they were still in Africa.
They call the maman by name, or else Sister. Momi. Mamma.
She is the absolute boss of this little closed community that has no
contact with the outside world. And woe betide anyone who gets out
of line. [...]
The ones who don't believe in voodoo maybe go to church. Not the
Catholic Church, though. In Nigeria there are stacks of Christian
churches, Pentecostalian, Evangelical; the Adventist church run by an
American preacher is also starting to catch on. And in Italy the girls
go to these churches organised especially for Africans. It's their only
distraction from the terrible life they lead. They meet two or three
times a week, Wednesday, Friday and then on Sunday, when there's a
service that lasts practically all day. They dance, they eat, on feast
days a hundred, even two hundred people may turn up, sometimes
even more.

The pastor is hardly ever a real pastor. To be a pastor in Africa all you need is a Bible; if you decide you're a man of God who's going to stop you?
And Europe is full of pastors like that.
Obviously the pastor is always in league with the maman.

8.
[...] You see, every night the girls go to work and in their heads there are only two thoughts. The first is: maybe tonight's the night I'll meet somebody who will help me. The other is: let's hope tonight nothing happens to me.
But to one or another something is going to happen. Always.

9.
[...]
As for gang rapes. They happen. Often.
[...] I can tell you this: the first rape is the hardest to get over.
But you console yourself by saying: I thought I was going to die, but I'm still alive.
The second time you're raped you say: it happens.
The third time you say: it's normal.
After the fourth you stop counting.

10.
[...] Getting used to that kind of life is impossible.
And yet you get used to it.
You start having a little money, you buy yourself a pair of shoes or a phone card for the mobile. A dress. An ice-cream. And when the maman sees that you're starting to get a taste for money she knows the worst is over, at least for her. She looks at the first pair of shoes, the first dress.
She says: Good girl.
And meanwhile she's thinking: it's done.
The families are pleased, too.
And they spend the first money that arrives from Italy straightaway, so they can show people they've turned the corner. They buy a car. A fridge. A television. They buy clothes and shoes and go around so dolled up you wouldn't even recognise them.

The money from Europe disappears in a flash, as if they'd burnt it.
Nobody puts any money aside.
[...] The girls say, that's it, I'm not sending any more money.
And so they start to phone saying your father is ill, your brother has a
hernia, you sister has cancer. Your mother's in hospital and needs an
operation. Your son is dying. Send money.
[...] In Benin no-one ever asks you: but how did you make all this money.
The important thing is that you keep the family, buy the car, give them
the money for a house. That's all fine. [...] But if that same girl who was
everybody's little shining star comes home forcibly repatriated, then the
family says: what have you done. You've brought shame on us. What are
we going to do with you?
And they immediately start looking for another journey to send her
back to Europe.
[...] The whole economy of the city is based on money from Europe,
all the businesses, the taxis, the hire scooters, the construction, the
schools, everything is based on money sent through Western Union.
But when the King of Benin makes his speech every year to Nigerians
overseas, he never ever mentions the girls.

12.
[...] To come to Italy they give you false papers for the journey, and if
they take them off you after you arrive, you find a way to get hold of
others. There are stacks of that stuff around; you just have to pay for it.
Passports, residence permits, papers that sometimes aren't exactly false,
but a few things have been changed here and there. There might be a
name and a surname you share with two or three other girls some-
where in Italy, and only one has the real document, and she may be the
one who sold it. The others have a copy. It usually works fairly well, at
least to a superficial glance. And having them means you're less anxious
when you're working.
[...] You end up living a double life, you become two different people,
and you no longer know which is which. Who something is happen-
ing to, and who is doing what. I think it's also a way of controlling
you, by stripping you of your name and your identity. A way of taking
everything from you. Of reducing you to a piece of meat for the
street. [...]

15.
But the girls, you say, don't they ever laugh?
Sure they do.
They laugh at the clients.
 The funny-looking ones.
The odd ones.
The ones who have no idea what to do with a woman.
A lot of them come to the street, especially the young ones. They don't
know a thing and you have to do it all for them.

16.
[...] The client doesn't always or only want sex.
On the contrary, sometimes sex is the last thing he's interested in.
And once you realise that, you're home and dry.
A lot of clients come to the street just so they can tell someone their
problems. They want company. They want to pour their hearts out to
somebody. They want to talk and to ask questions.
[...] And these love stories sometimes even end in marriage.
There are also the stories of the girls who take advantage, though, who
marry only for the papers and then continue living the same life as
before, with the difference that now they no longer have to worry about
being illegal.

19.
In other words, it's not easy to get out of the scene.
A lot of girls no longer work on the street, but the street continues to be
their point of reference. Their friendships are all there. They haven't
settled in here, in any sense. They live in Italy but keep on living their
African lives, no regular hours, living in the here and now. They have
relationships with Italian men, but instead of those men helping the
girls become more Italian, the men become more African. [...]

20.
So, if you talk with the girls and you ask: what do you want? What do
you need? They'll tell you one thing only: papers.
Without papers you can't do anything, you can only stay on the street
and whore for a living.

21.
You say: you can report it to the police.
But a lot of women can't.
Think of Osas, whose brothers were kidnapped just because she
couldn't stand it on the street anymore.
[...] What's more, the girls don't like entering a rehab community.
After years of slavery they can't stand rules, and impositions, and prohi-
bitions anymore.
They say: we're already prisoners, we don't want to go to another jail.
[...] The client, like it or not, is often the only resource we girls have.

23.
This is a very sad ending, where justice doesn't triumph and innocence
is not rewarded [...]. And, moreover, the victim turns into an execution-
er.
But what can we do about it?
Everybody would like the victims to always be good, always be saintly,
innocent little lambs, meekly deserving of our most earnest compas-
sion.
Instead, well, you've seen it for yourself. The girls from Benin City don't
want to know about sainthood.
They're ordinary people.
Good and bad.
Loyal and dishonest.
Sometimes even hypocritical, lazy, and cruel.
There are also the girls who steal and who lie, who deal drugs and laugh
about it, who've made a kind of flag out of their lives on the outside.
They no longer look for pity nor want to be redeemed.
They want only the maximum for themselves, whatever it costs.
Telling you about it, I feel ill at ease.
[...] Life on the street is violent, I've already told you that. But often the
girls themselves become violent. They beat each other up. A lot of them
beat up the clients, too.
[...] You have to think of it as a parallel world.
Submerged, indeterminate, where anger is the rule, anger and igno-
rance. Where nothing is ever certain, anything is possible, where
everyone is the aunt or the niece or the cousin of somebody else. And

they wheel and deal and sort each other out, and in the end they go
around with each other's papers, and then say she's my sister or my
aunt, even if it isn't true [...]
They all live this way, ripping off the Italian boyfriend for a while until
he dumps her, working the street for a while, ripping off the roommate
who then in turn starts ripping her off, and so on and so on and so on, a
thousand times over. Always chasing that one mirage, of getting rich
and going back to the village as a madonna. Always looking for the big
break, they can strip off everything he has and more. [...]
Thinking only of today, or at most, tomorrow.
For them the day after tomorrow is already inconceivable.
It's a kind of self-segregation, you see.
A way of saying to the whites who reject them: we're rejecting you,
now.

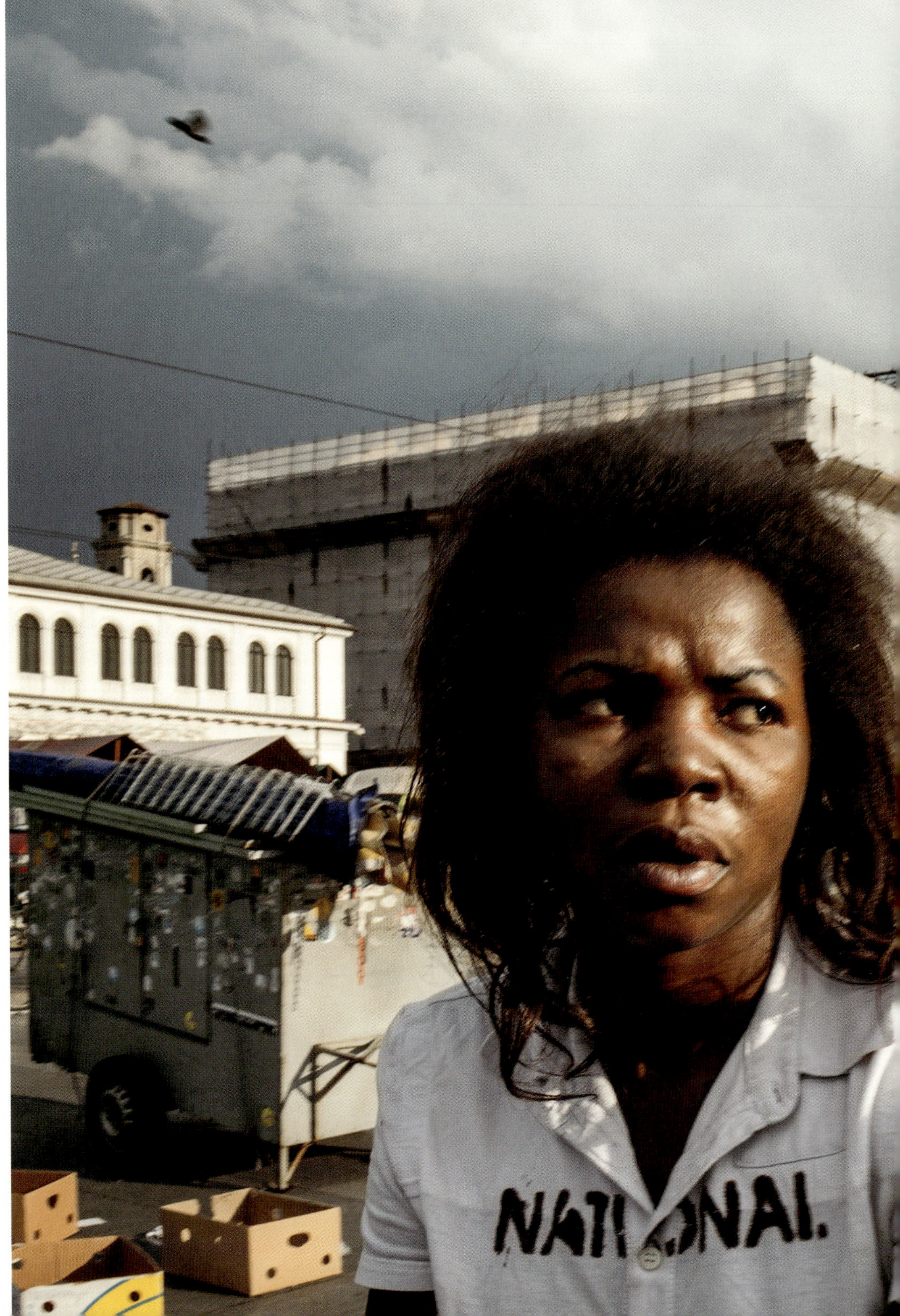
NATIONAL

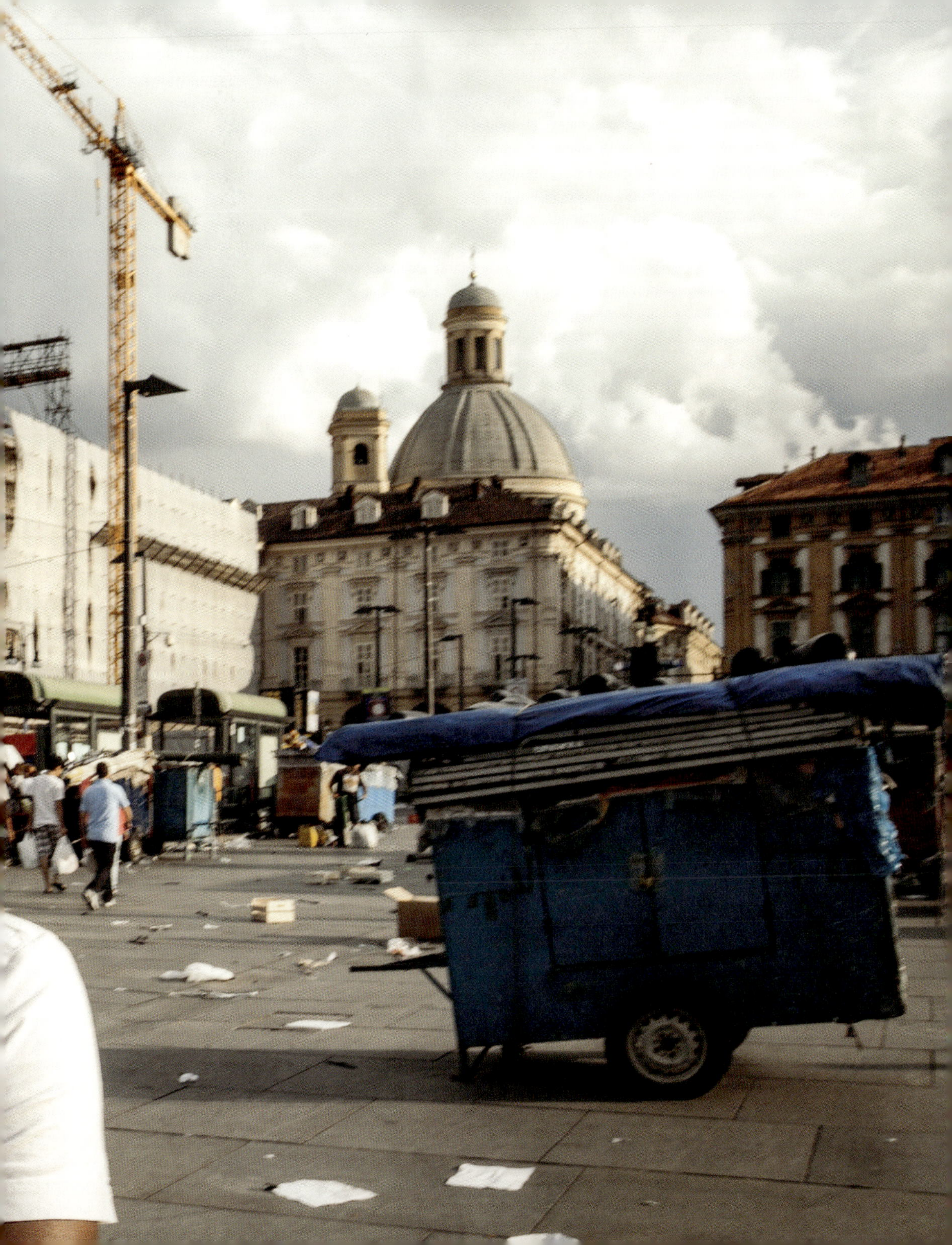

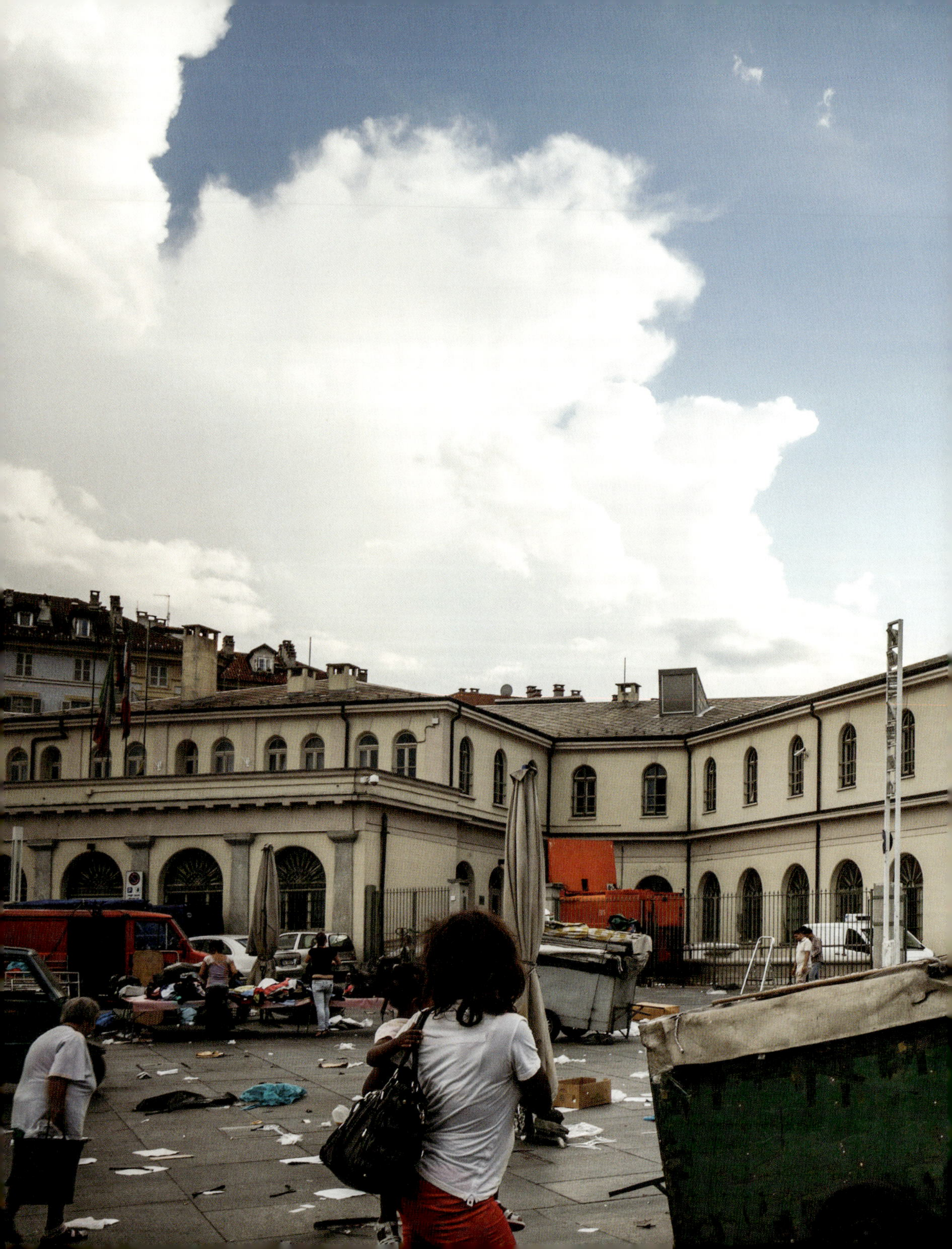

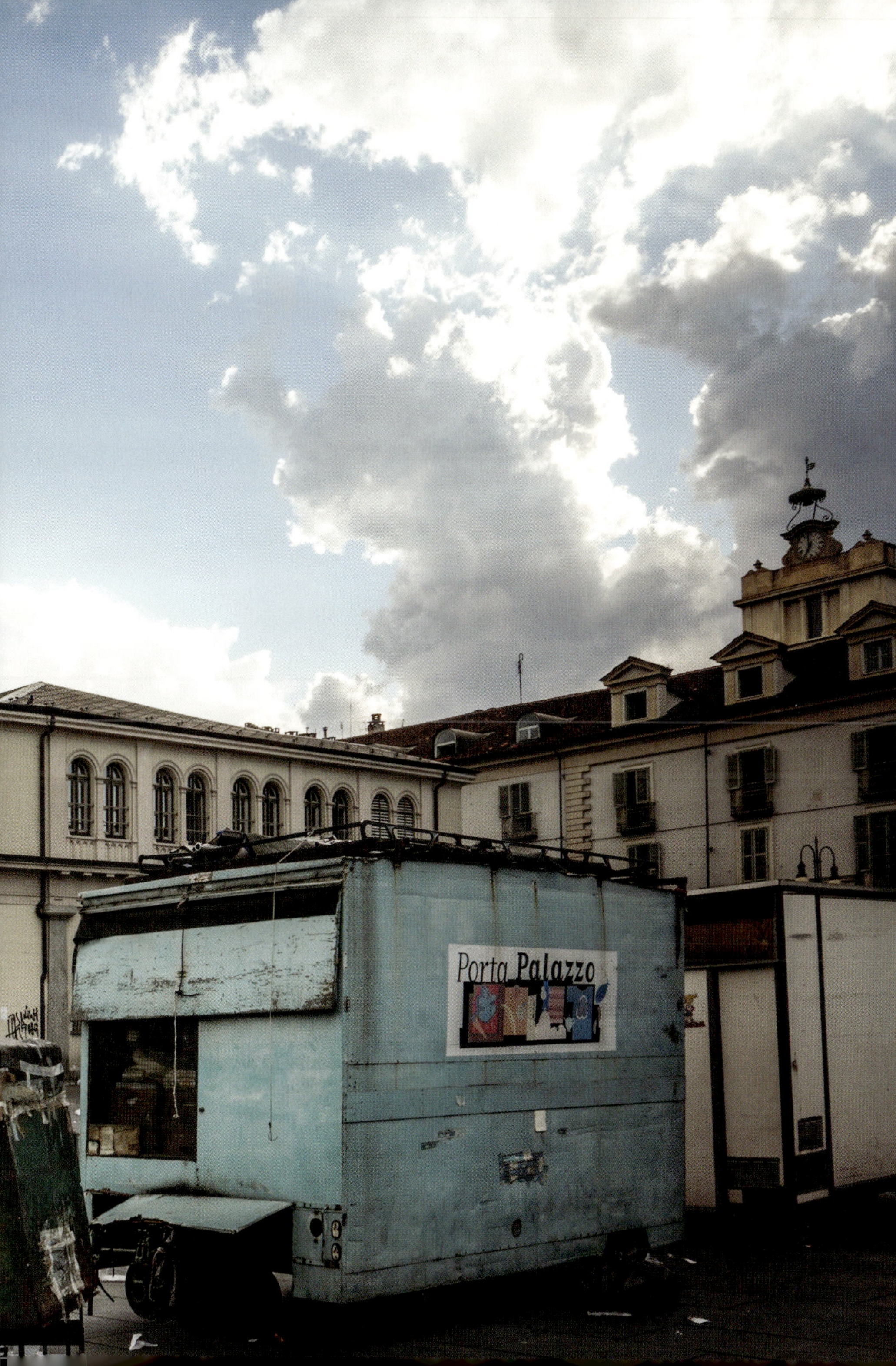
Porta Palazzo

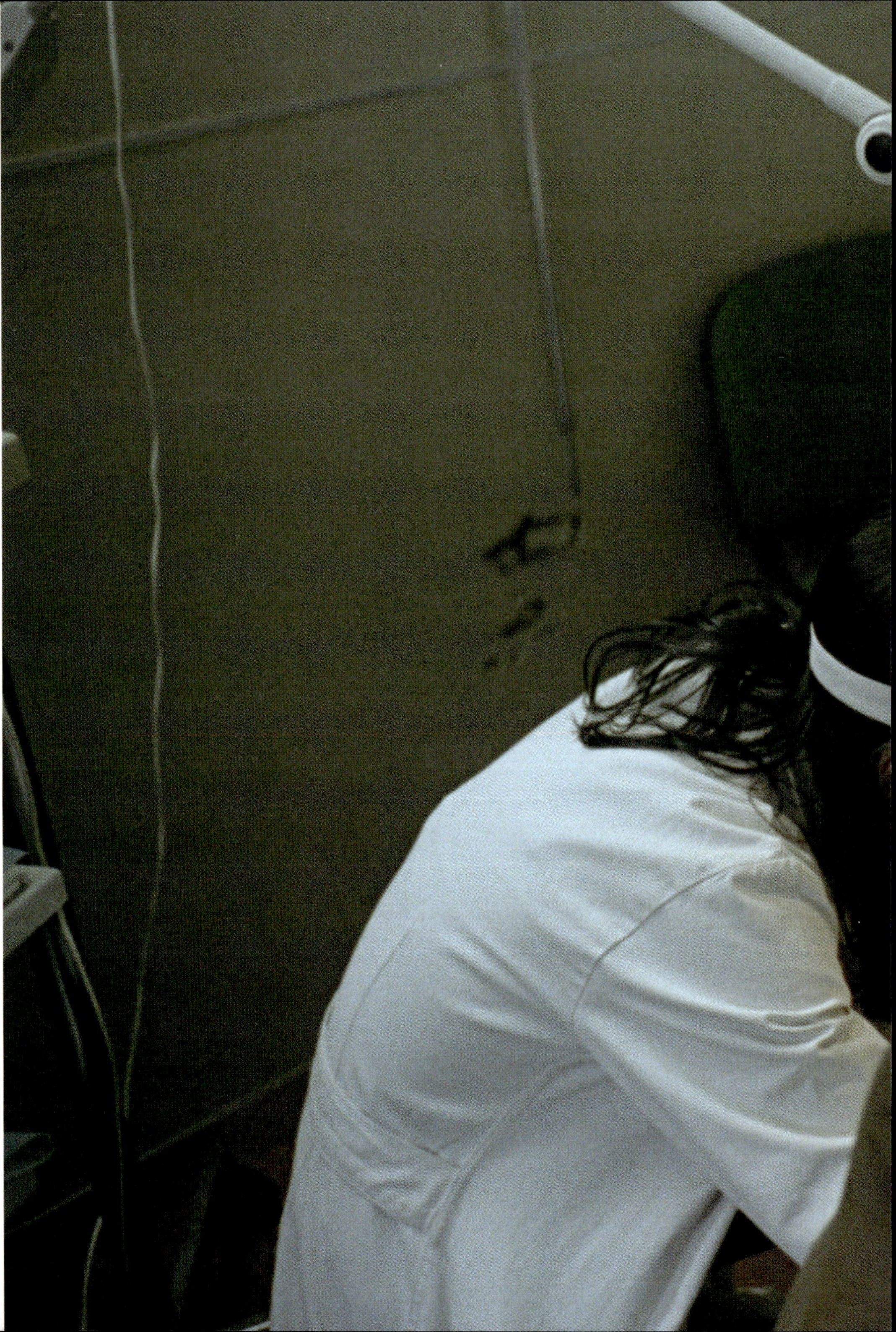

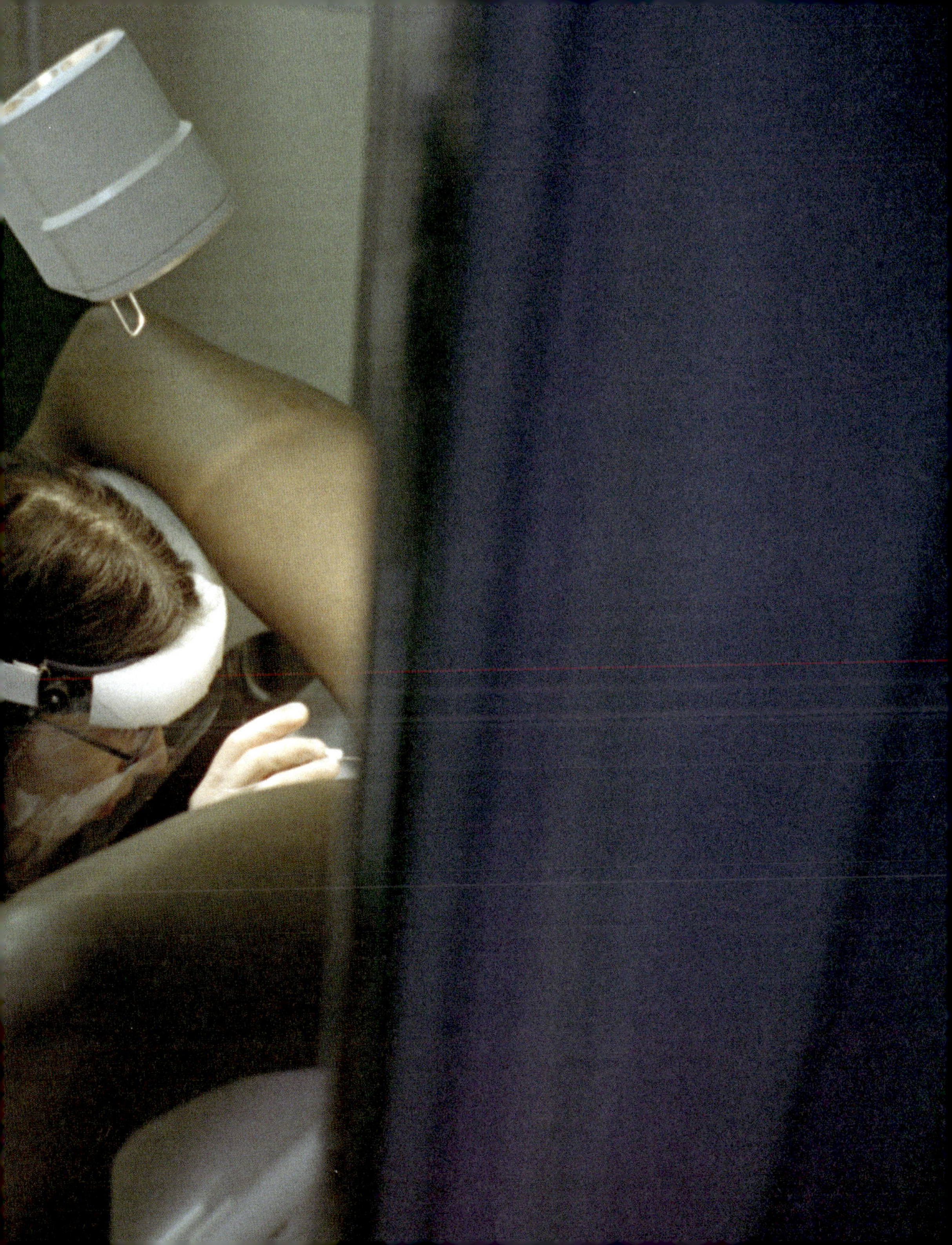

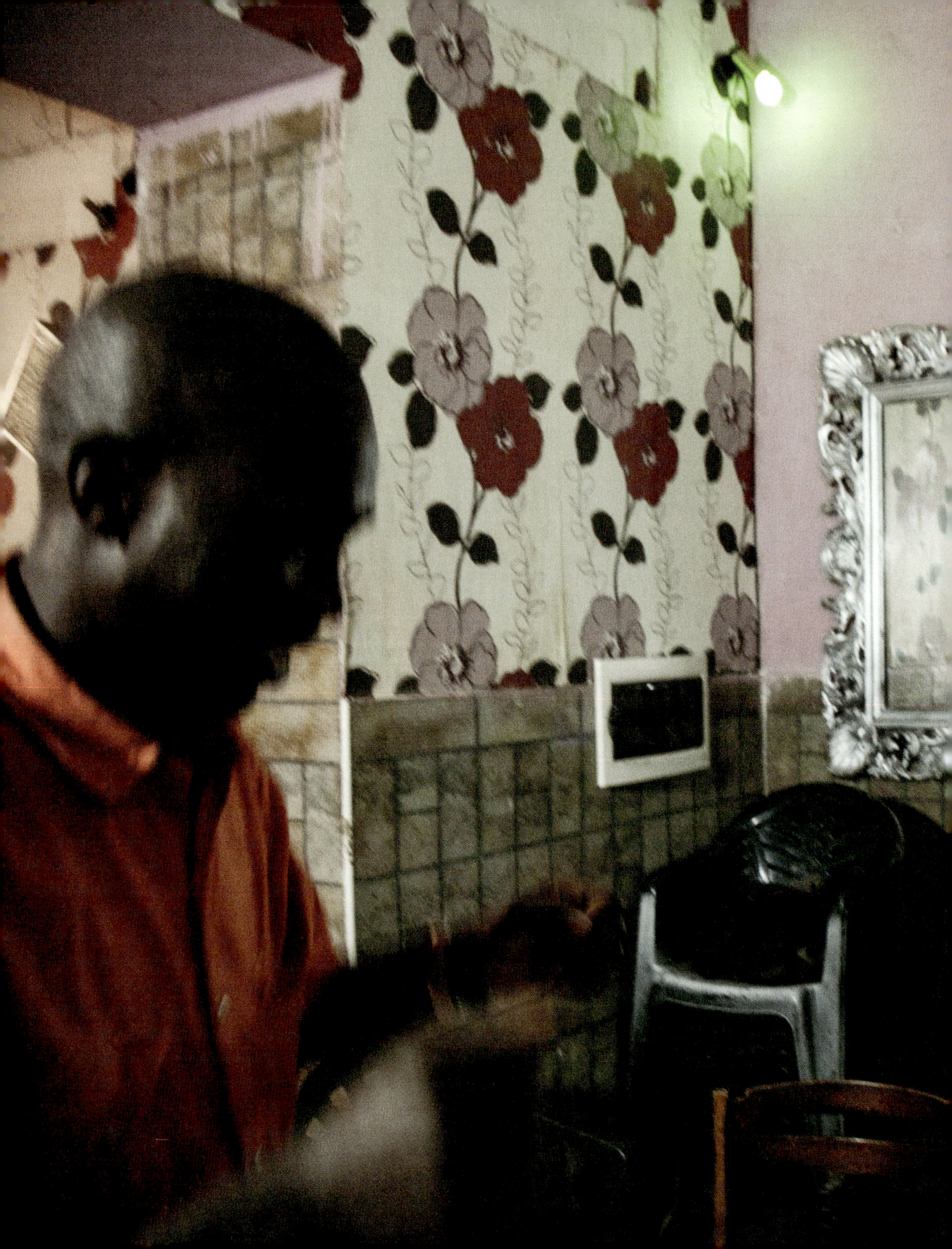

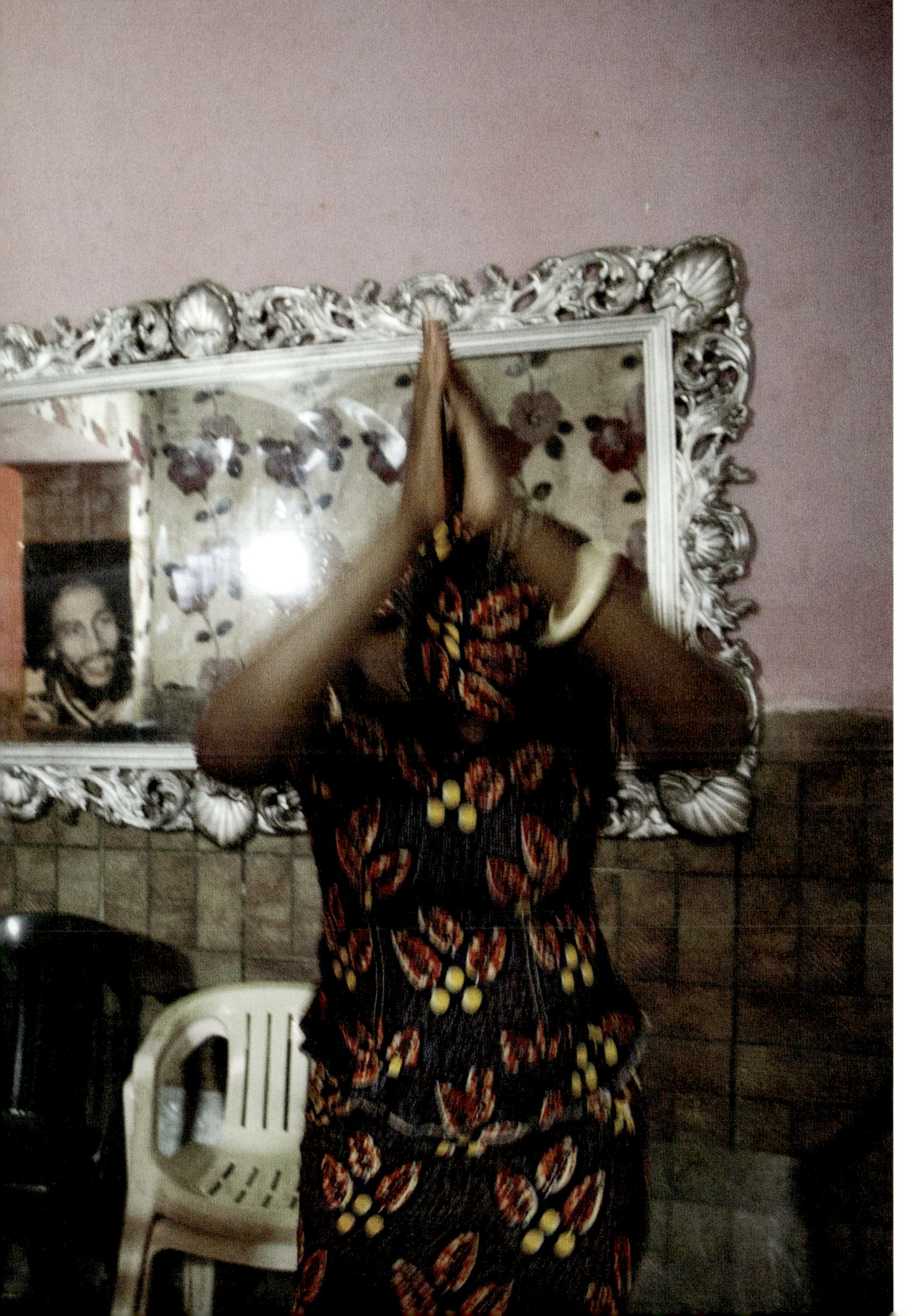

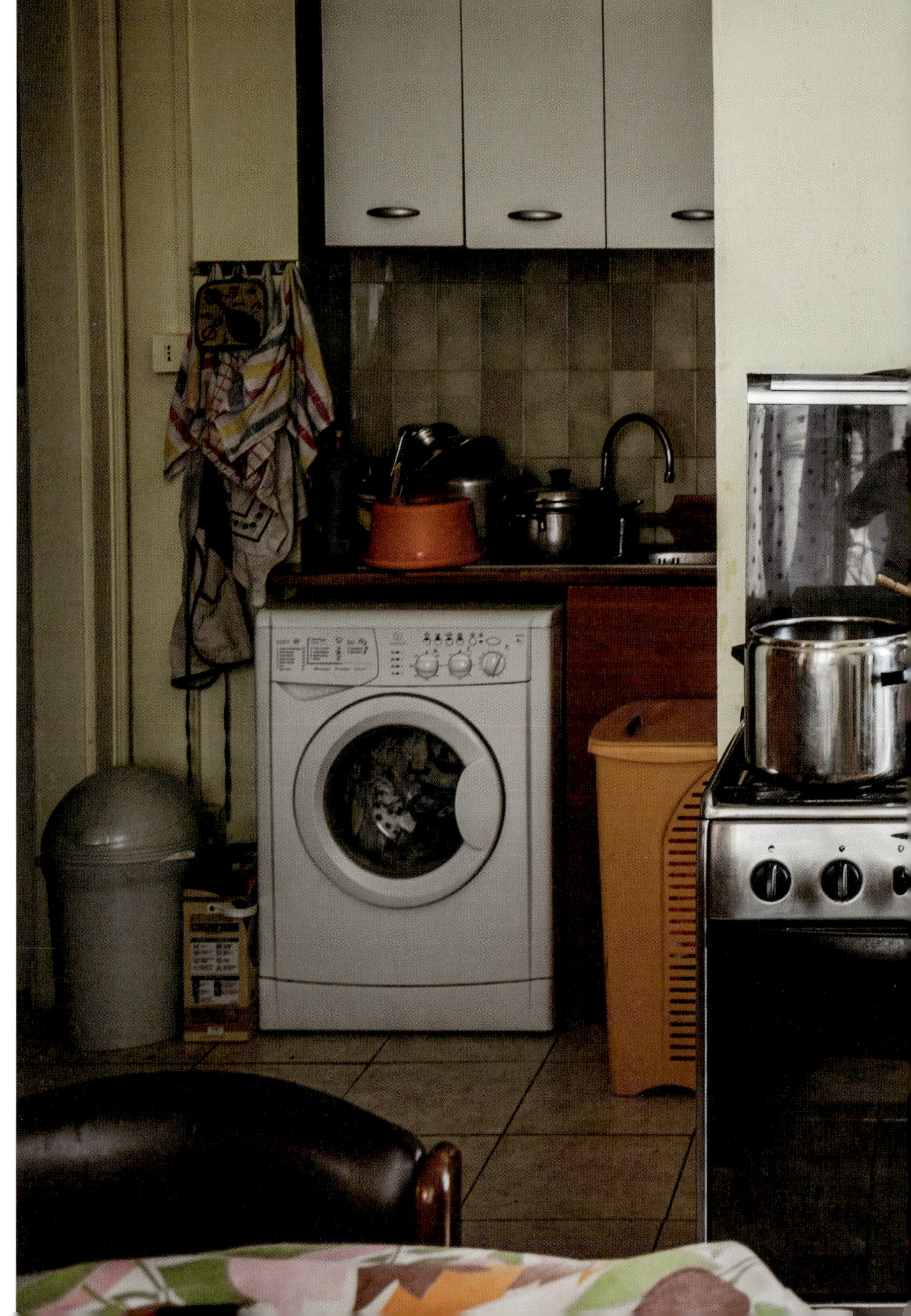

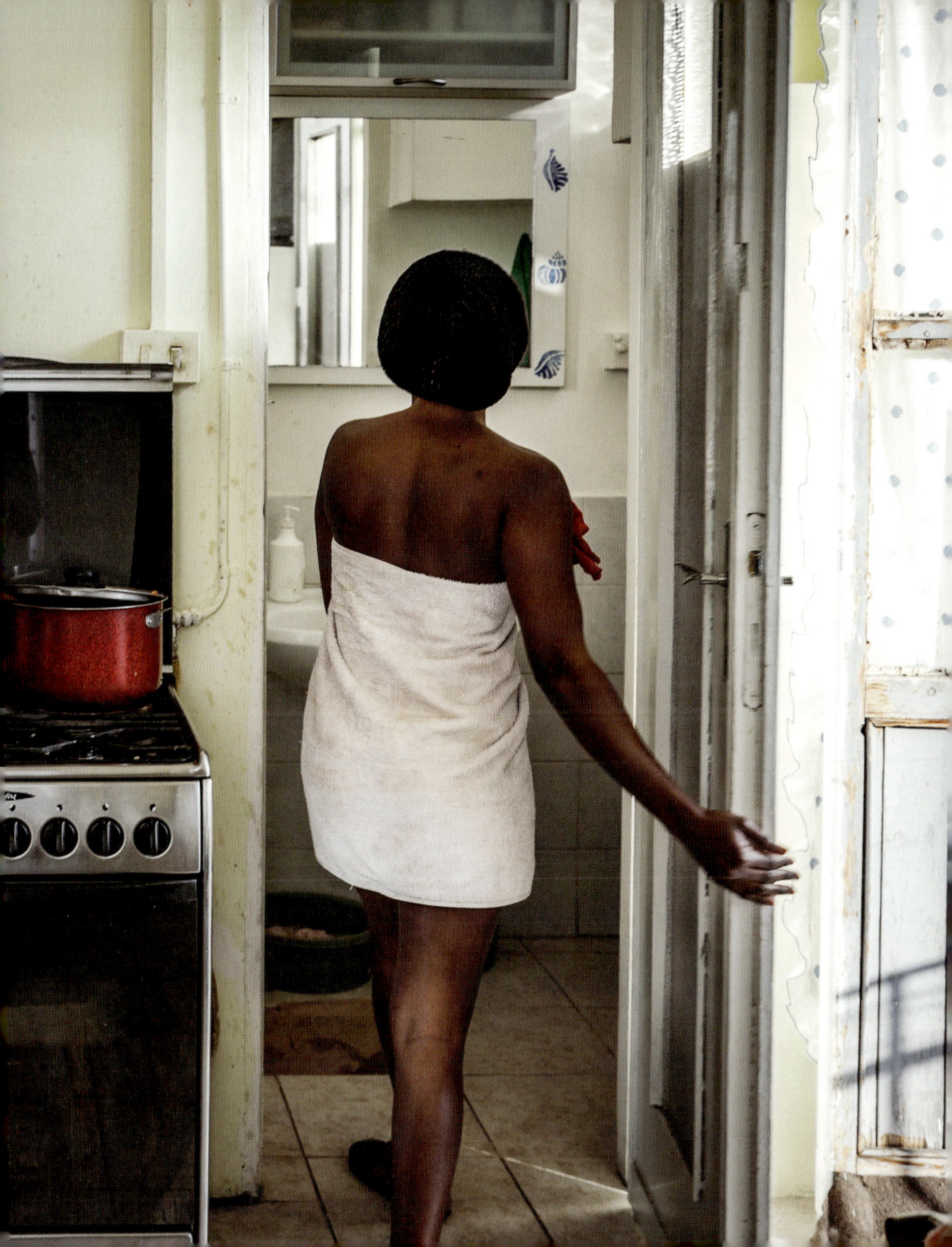

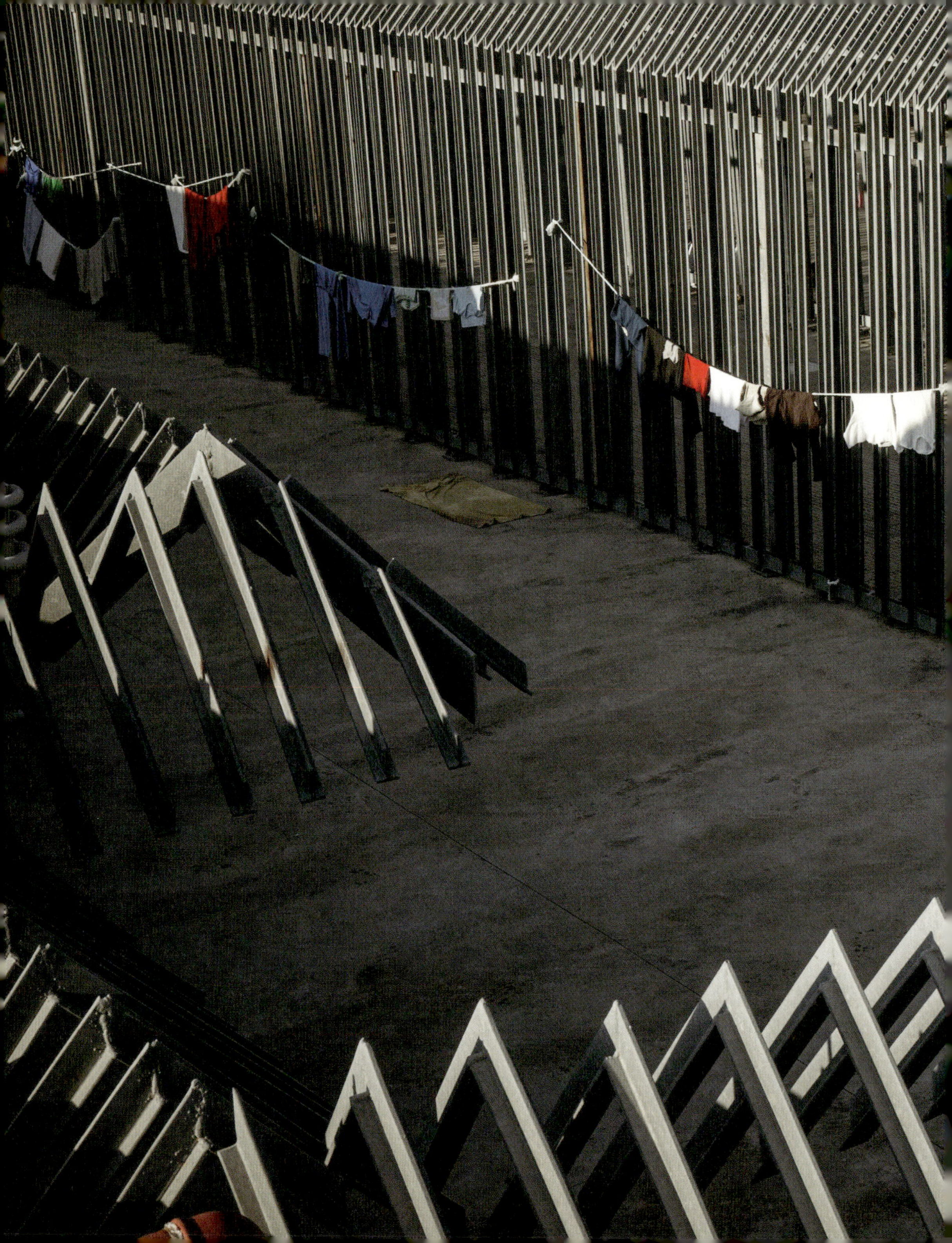

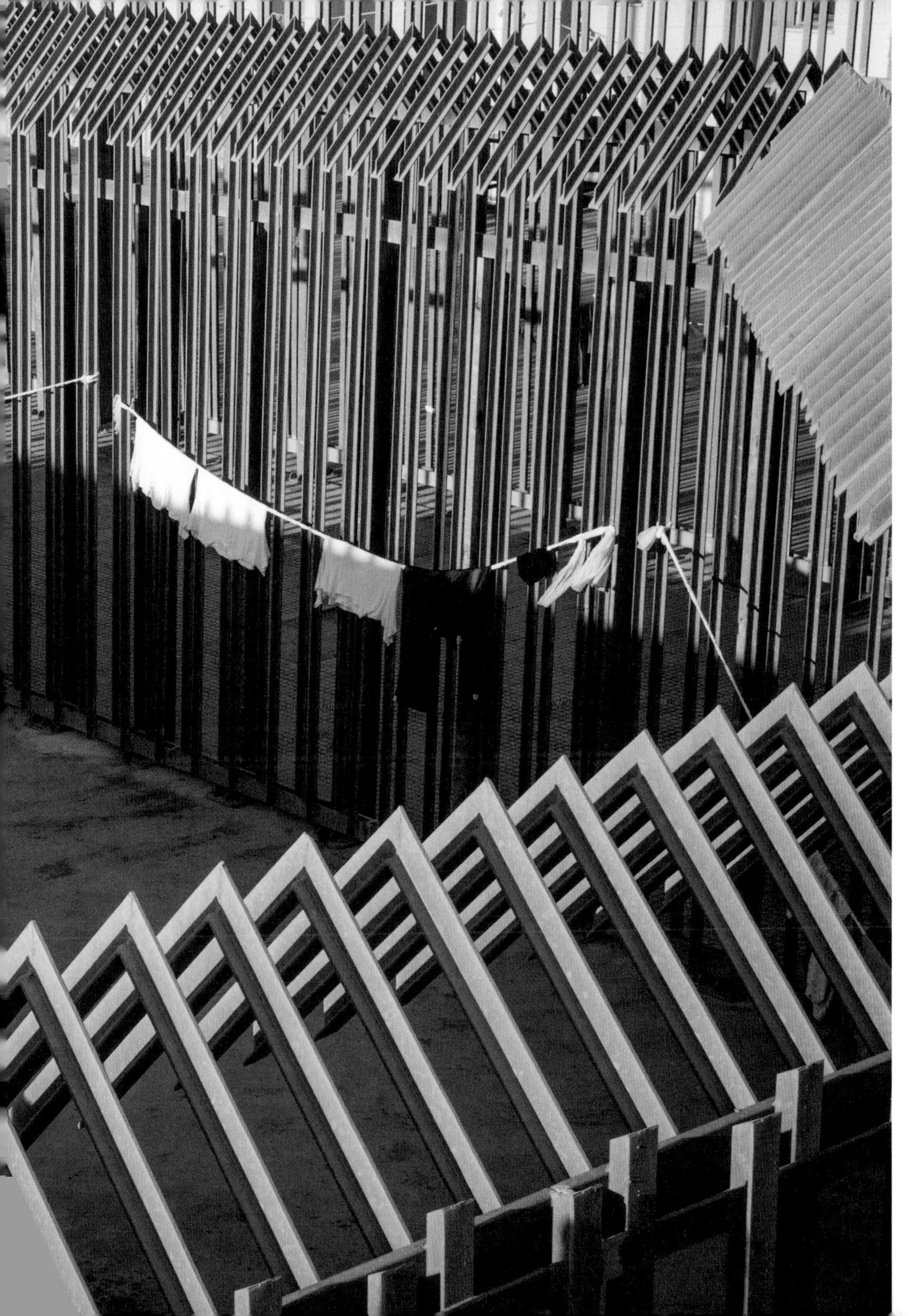

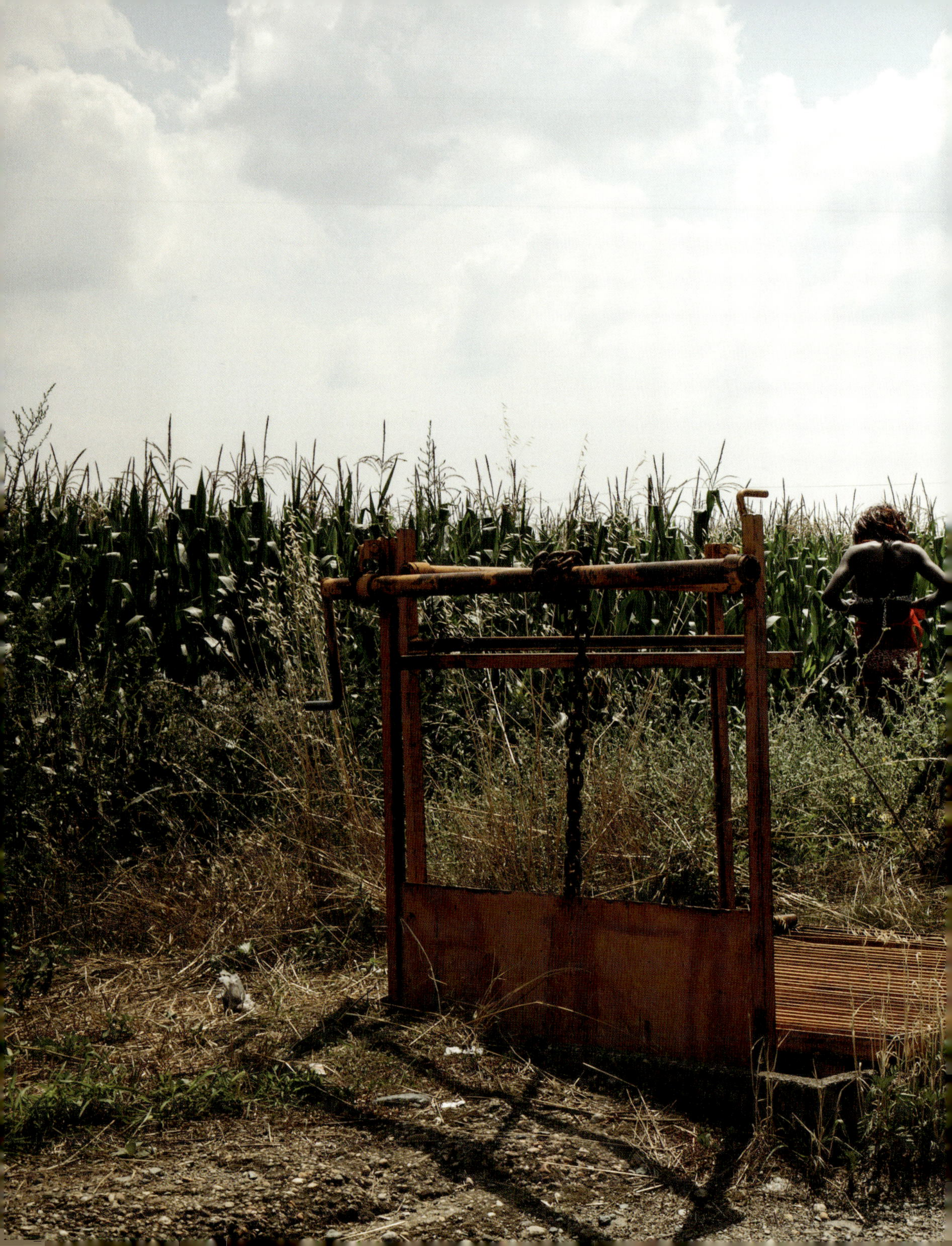

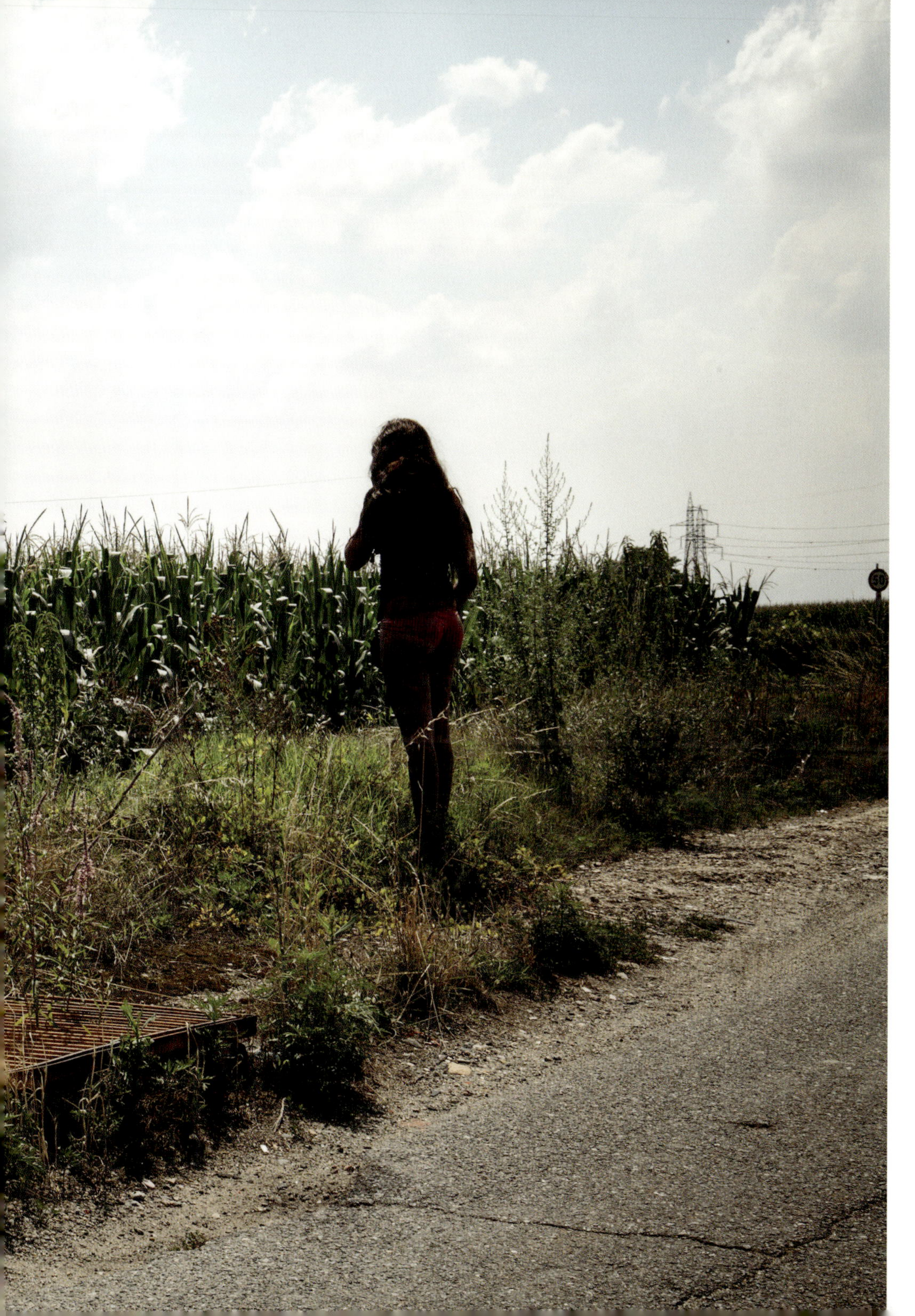

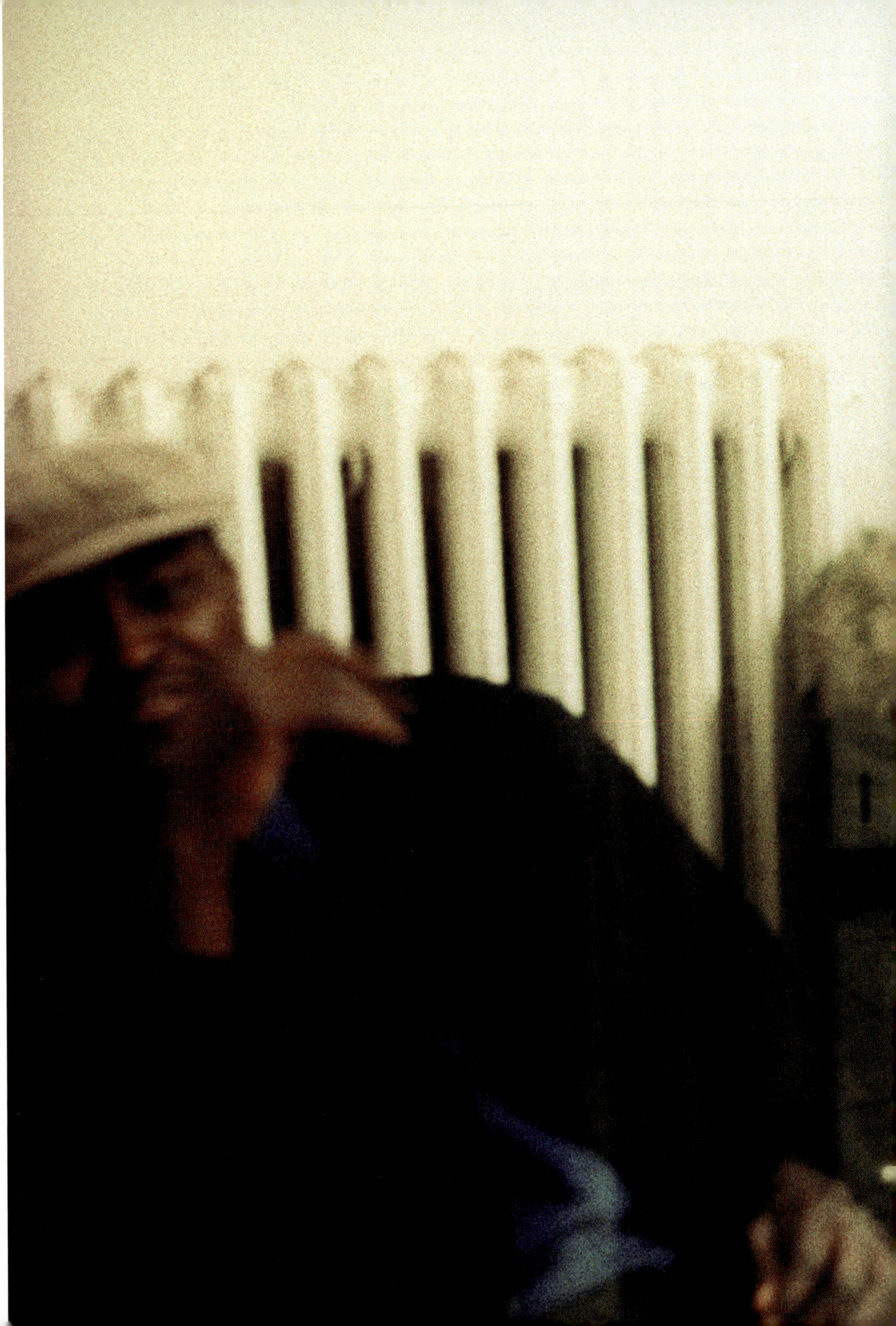

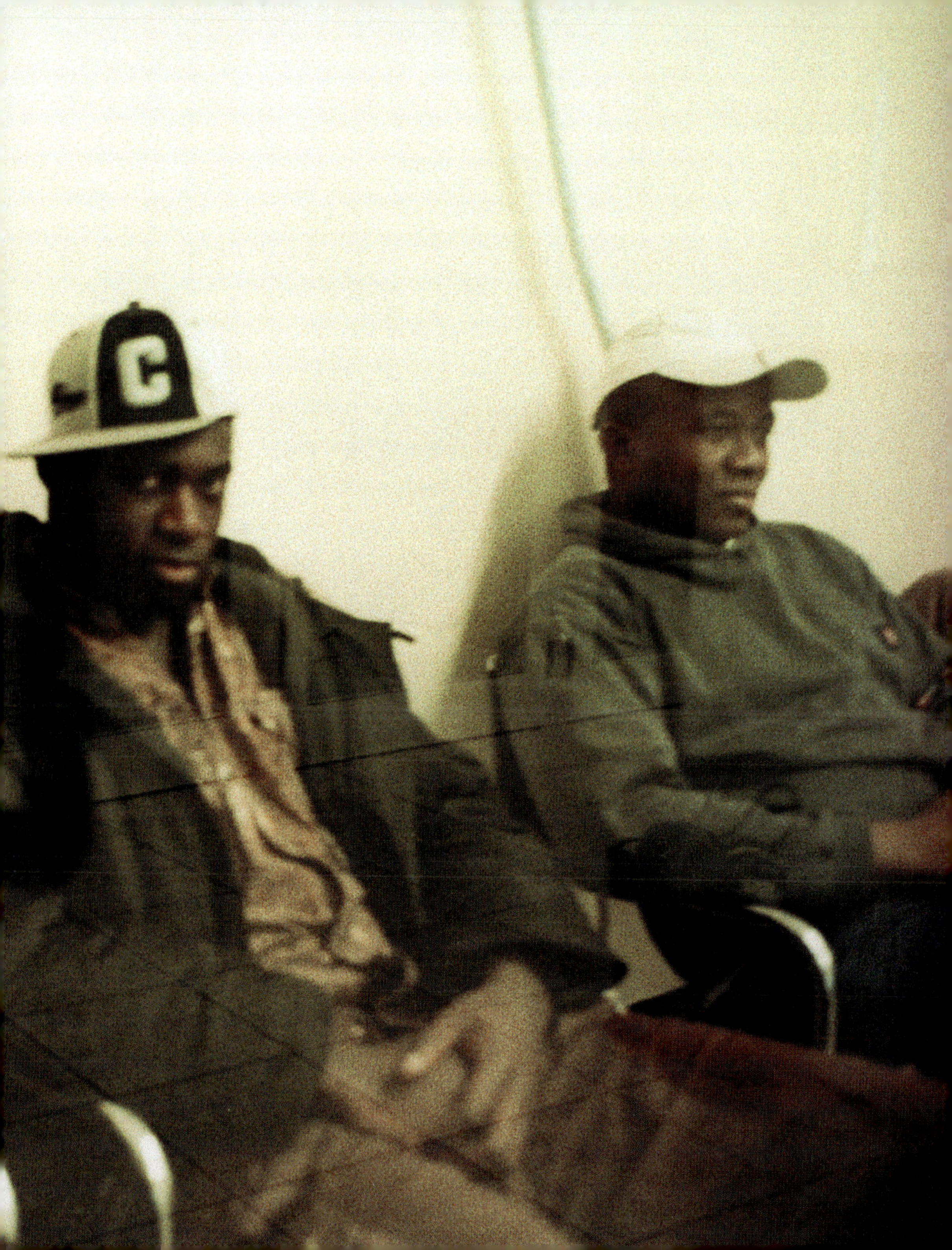

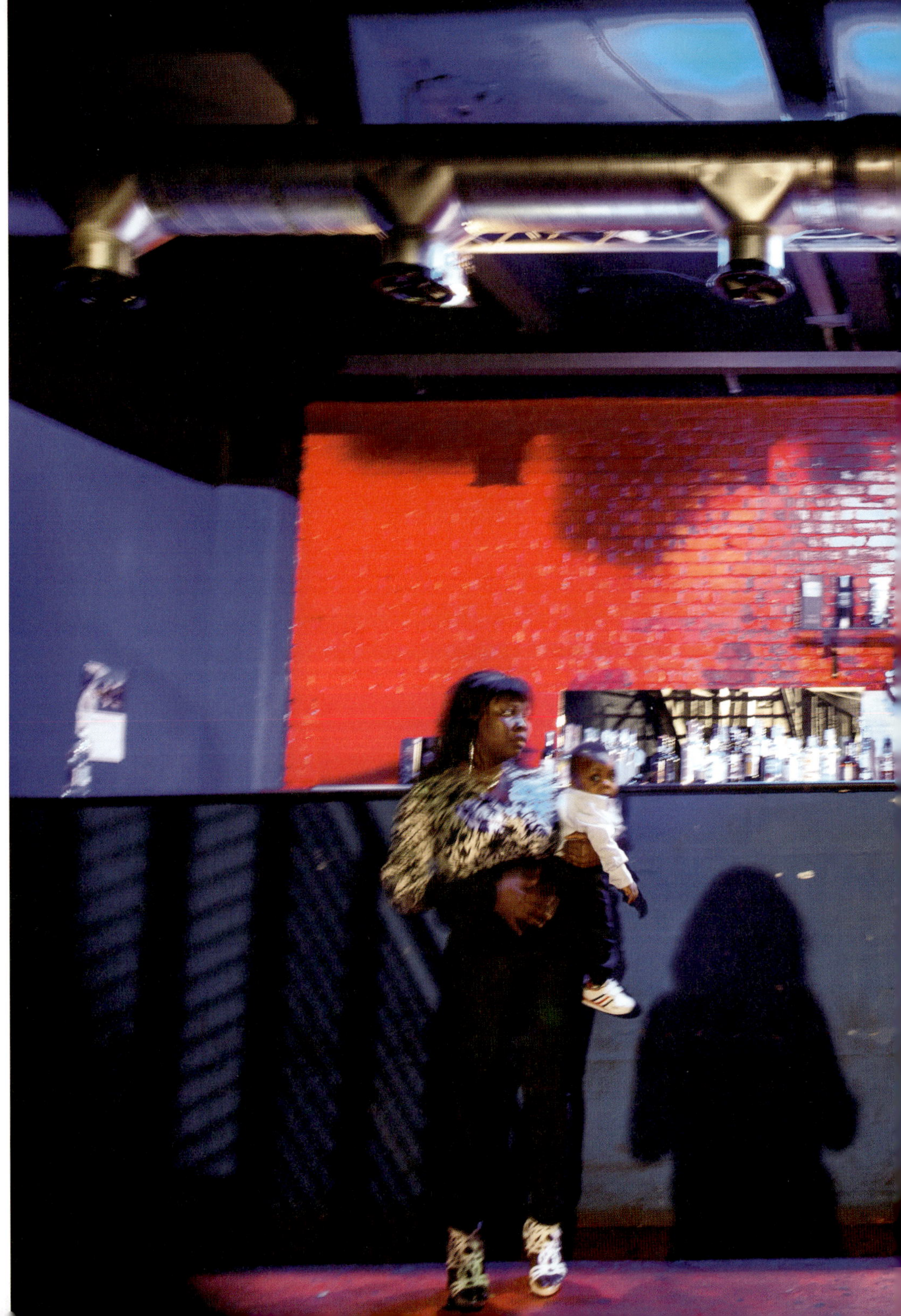

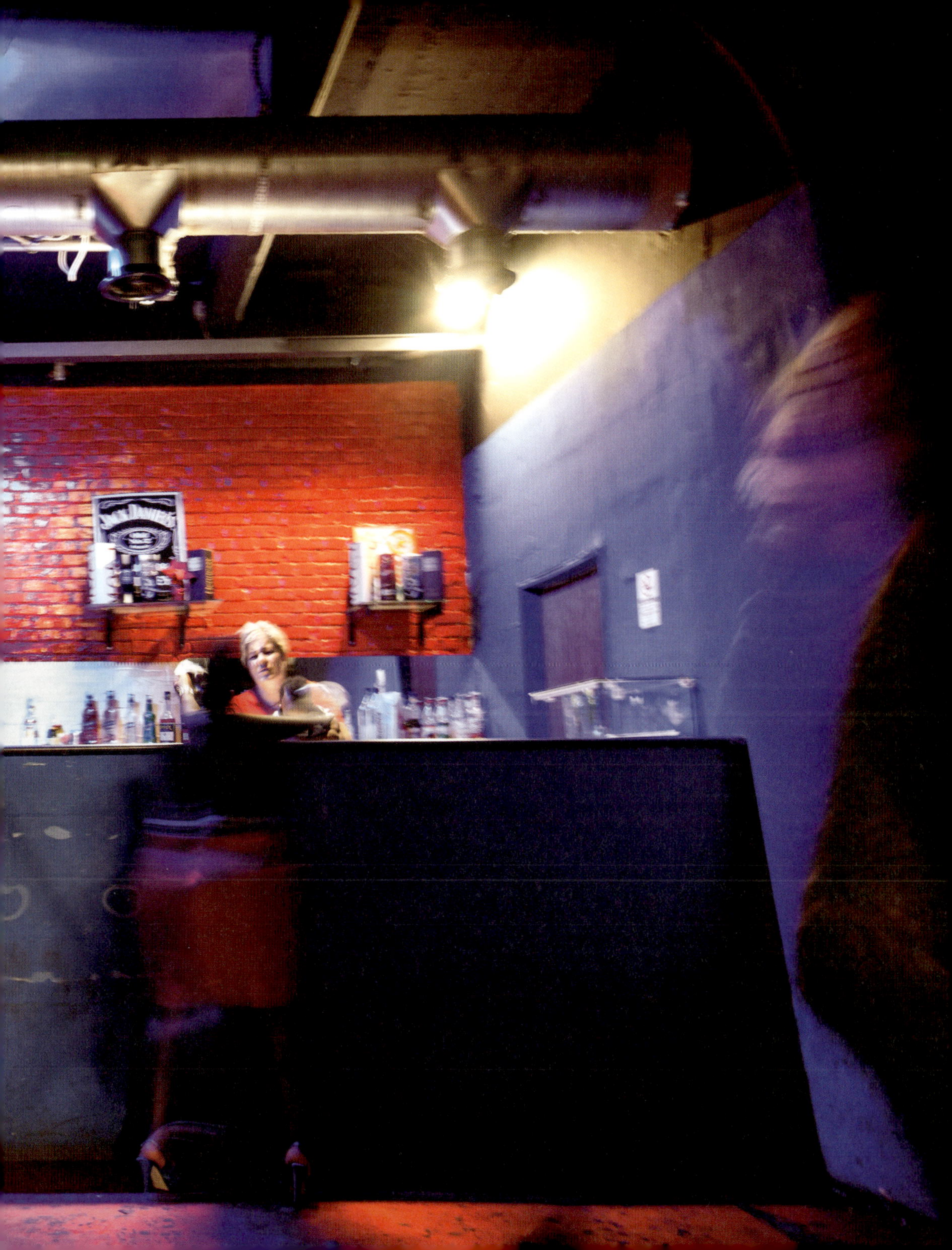

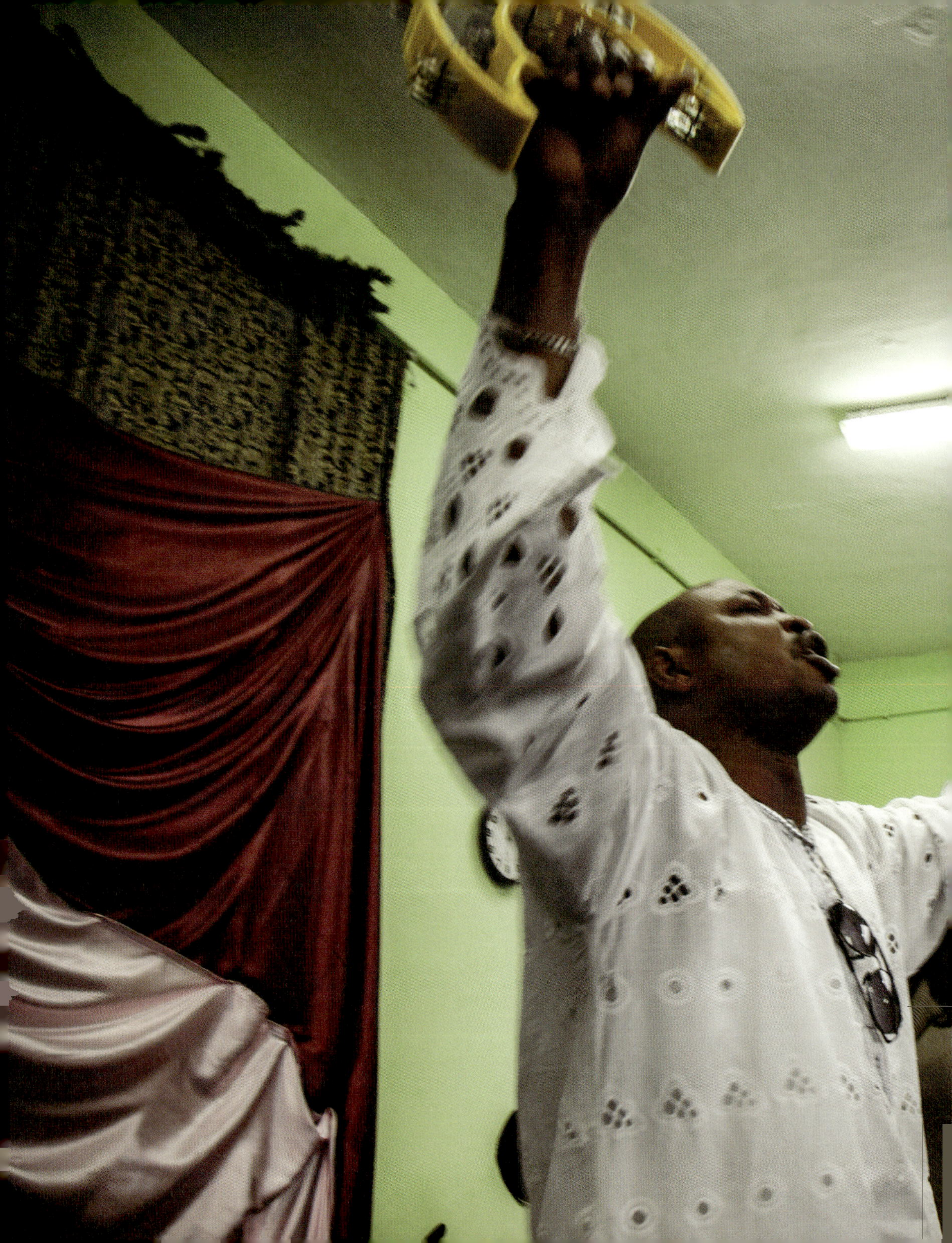

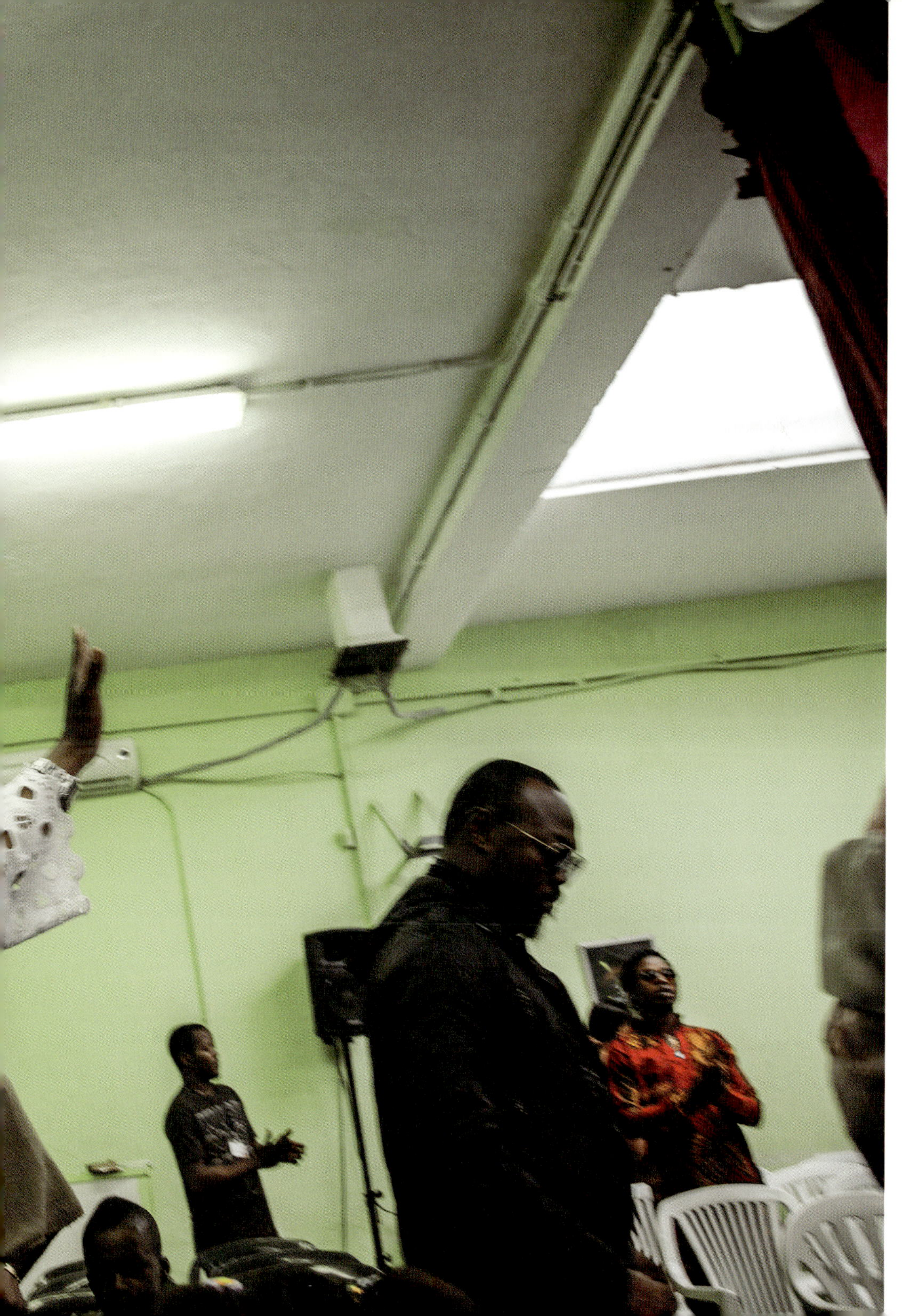

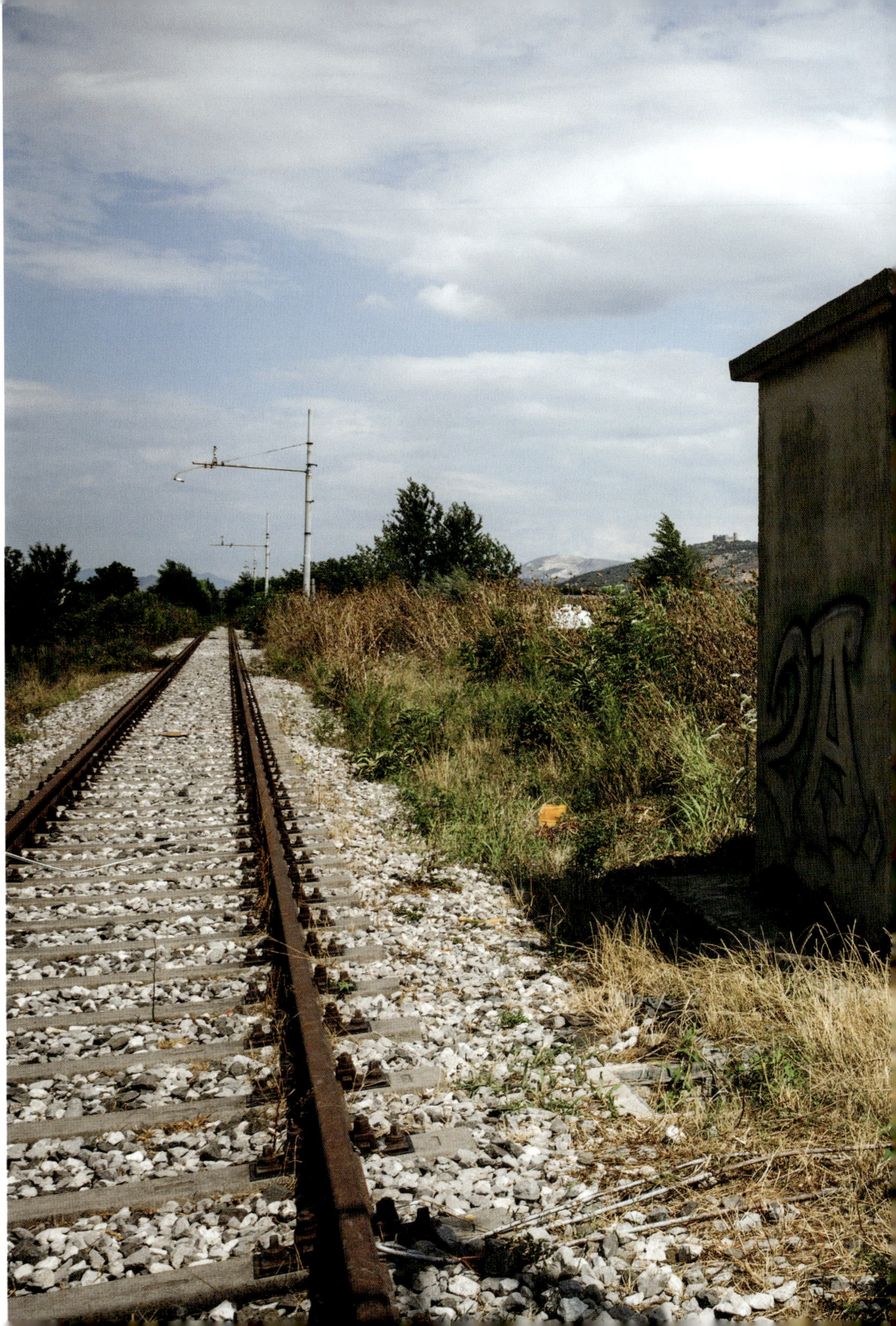

116

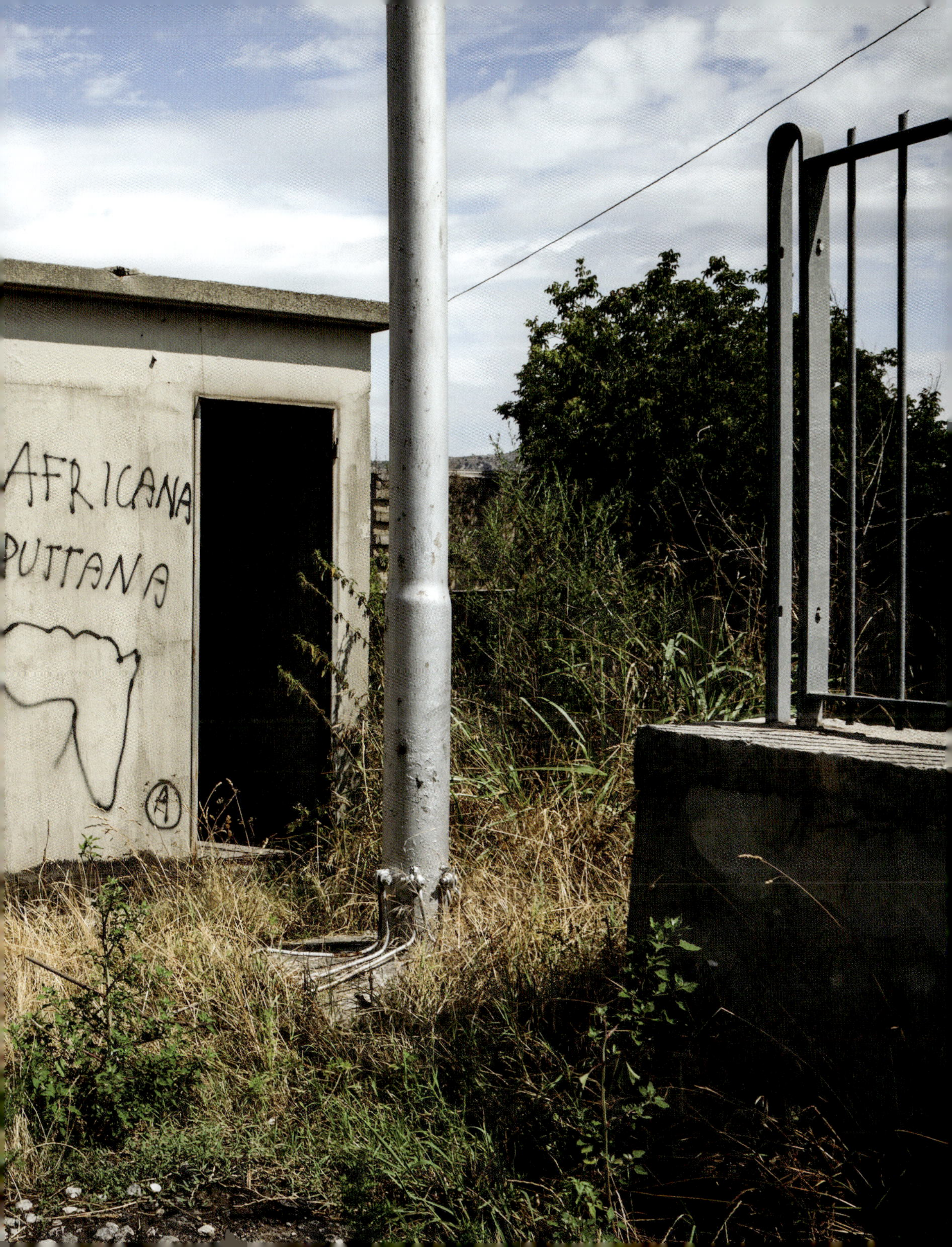

AFRICANA
PUTTANA

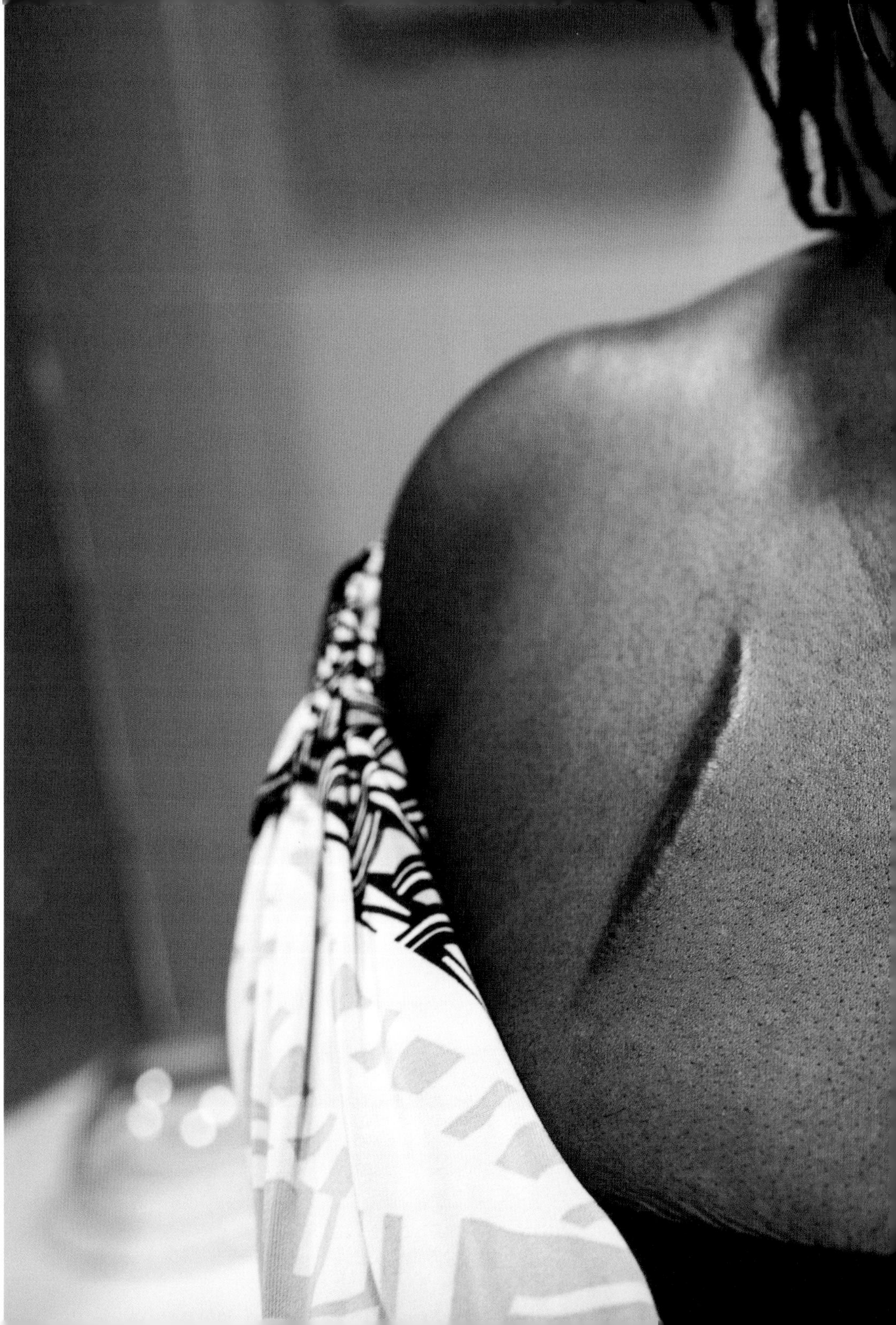

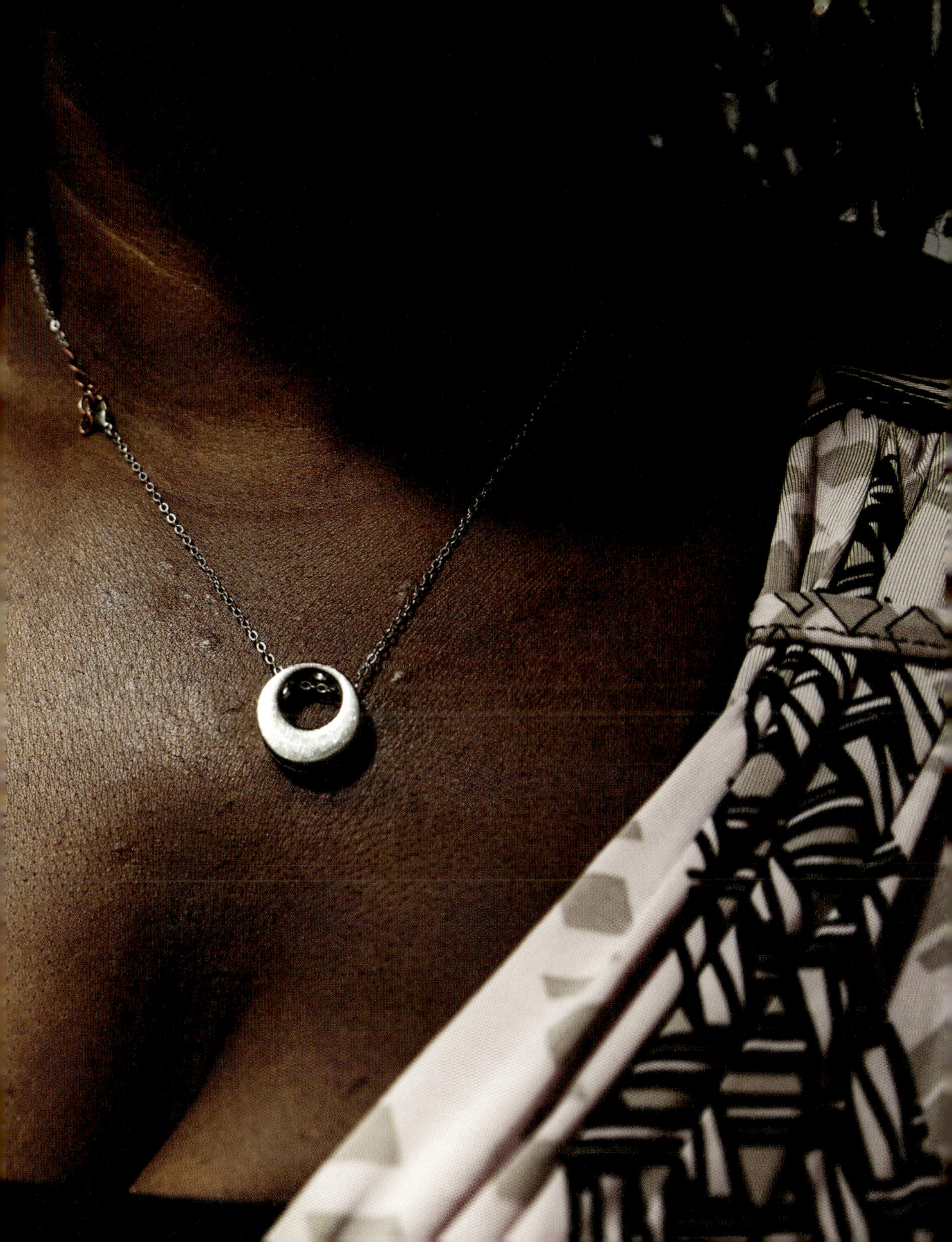

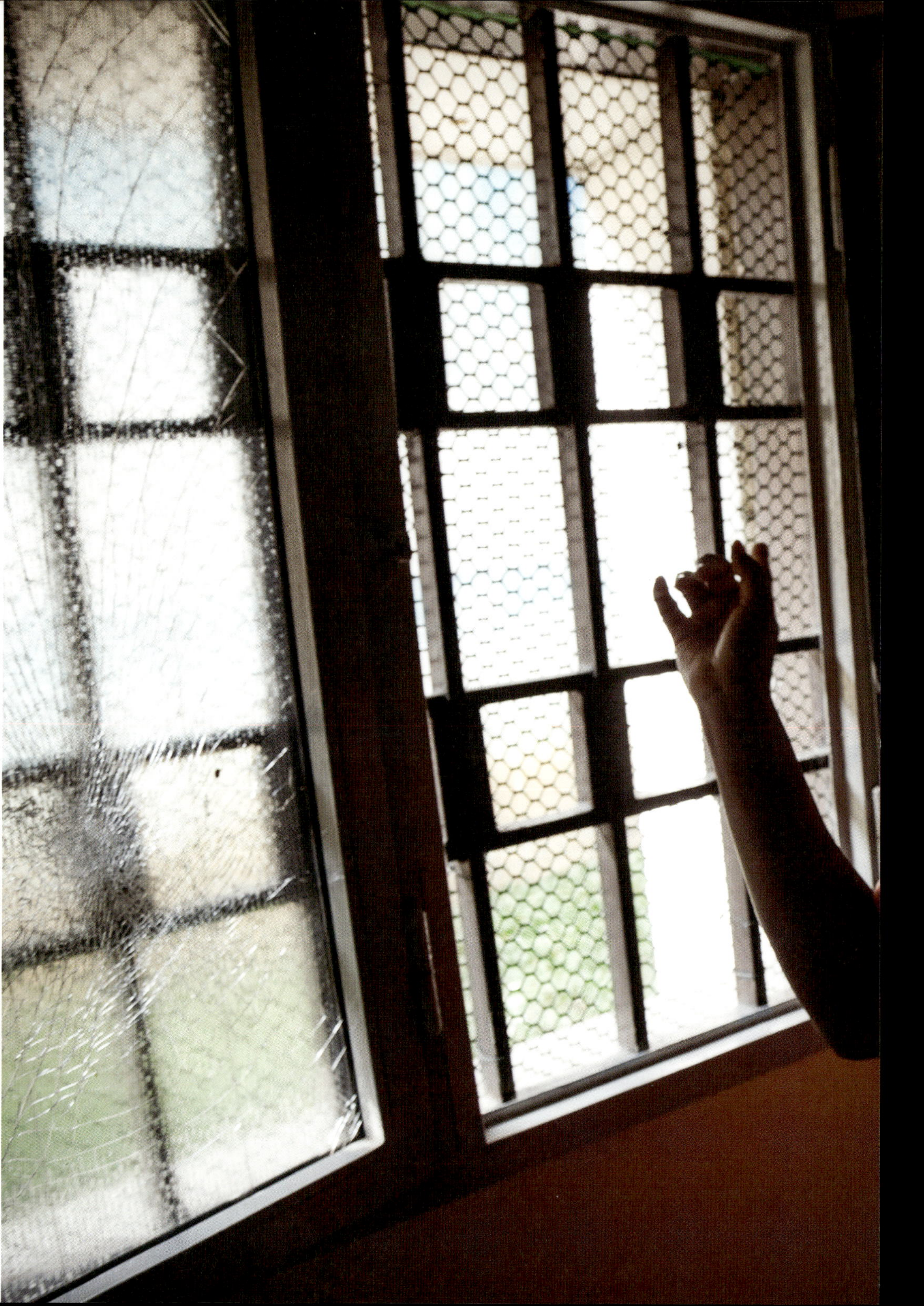

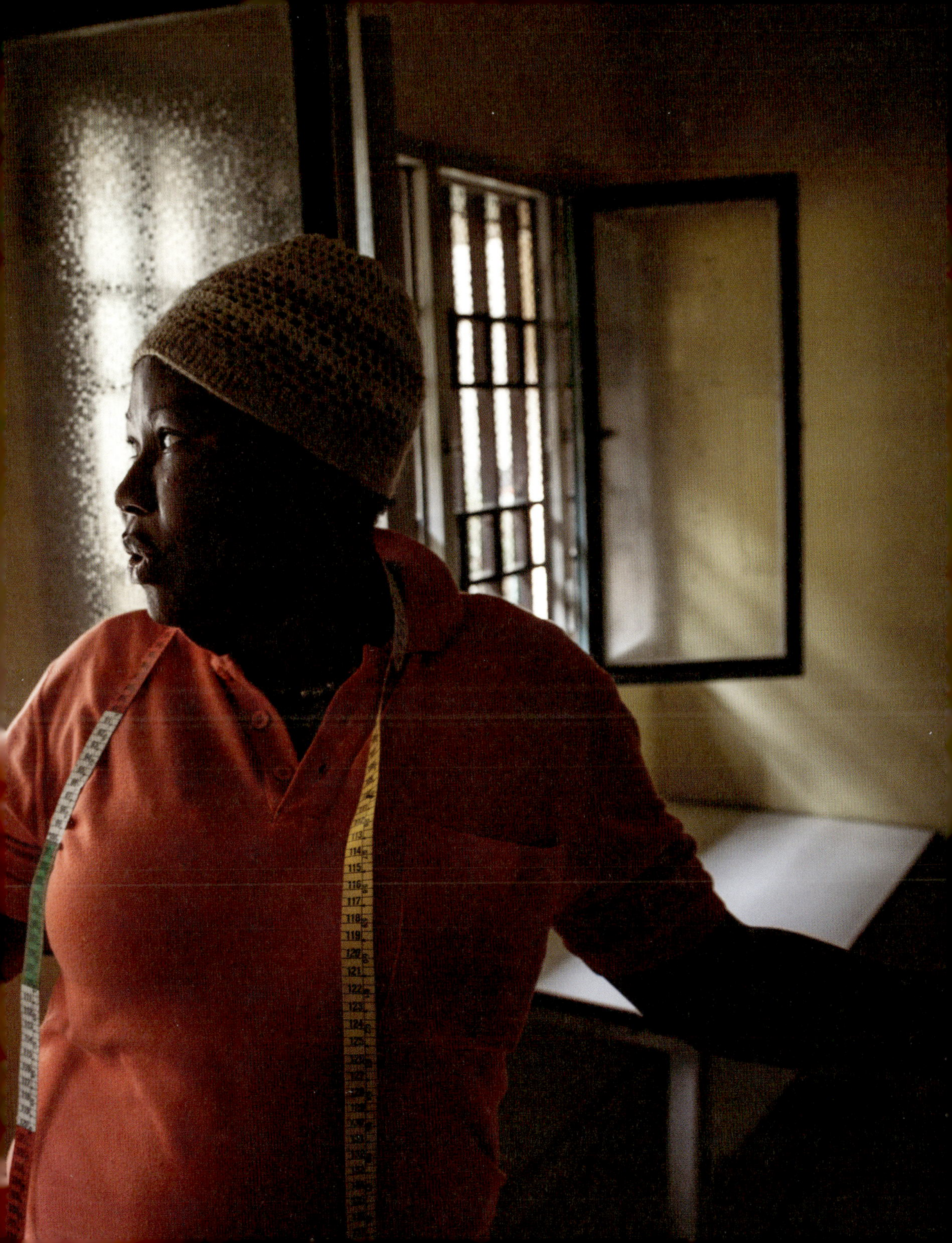

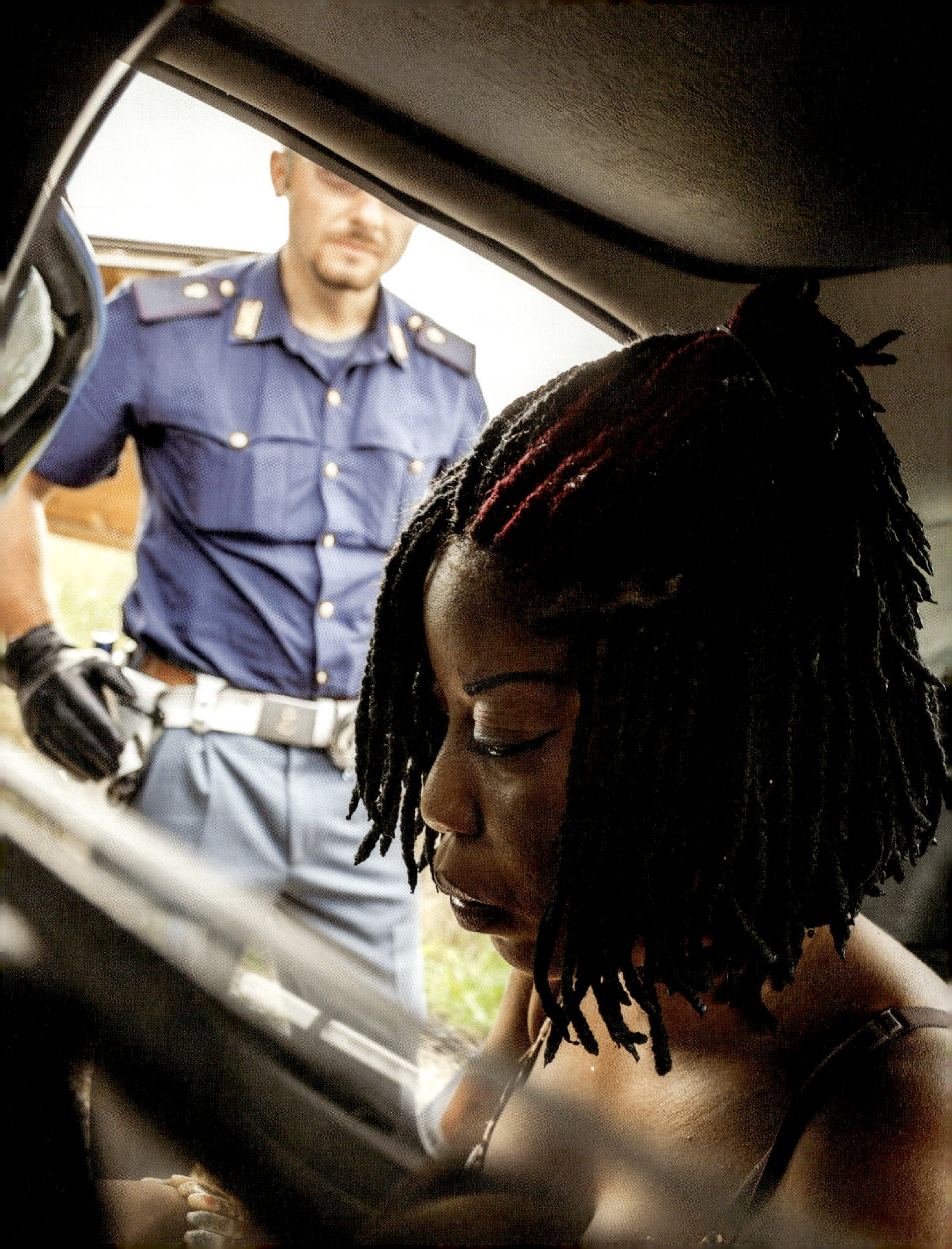

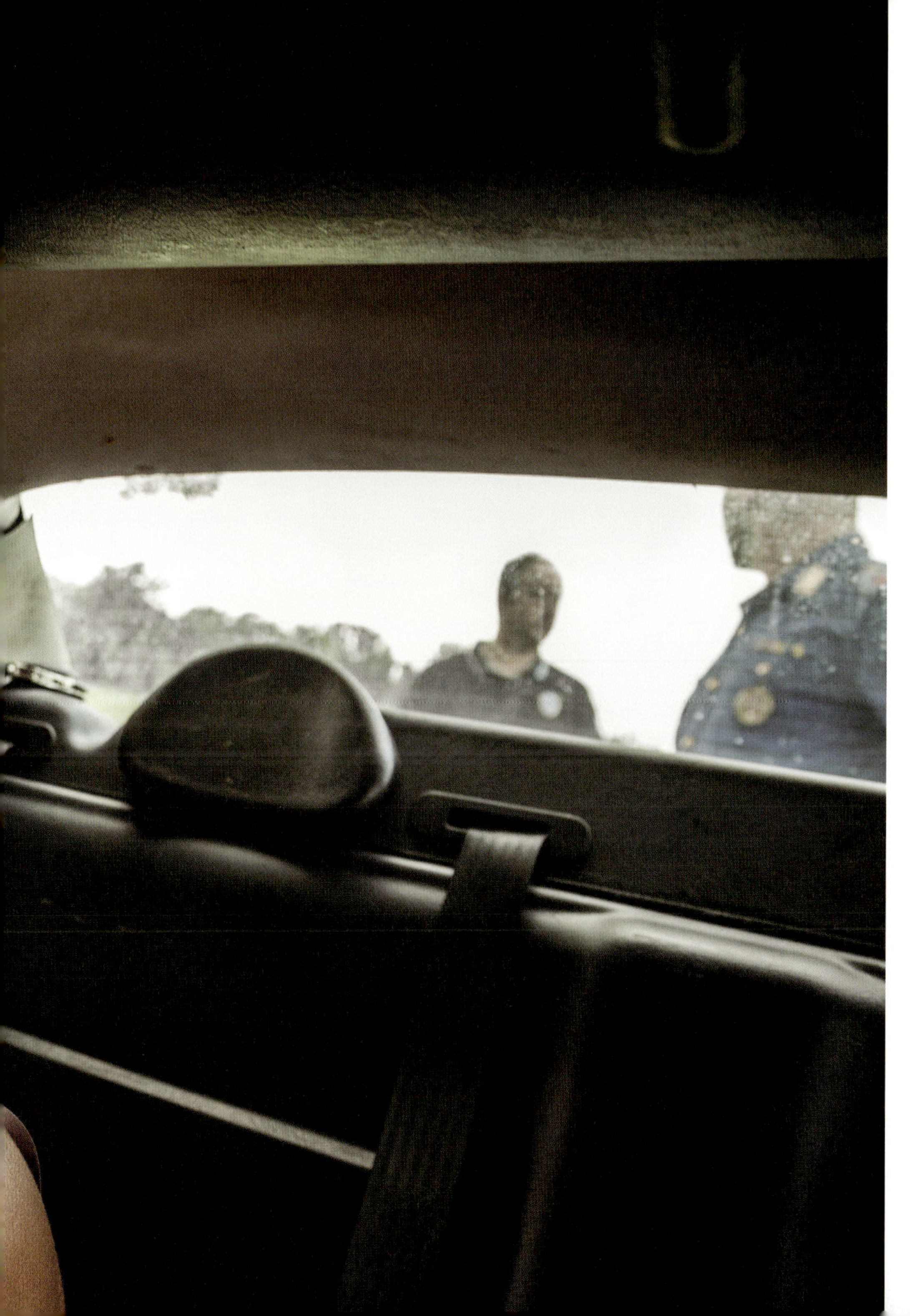

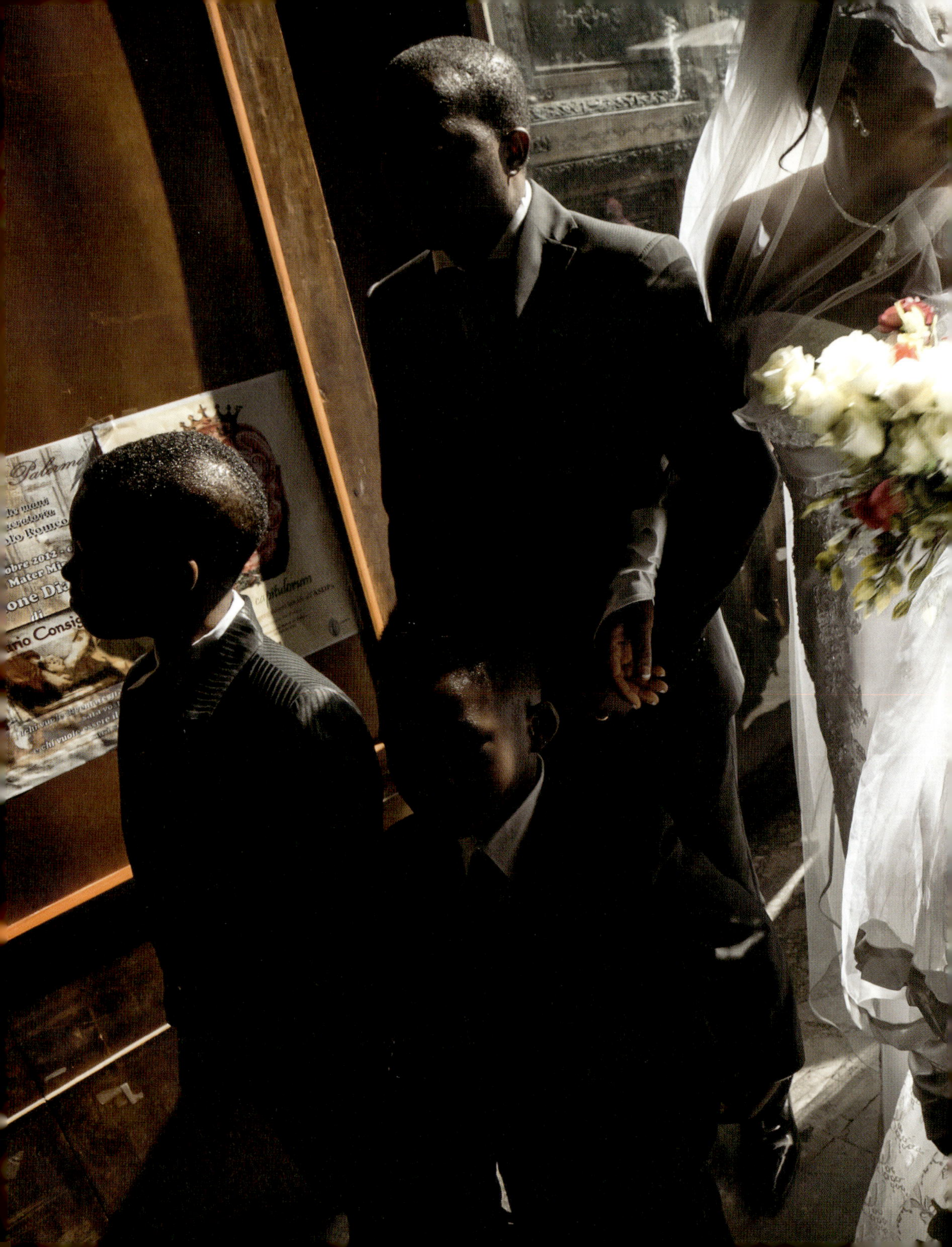

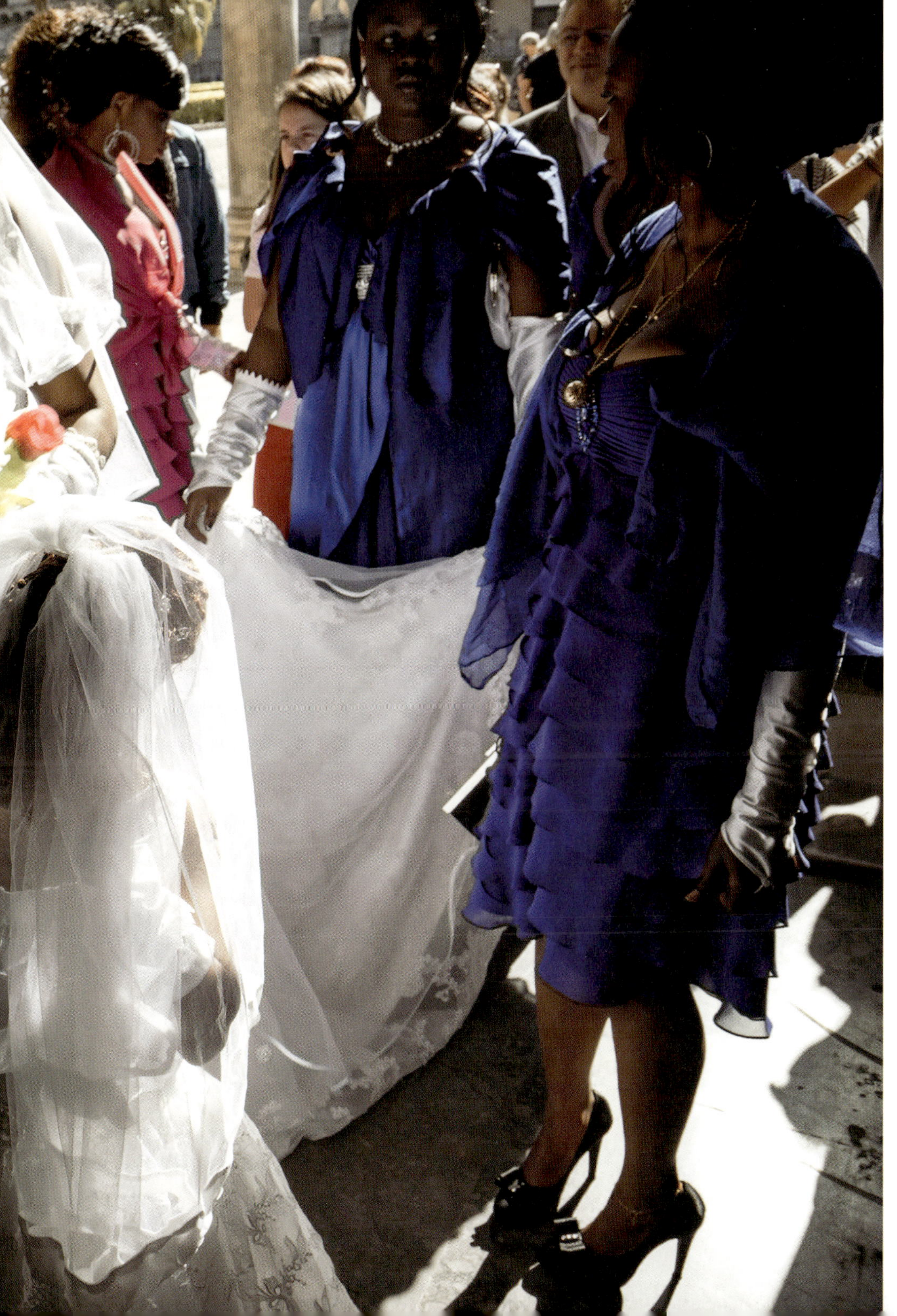

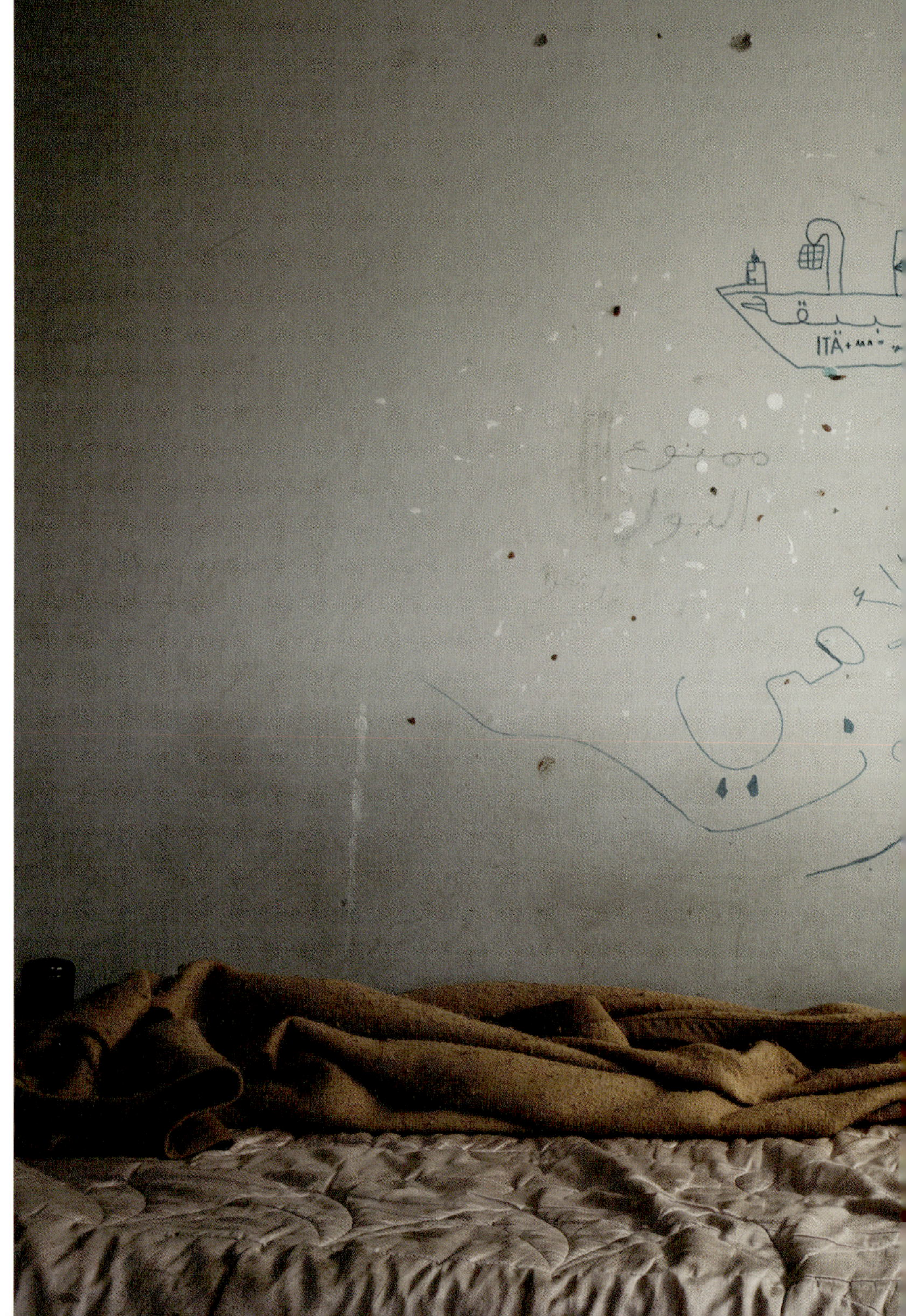

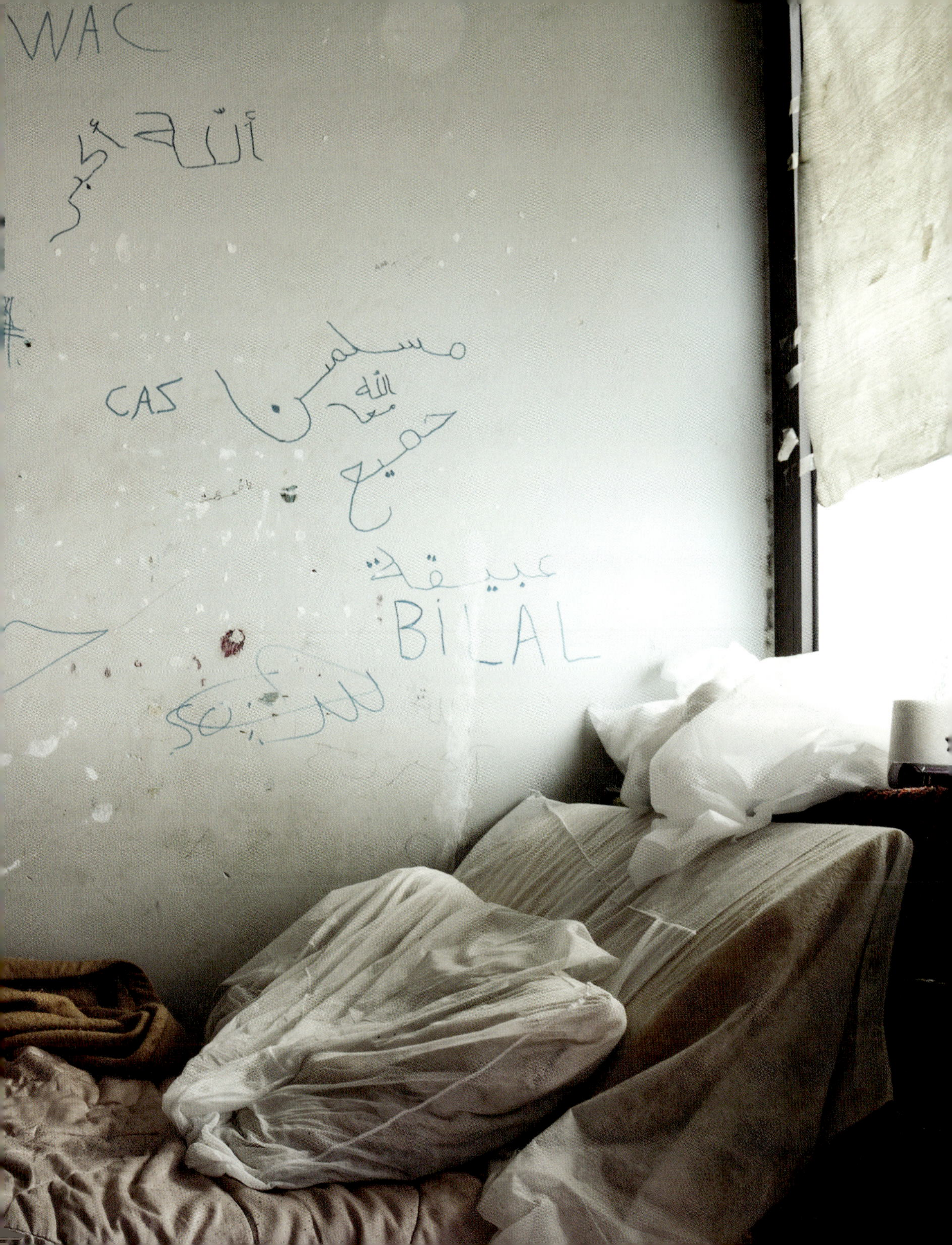

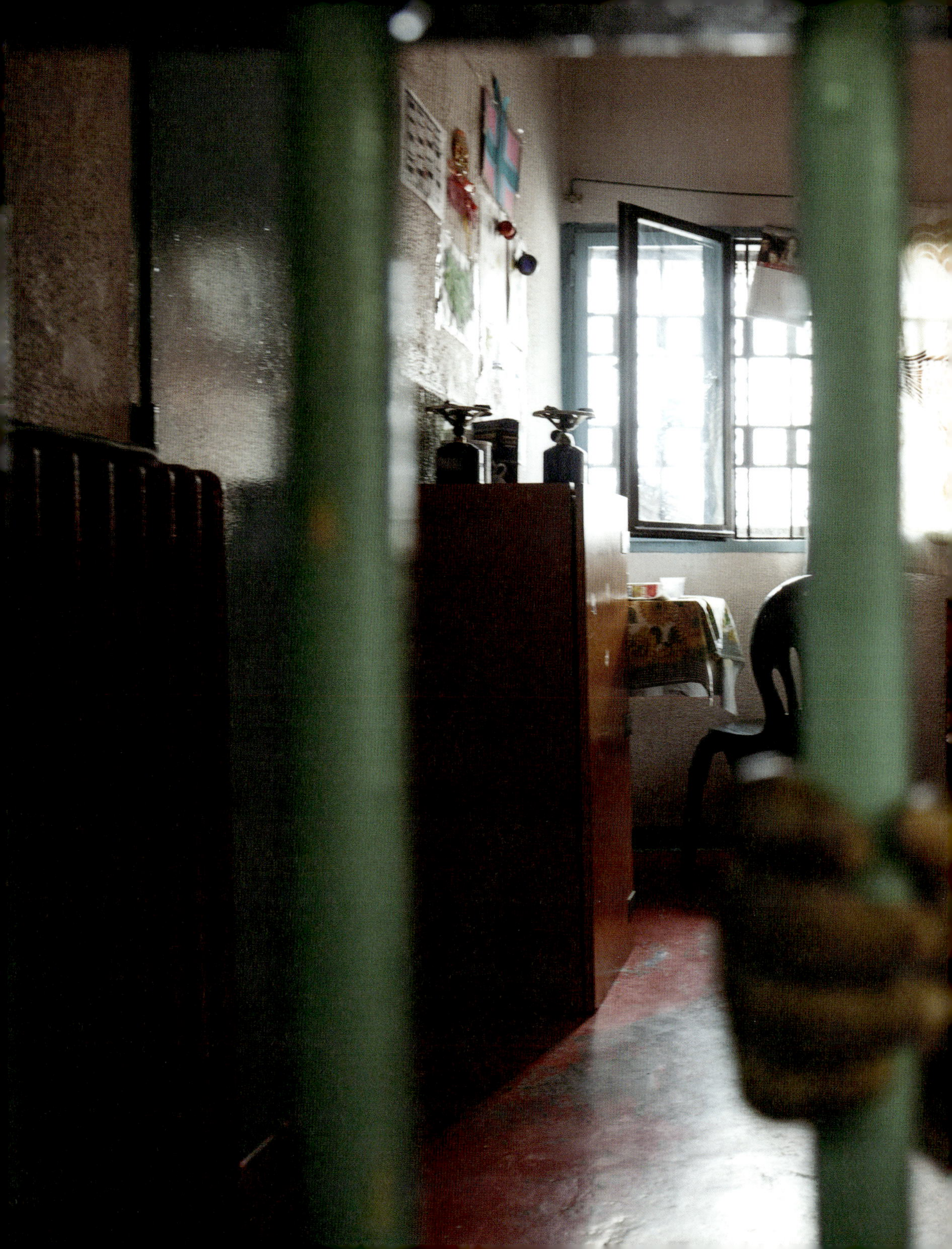

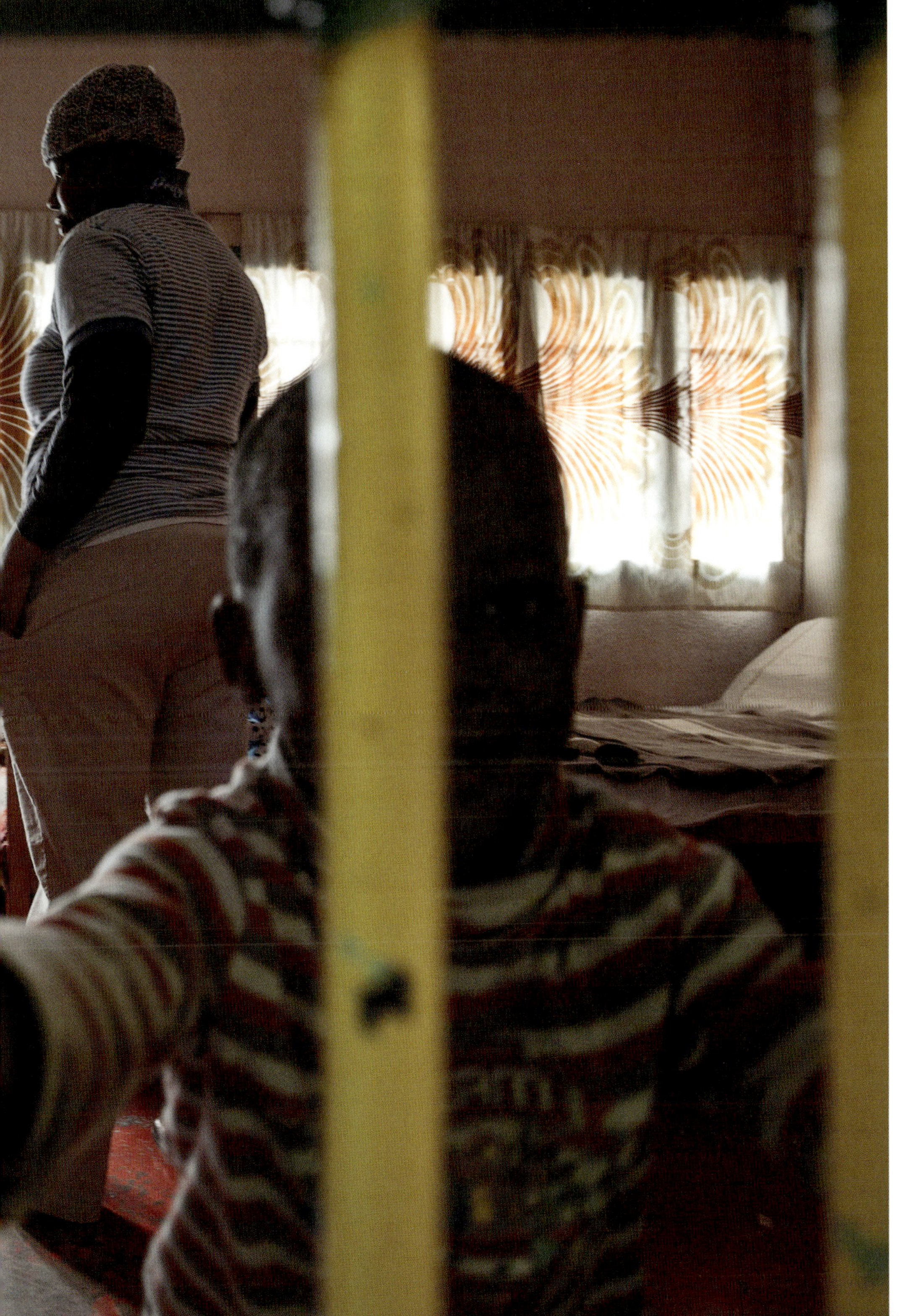

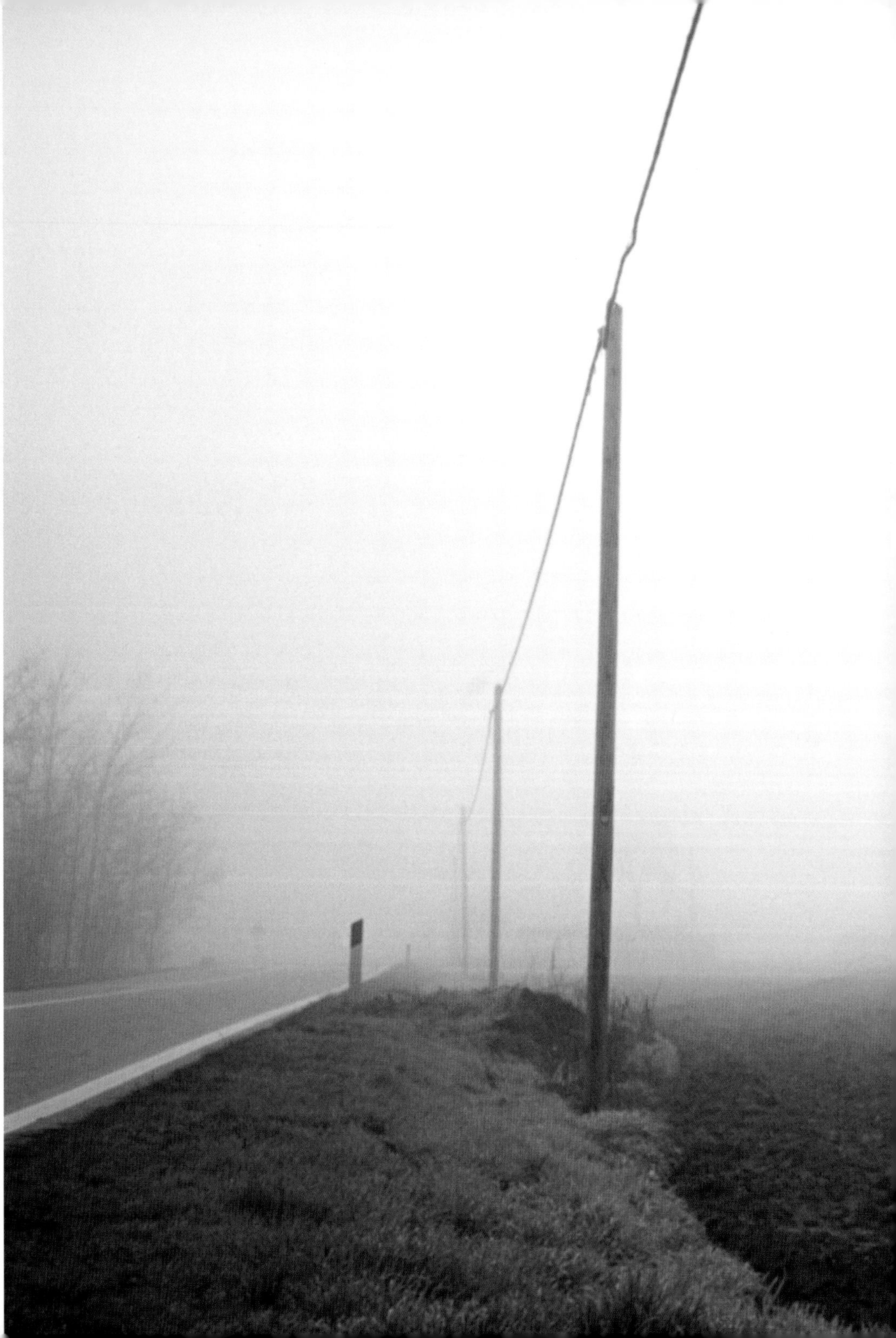

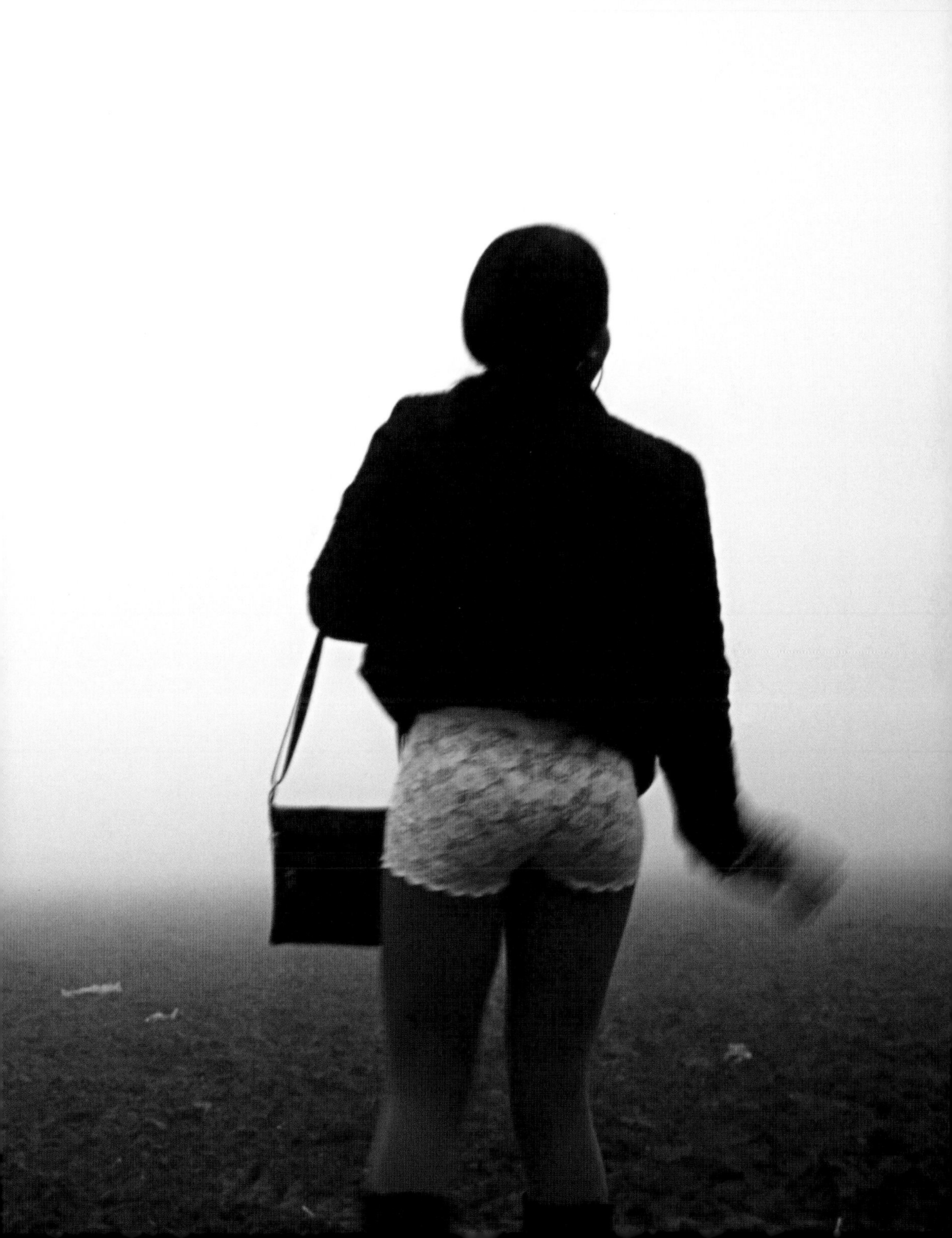

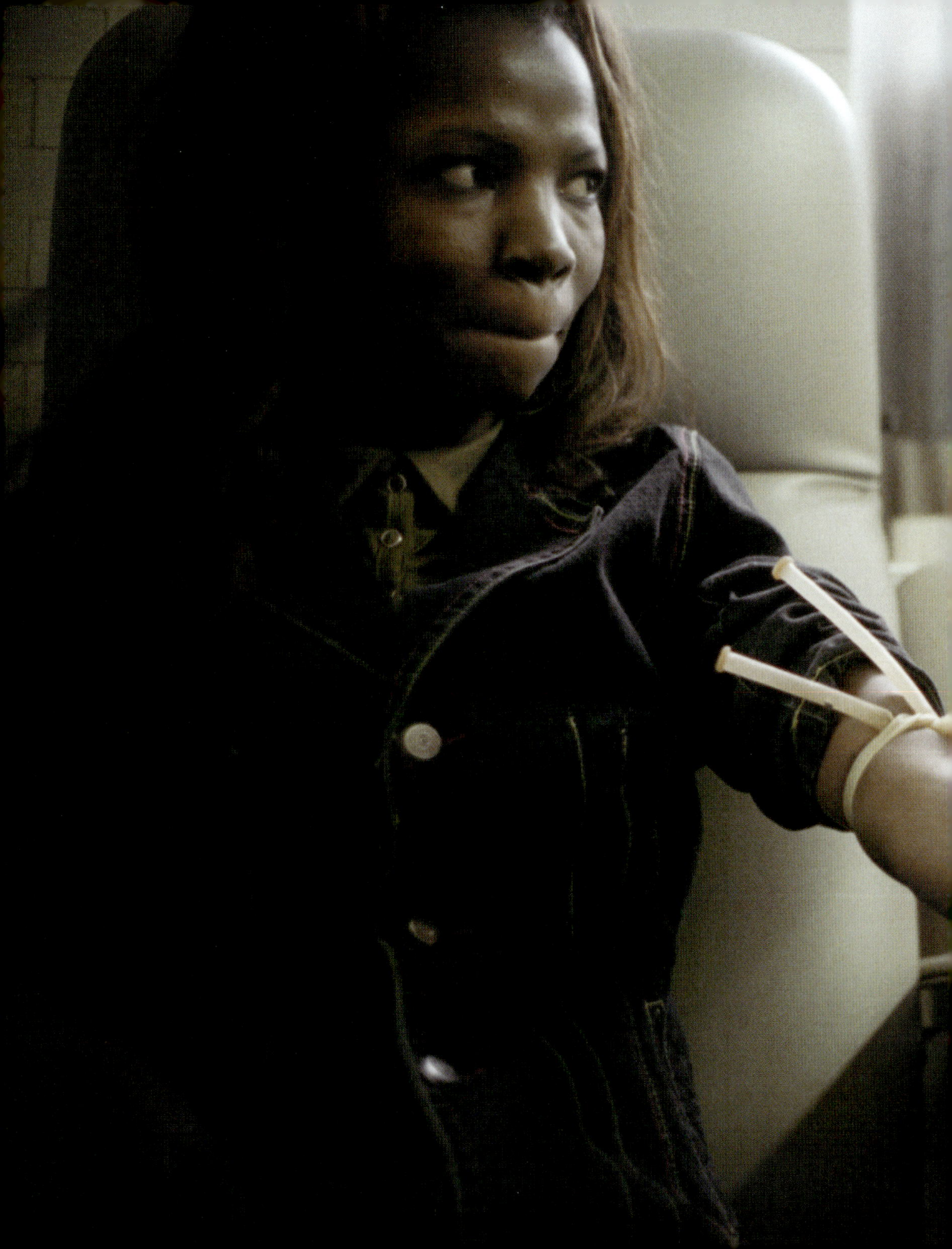

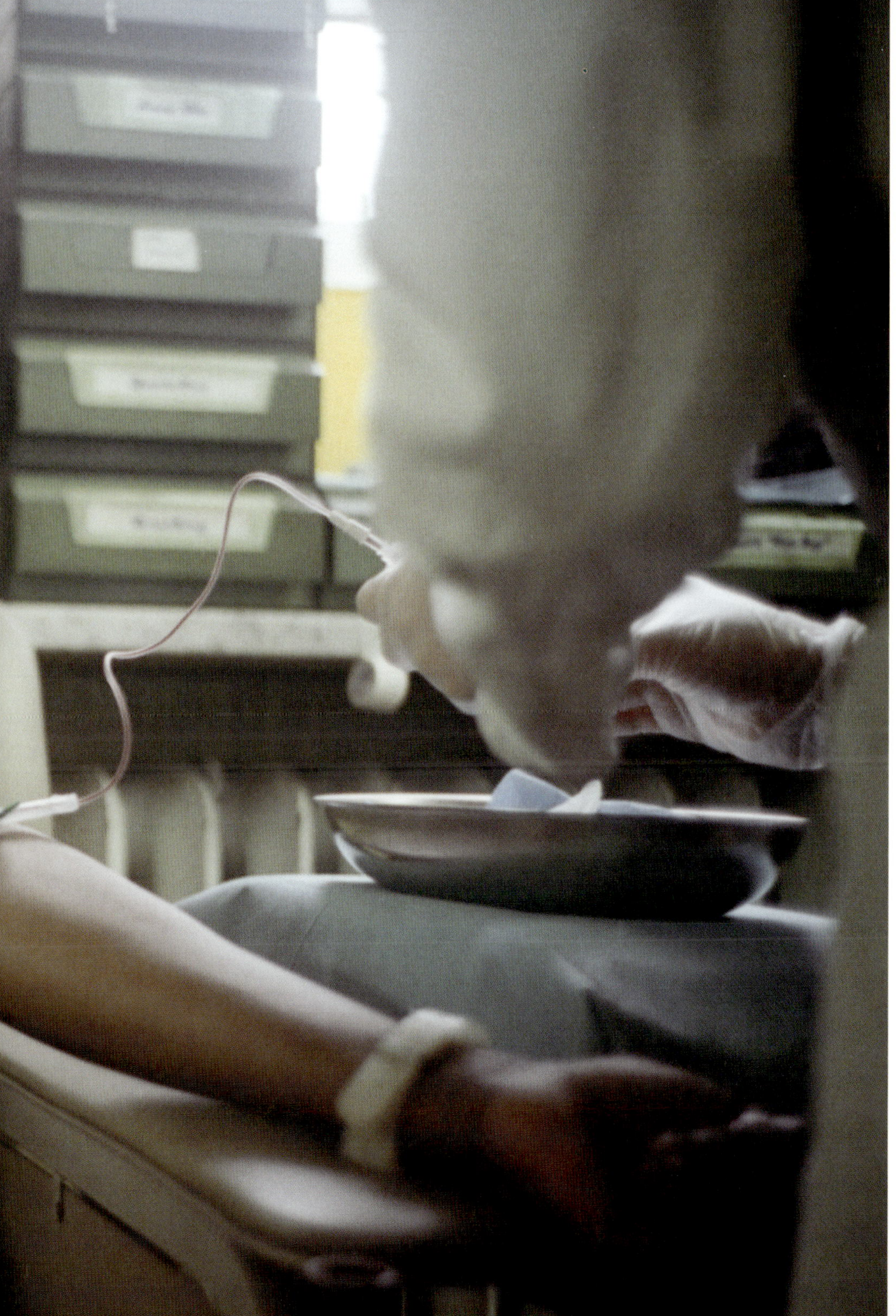

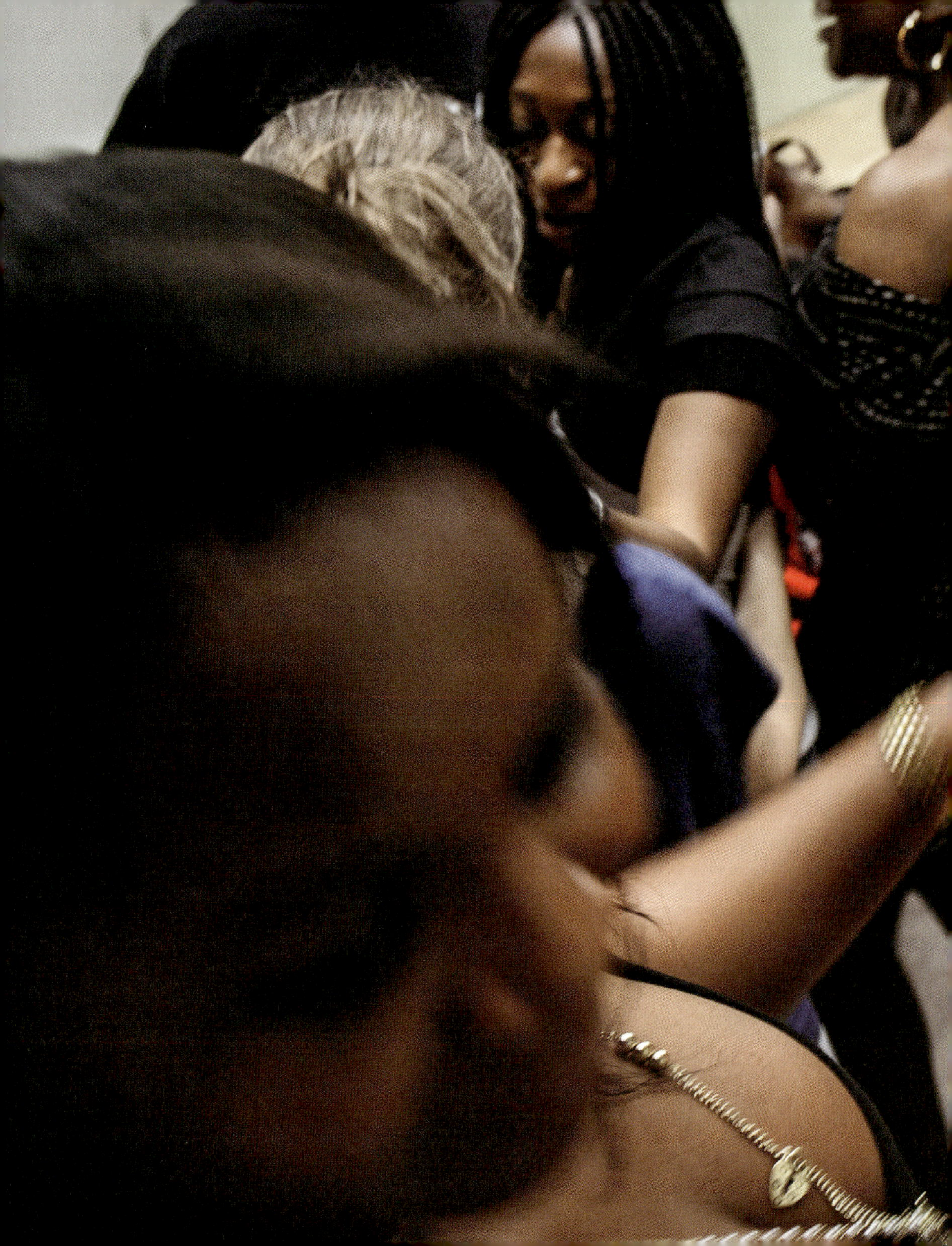

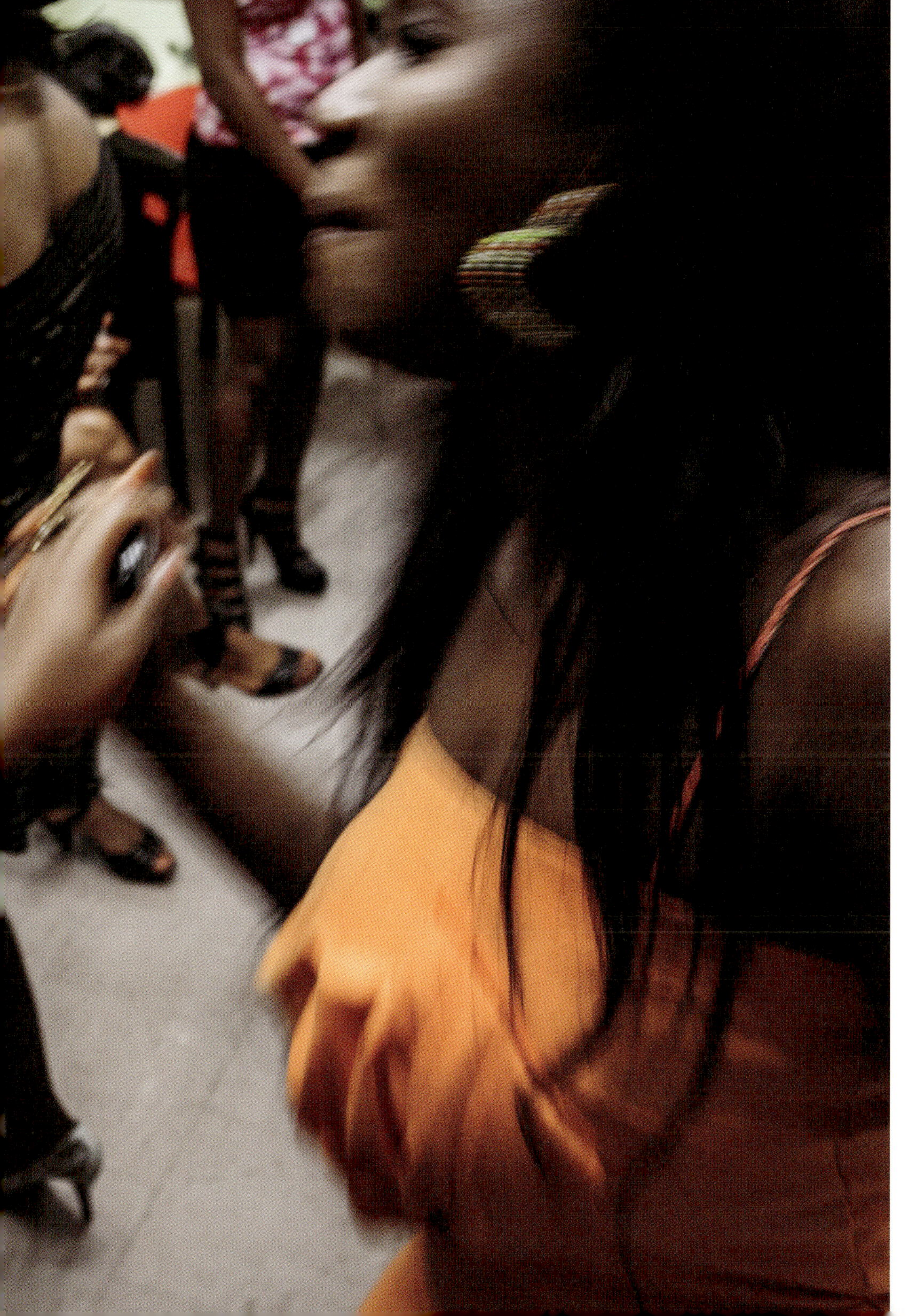

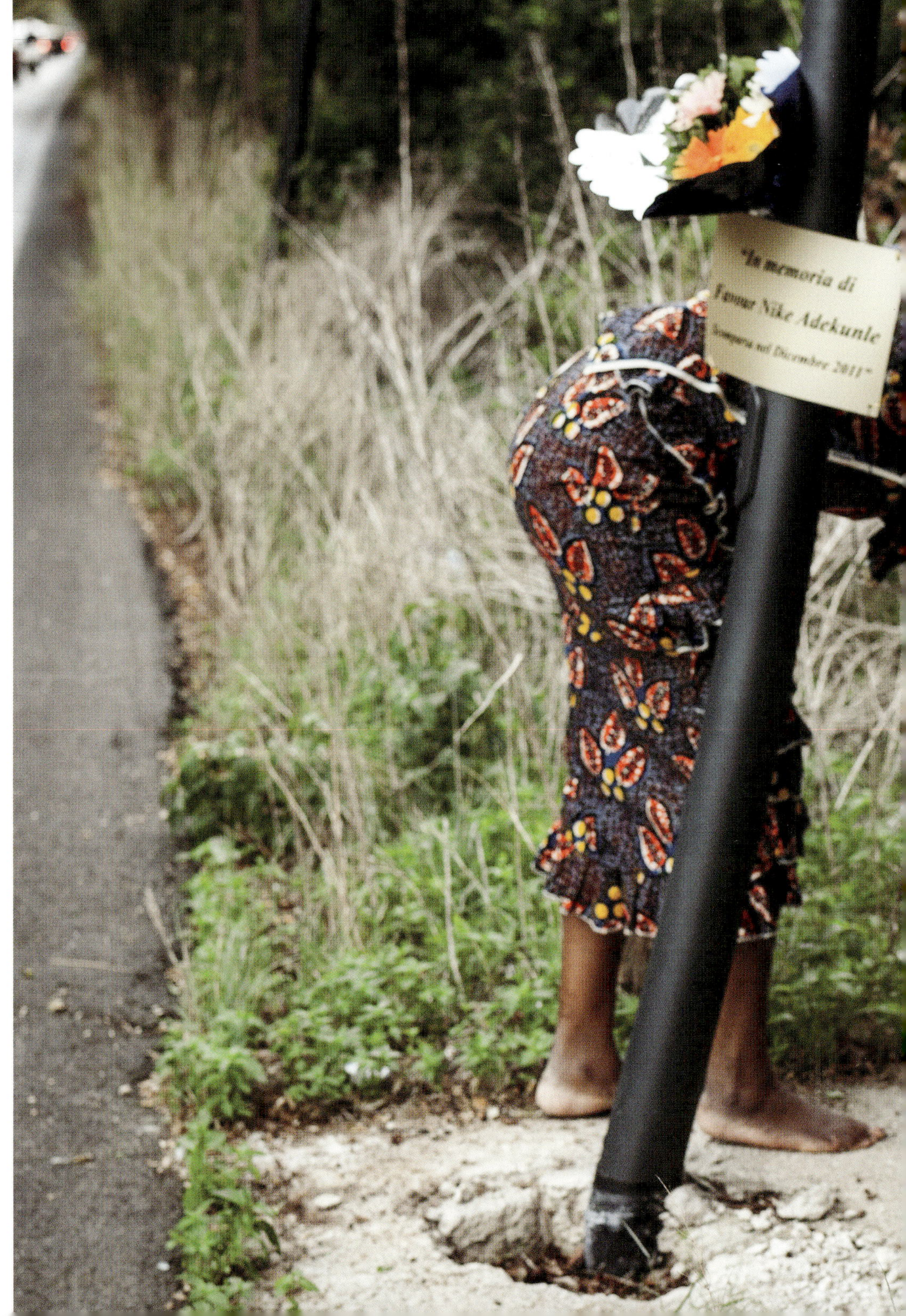
"In memoria di
Femur Nike Adekunle
Scomparsa nel Dicembre 2011"

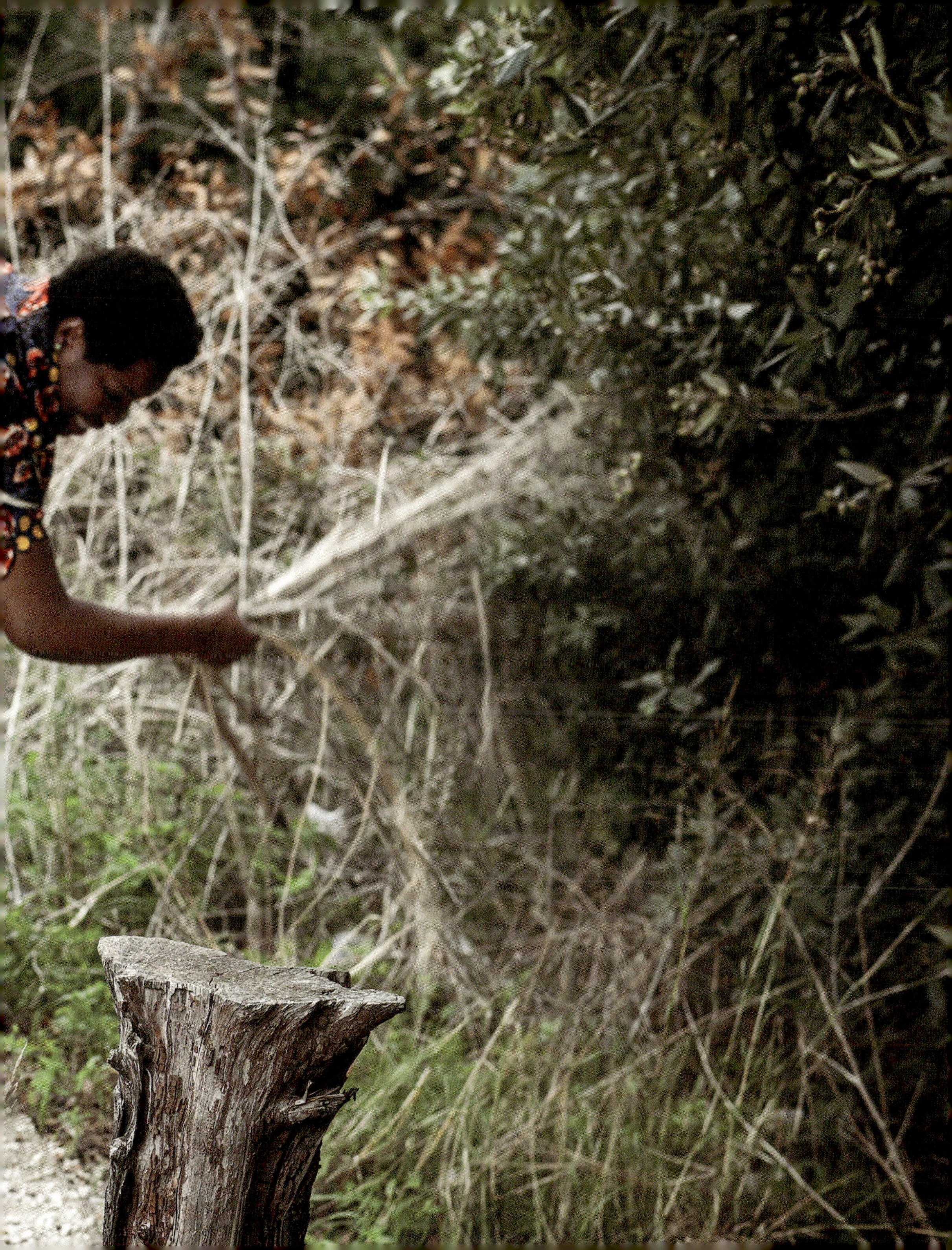

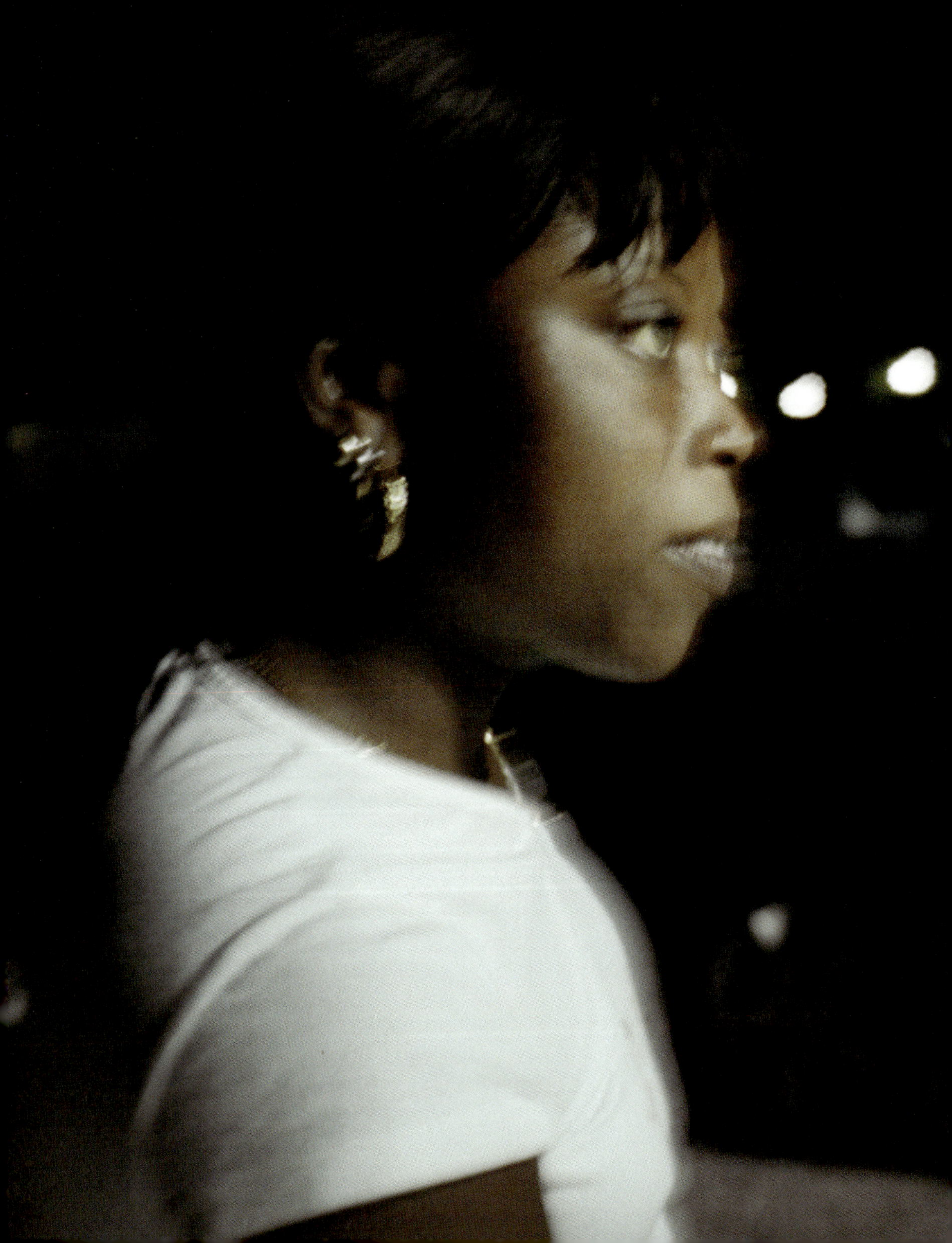

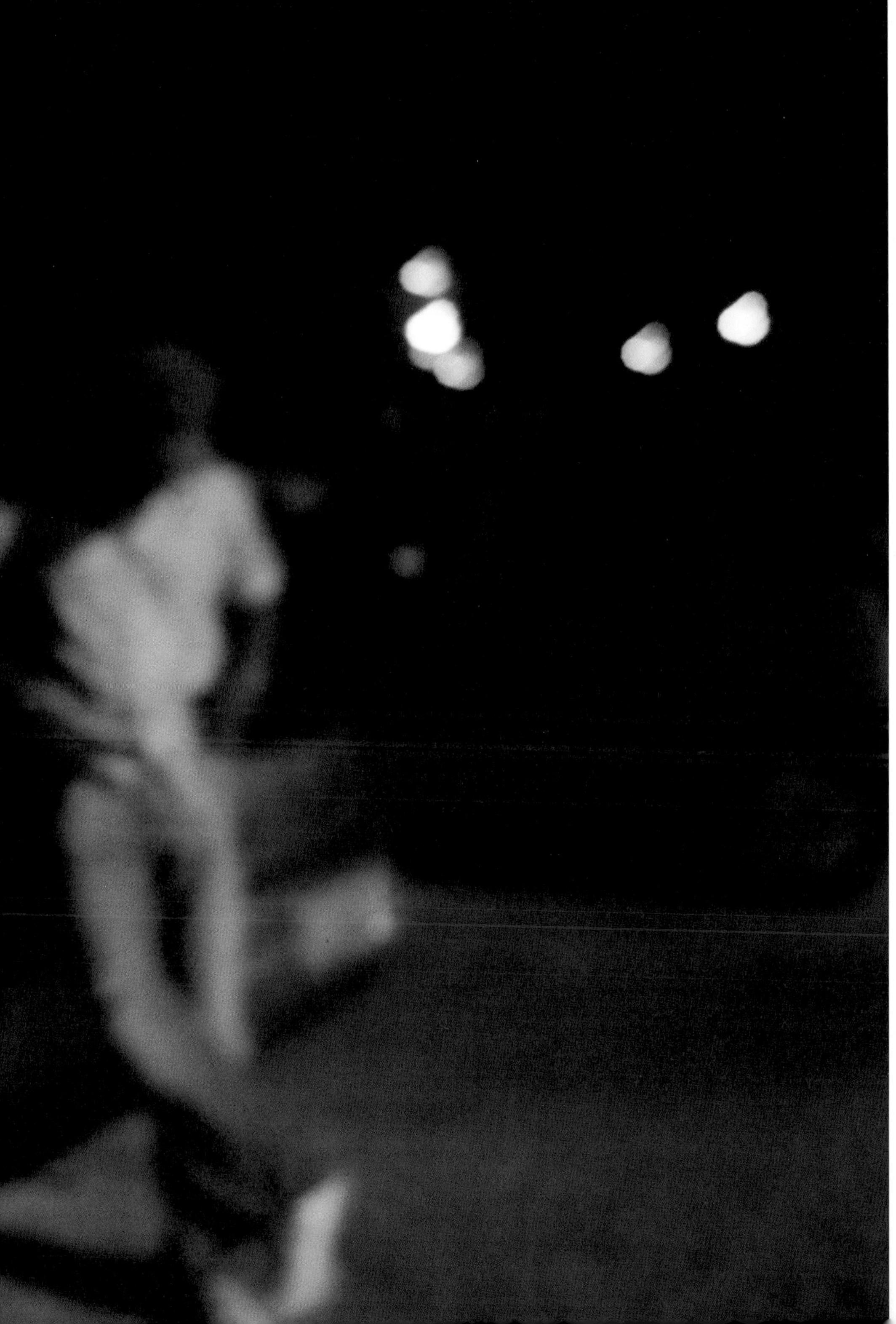

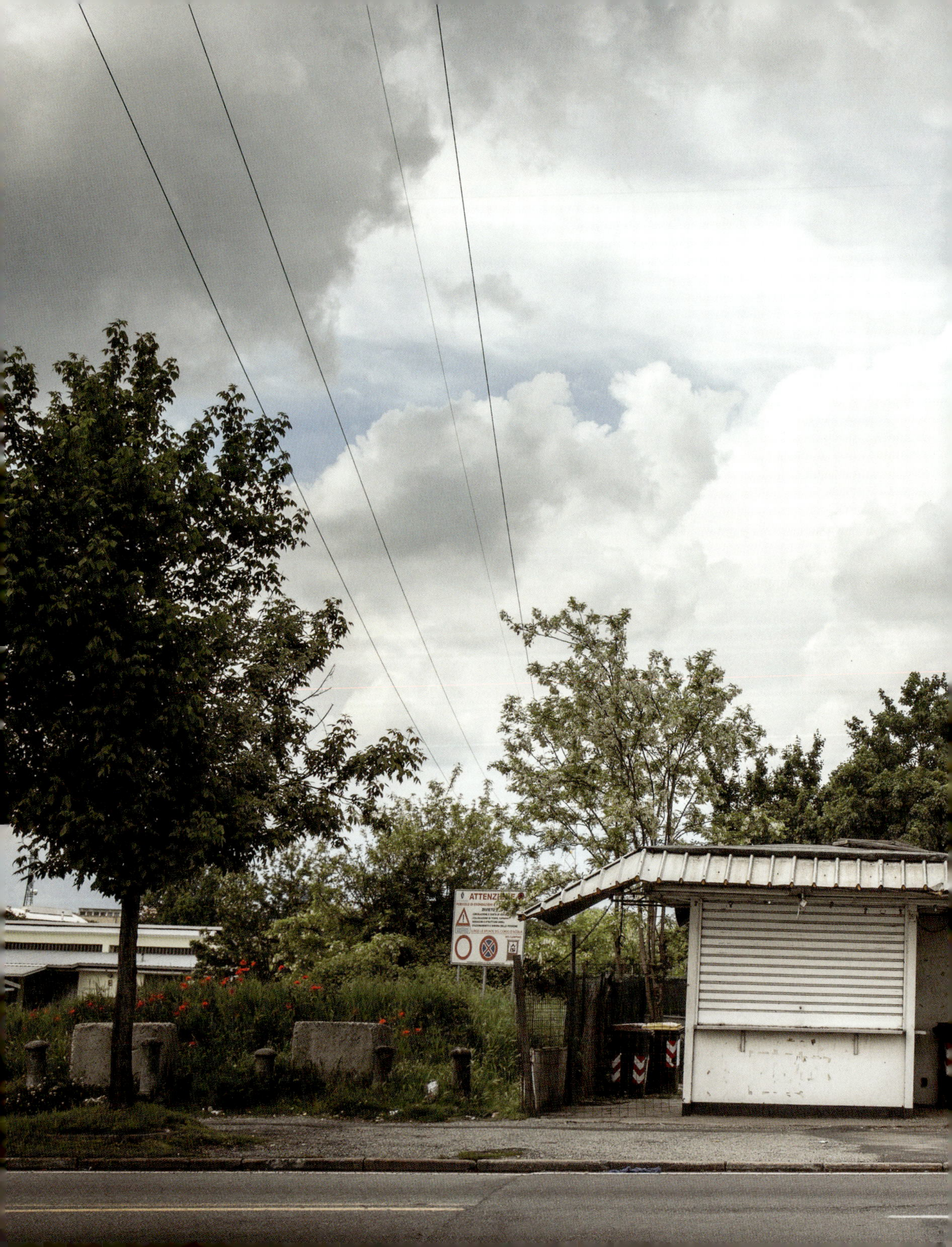
ATTENZIONE

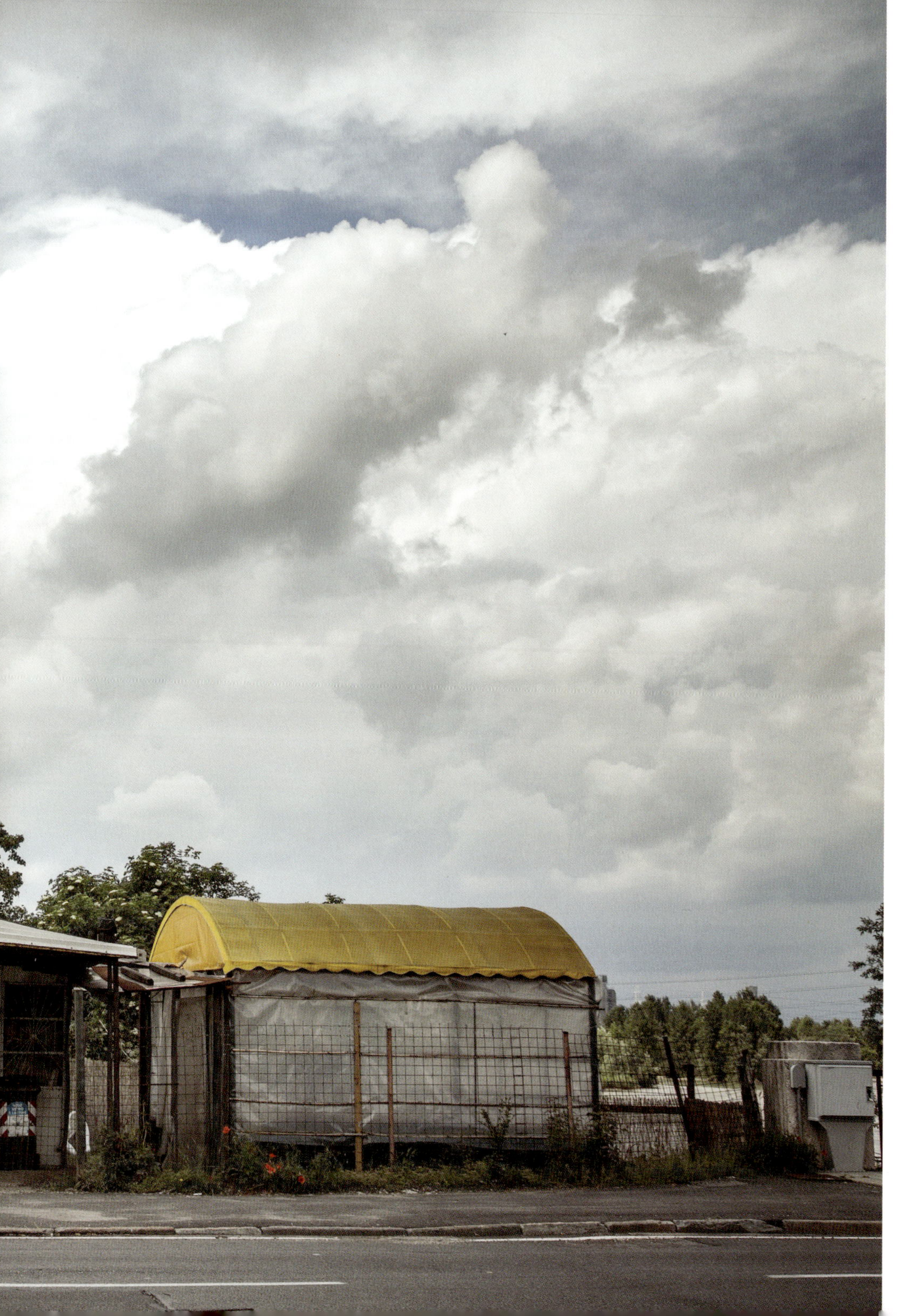

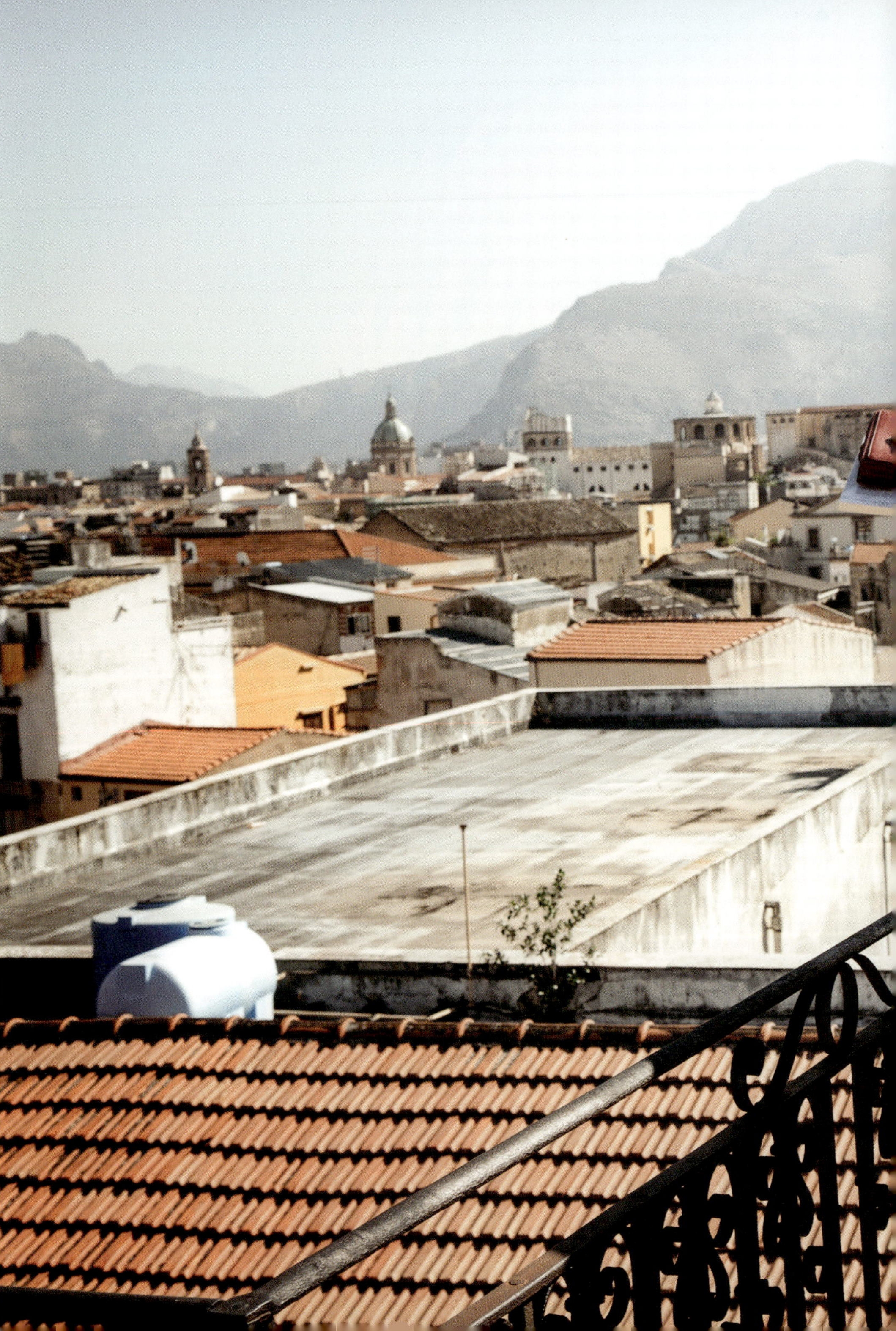

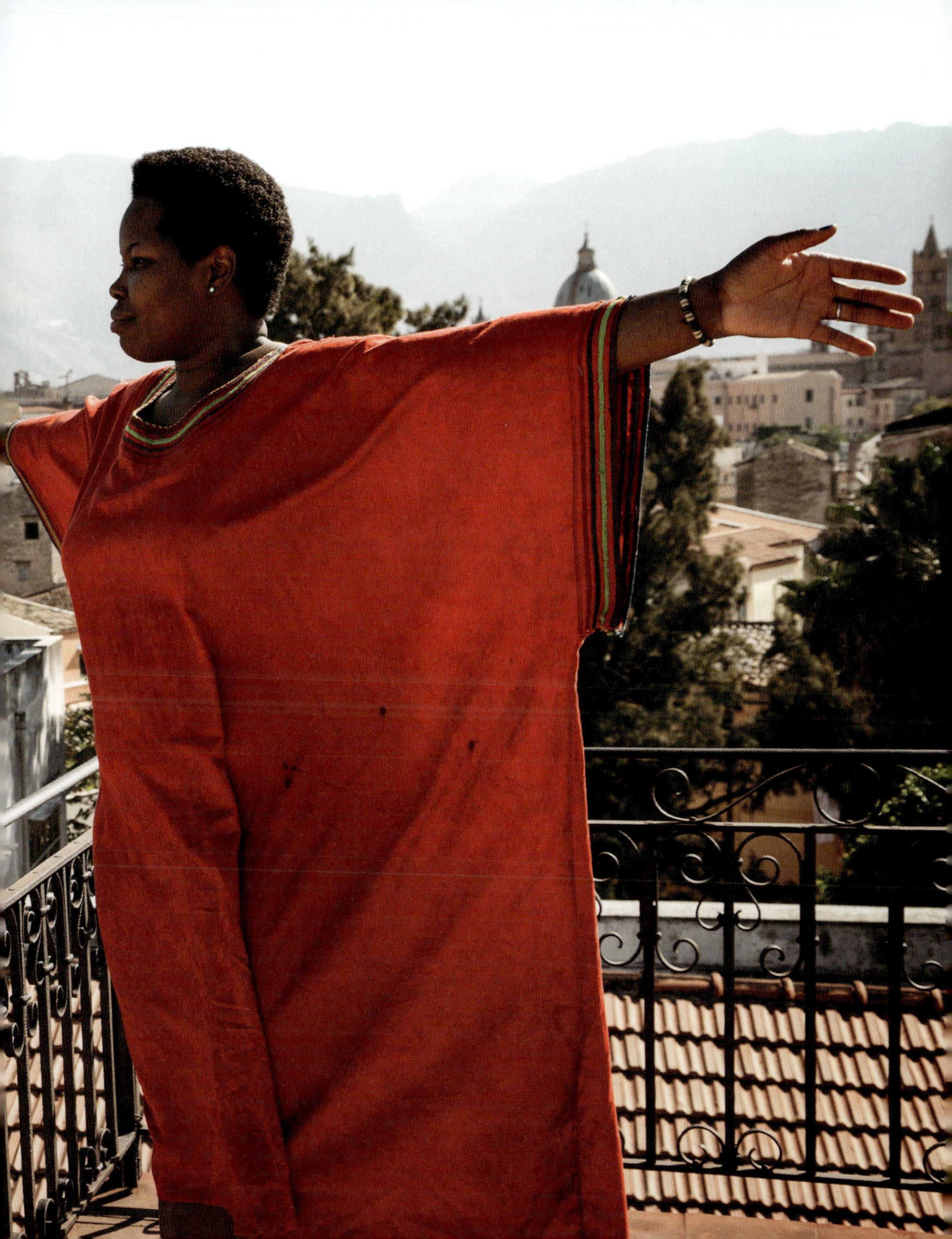

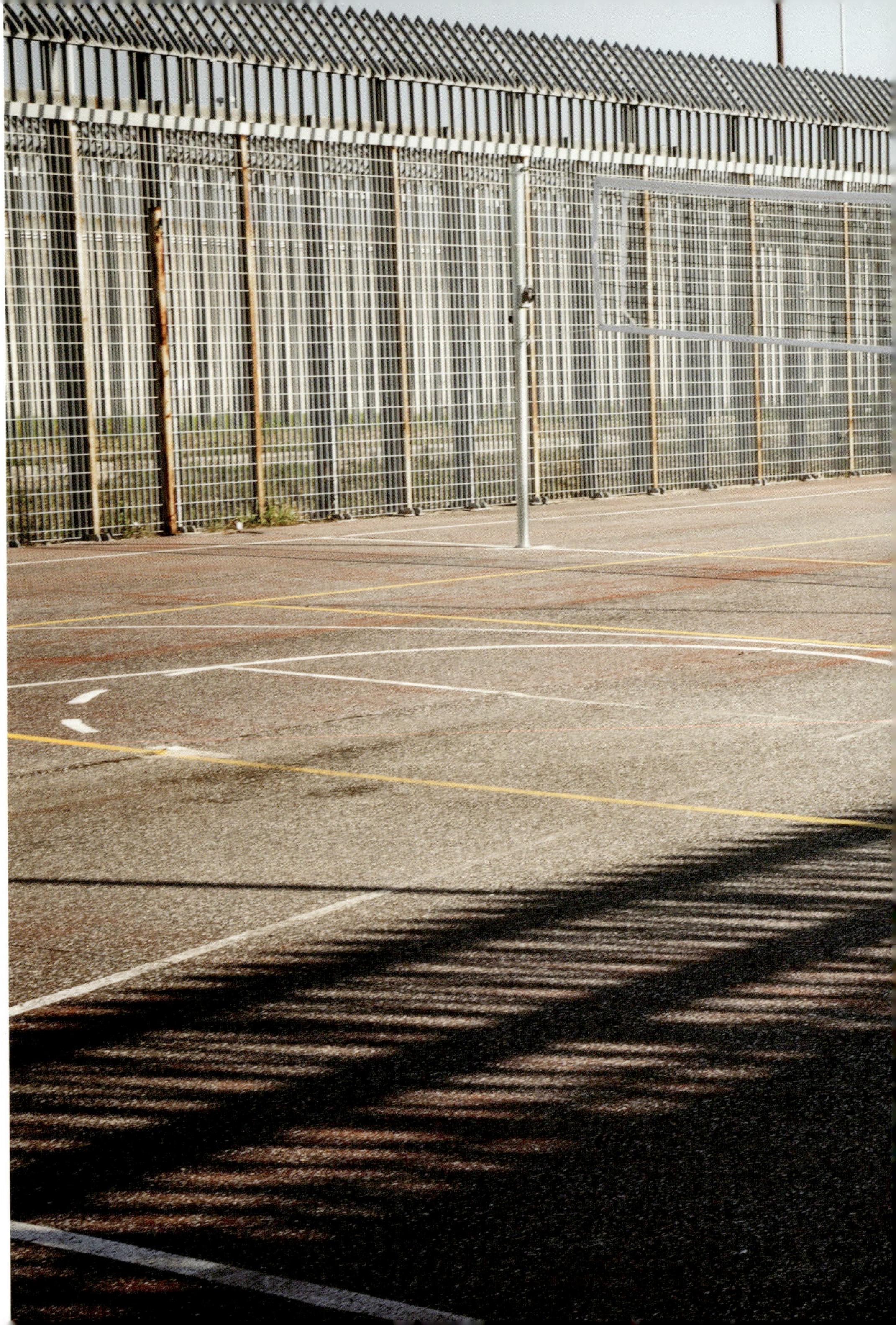

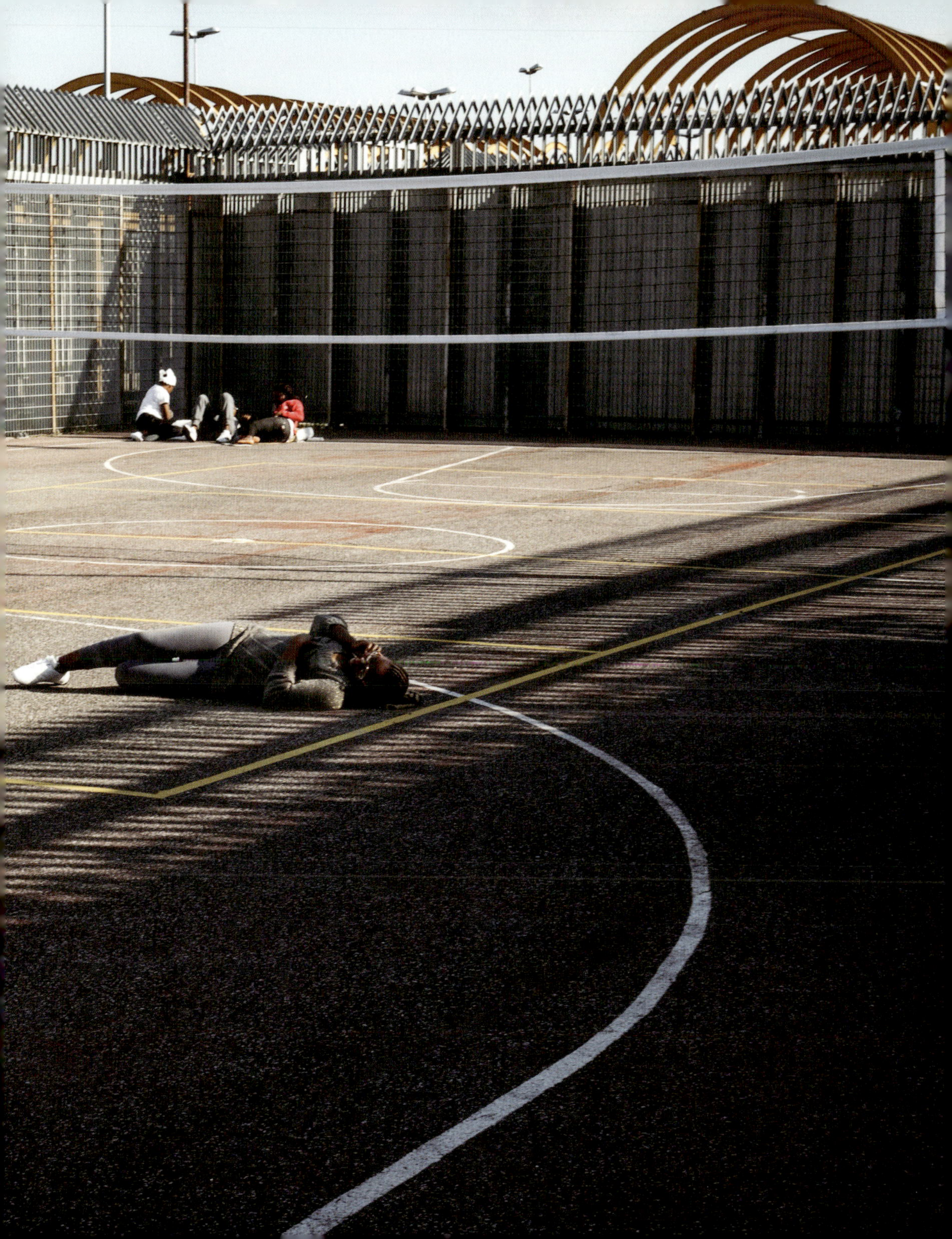

Part three

21.
[…] It's time to put a stop to the segregation. It's time to start going
to the supermarket and the dentist, to the bookshop and the health
centre.
During this process they can be supported by the ex-clients who have
now become their partners. But they, the men, will have to take a step
back. […]
Because the real work you do with the girls is what happens inside.
You have to break with the street and the friendships on the street. […]
And above all: break the shackle that is sending money home.
Because this, perhaps even more than the debt, is the most difficult
chain for the girls to break. The chain of a thousand family obligations
and the thousand responsibilities that come with them. Of affection.
Of pity. Of the desire to be accepted at least. […]
And it's very difficult to say: Enough.
But if you want to save yourself, you have to do it. […]
You have to find the guts to say: my journey has been a total failure.
And then, you see, out of that failure a new life can be born.

22.
[…] Trafficking is not just a question of sex, of whores and clients.
Trafficking is first of all a colossal business. A business. It's a form of
slavery that makes a stack of money, and whites and blacks share that
money, in perfect harmony.
Fortunes are made off the backs of us girls, and not just the fortunes of
people like the maman I saw in the paper, sitting on a divan in Benin
City, surrounded by piles of cash that high.
There are also the respectable whites, the ones who never beat their kids
or their wives, who probably go to church on Sundays, they've got a
beautiful dog, nice neighbours, a reputation with never a shadow of a
stain on it. They're the ones who sell the visas, who organise the journeys, who let you through at the airport without anyone noticing.
They're the cops on the take, the maman's lawyers, the intermediaries,
the landlords. A lot of oh so upright citizens have made their fortunes
thanks to the traffic in girls from Benin City. […]

24.
The last story I'm going to tell you is my sister's story.
My younger sister, the one who's now just over twenty. She was four-
teen when I left. I barely remember a skinny little thing with very long
legs. Braids in her hair. Big big eyes.
A few months ago she told me she was pregnant and that she wanted
to come to Europe.
She too had found a journey.
She said: I finally got my lucky break.
Her lucky break.
I shut my eyes and inside me a voice shouted: it isn't possible. When
will this story ever end. How many years, how much pain, how many
deaths are still needed before Nigeria stops sending its daughters to
the slaughterhouse.
I could hardly find enough voice to say: look, if you want to dream, go
ahead.
But the reality here is very different from the dreams.
Listen.
I took my courage in both hands and I started to speak. What traffick-
ing is. What the girls do. How they live. The horrible existence they lead.
It was the first time I found the courage to speak with someone from
my own family; to say it all, all of it! Without sparing a single detail.
You see: I couldn't keep quiet about it, not this time. And so, my mouth
dry, I explained everything just as it is. I told her about the cold and the
beatings and the ridiculous shoes and the fear. The twenty-five euros
and the Ditoi and Itohan found by a dog, all eaten by rats.
Don't think you're smarter than the other girls, I said.
Don't think you're different.
Don't hope it'll go better for you.
That's what I said to her.
She asked only: it happened to you, too?
I said: yes.
And she hasn't spoken since about coming to Europe.
Do I need to tell you how happy that makes me?

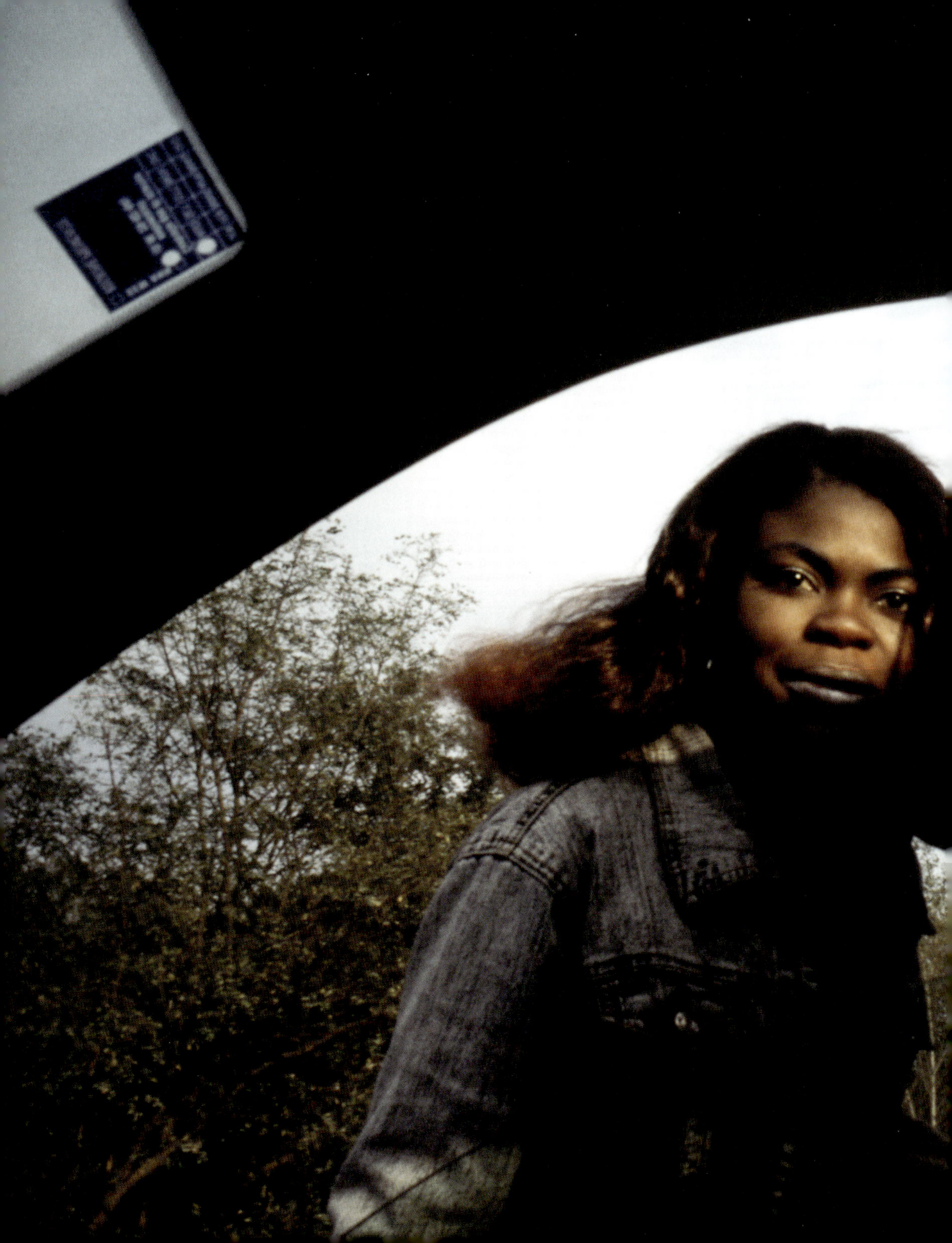

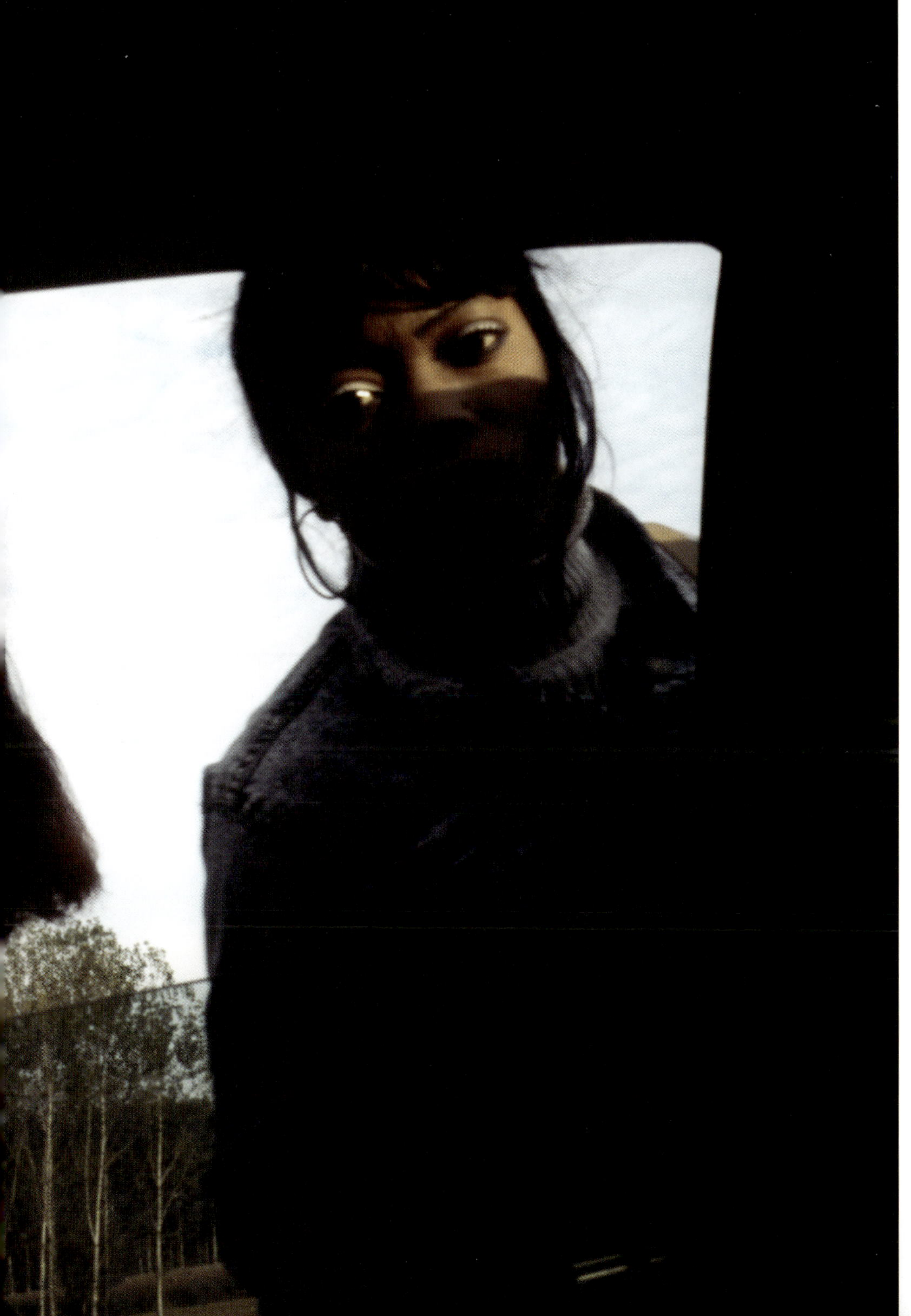

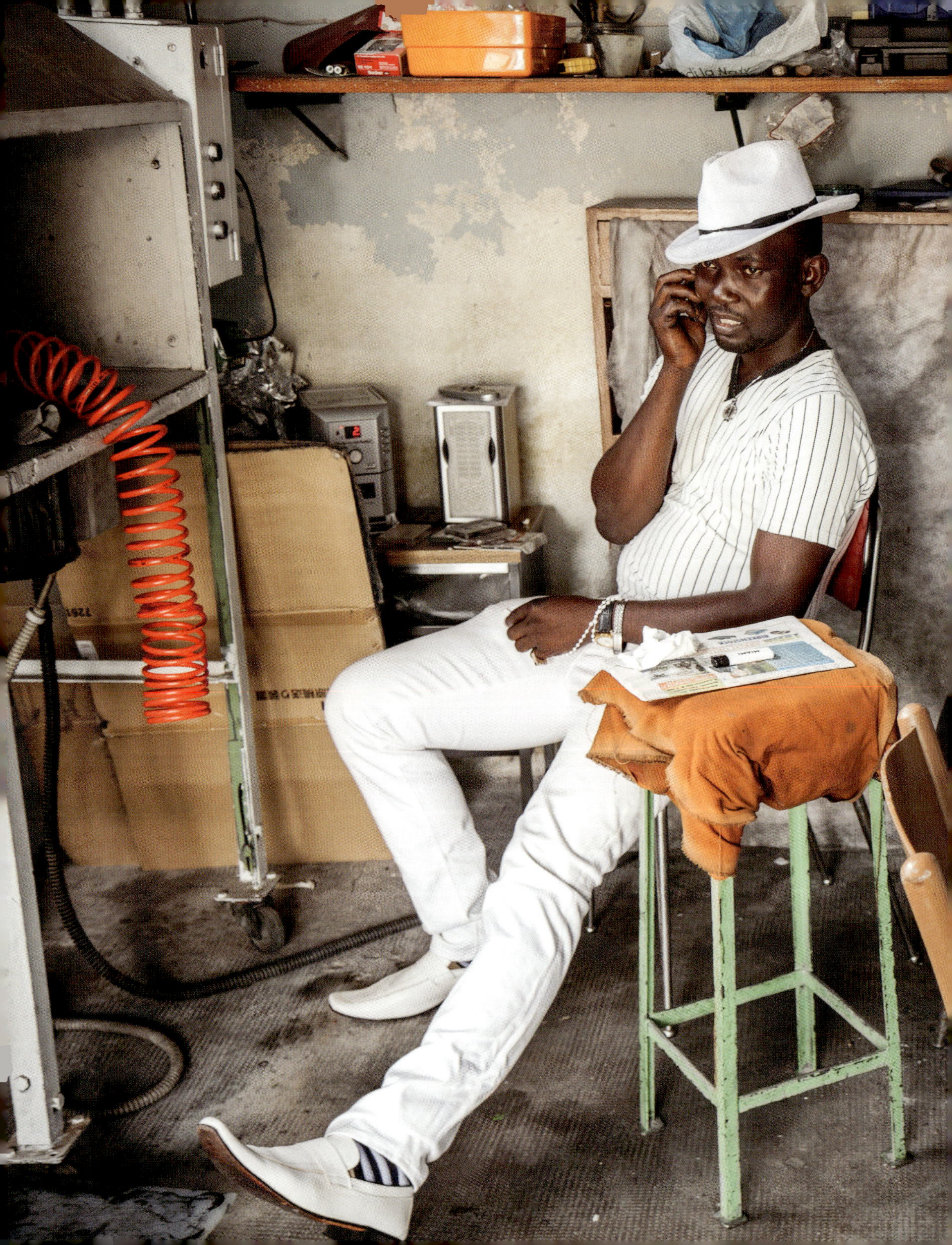

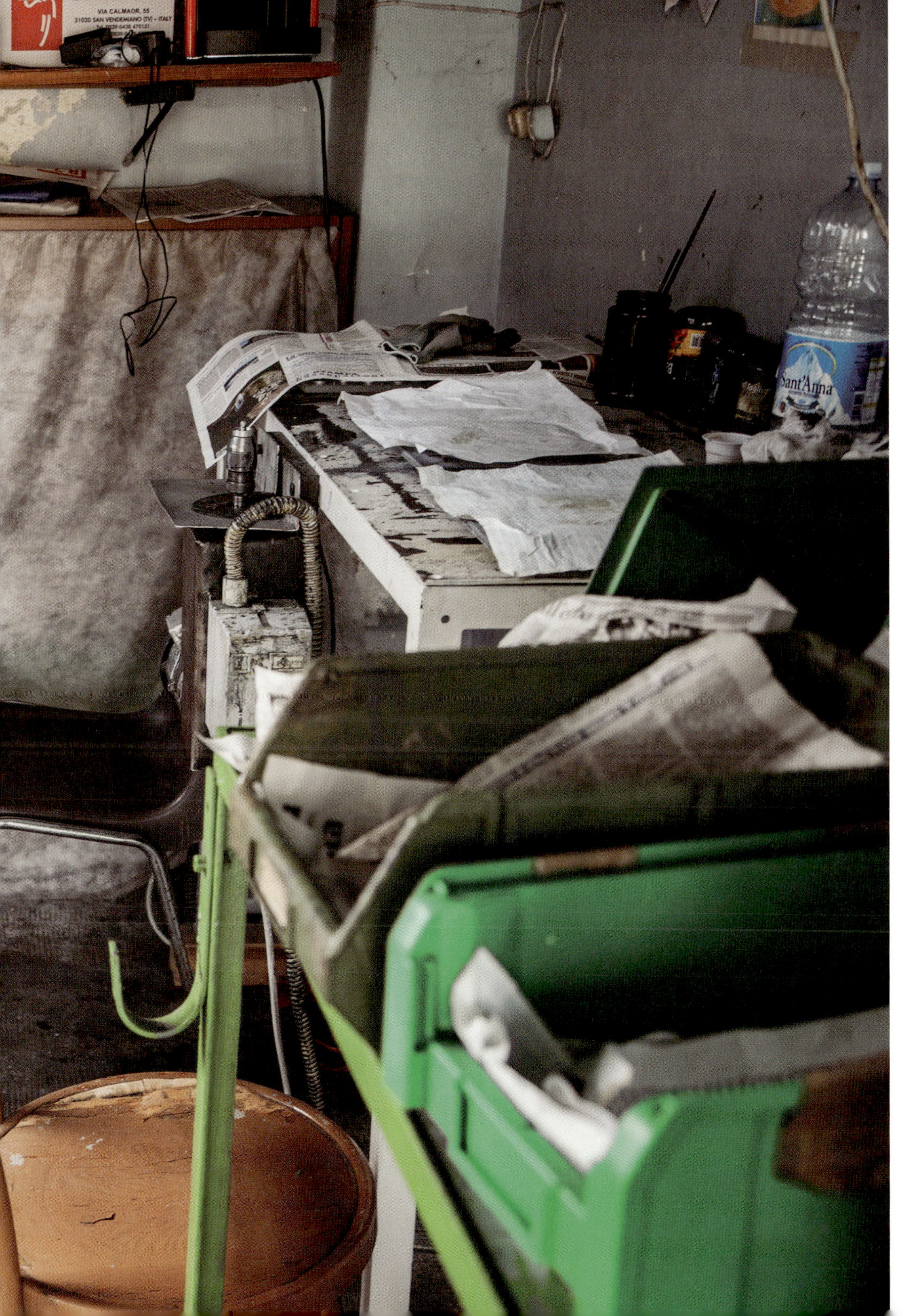

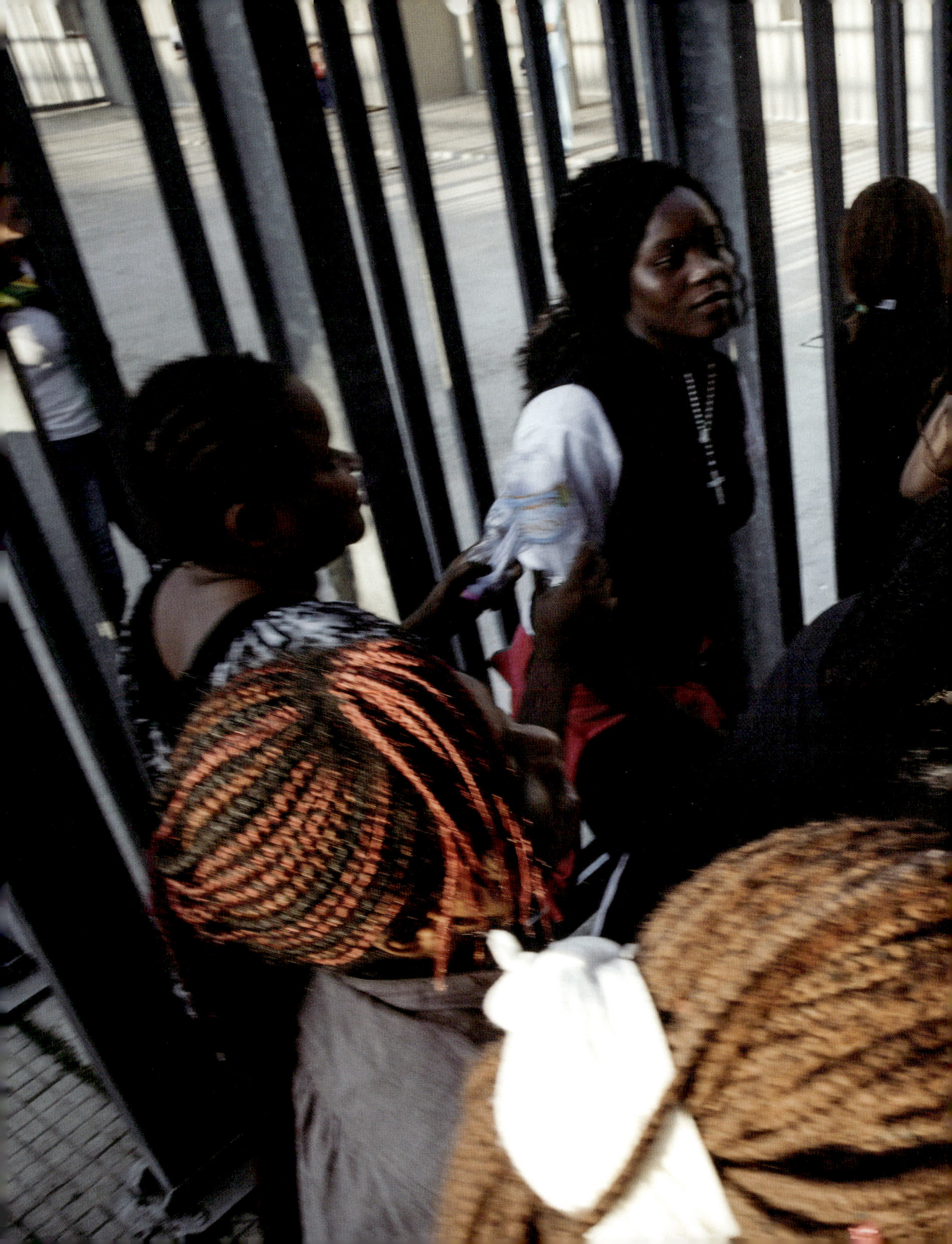

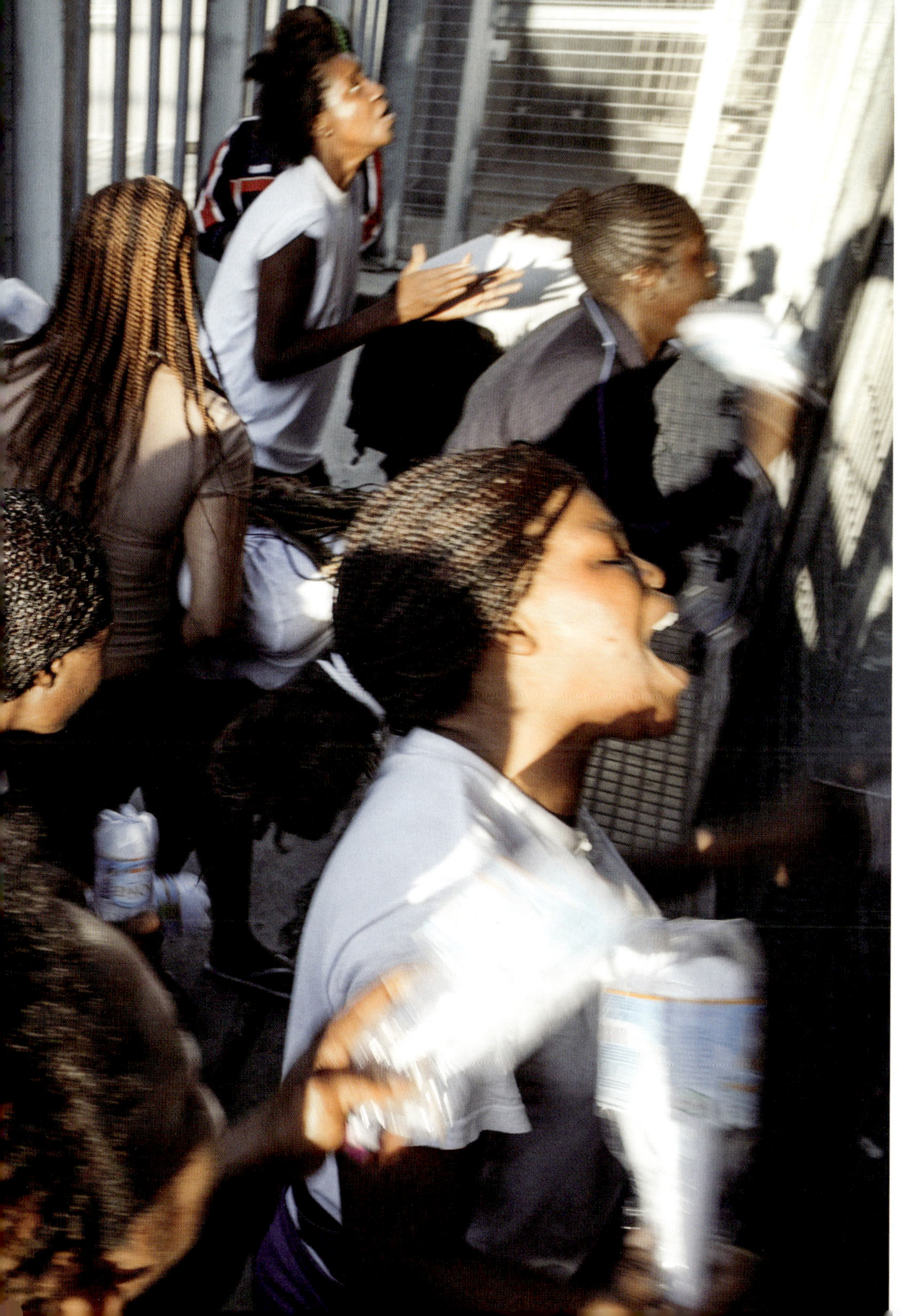

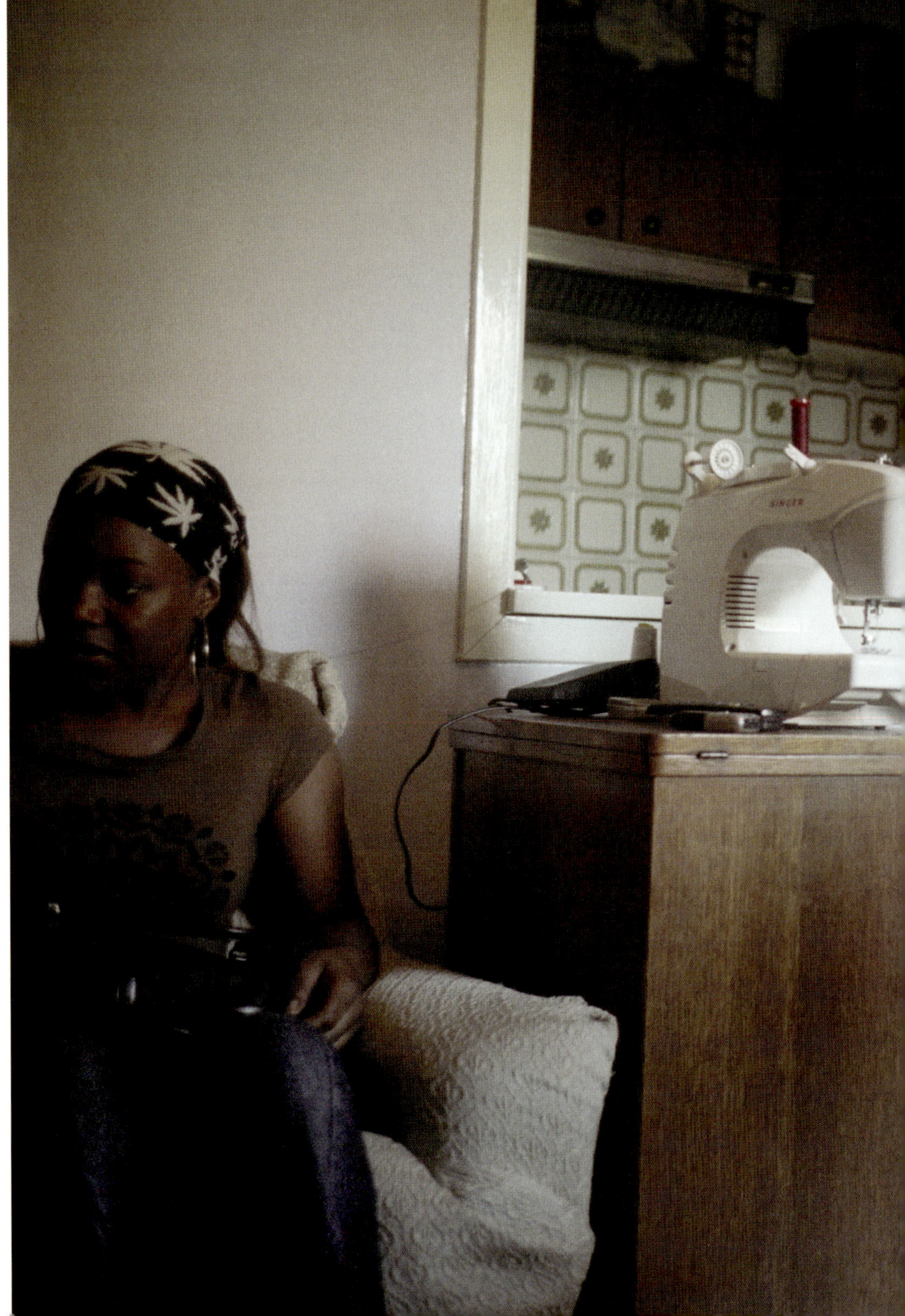

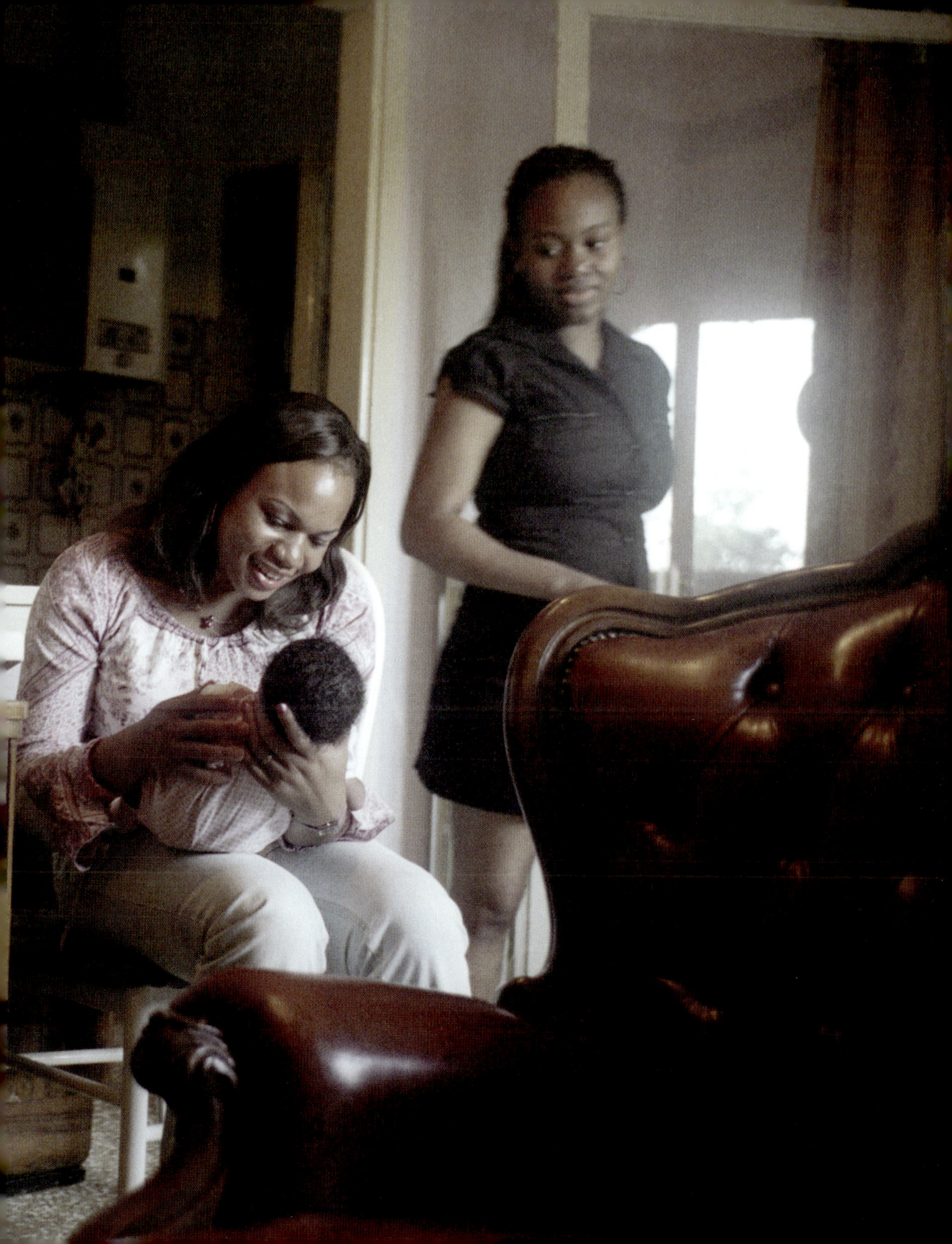

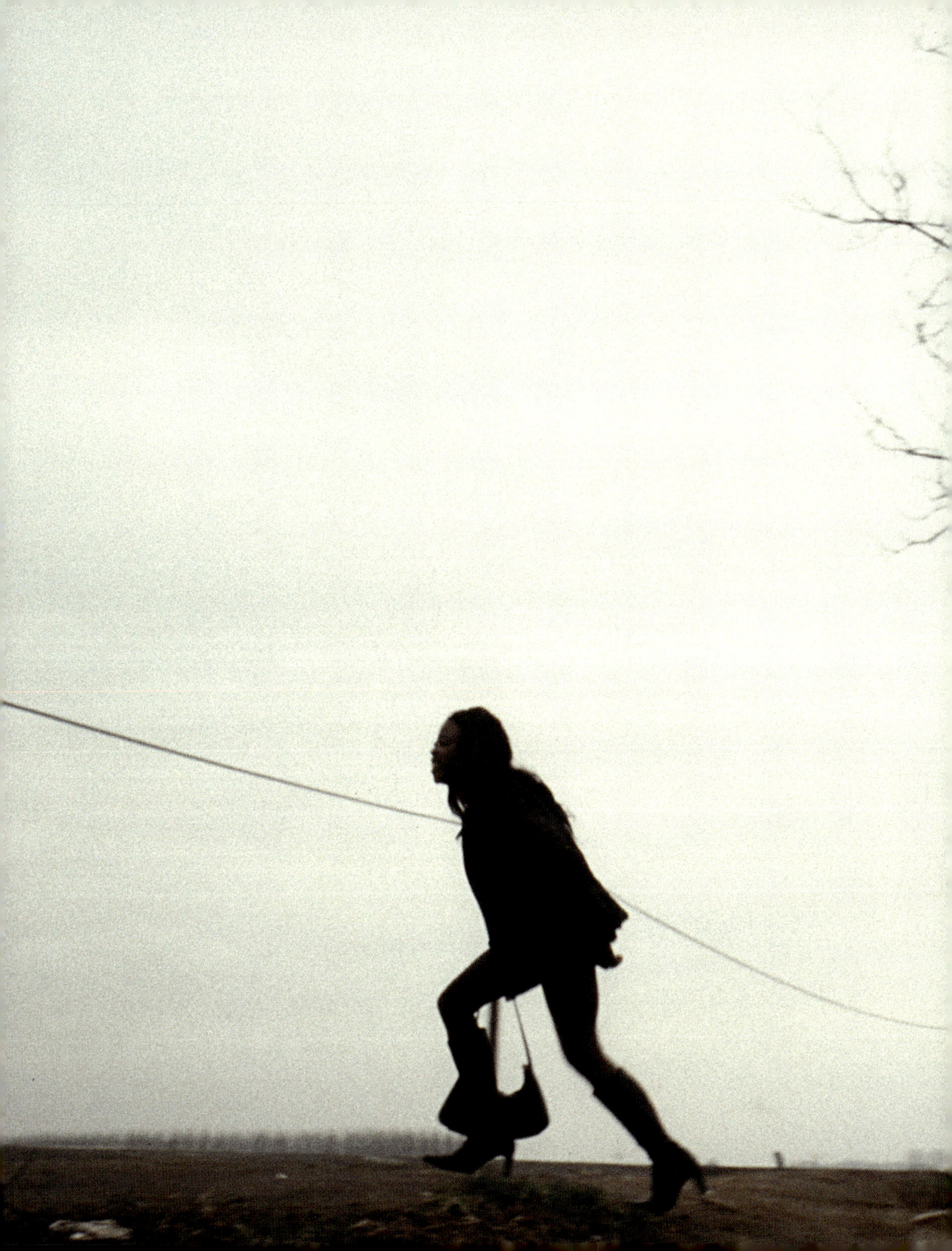

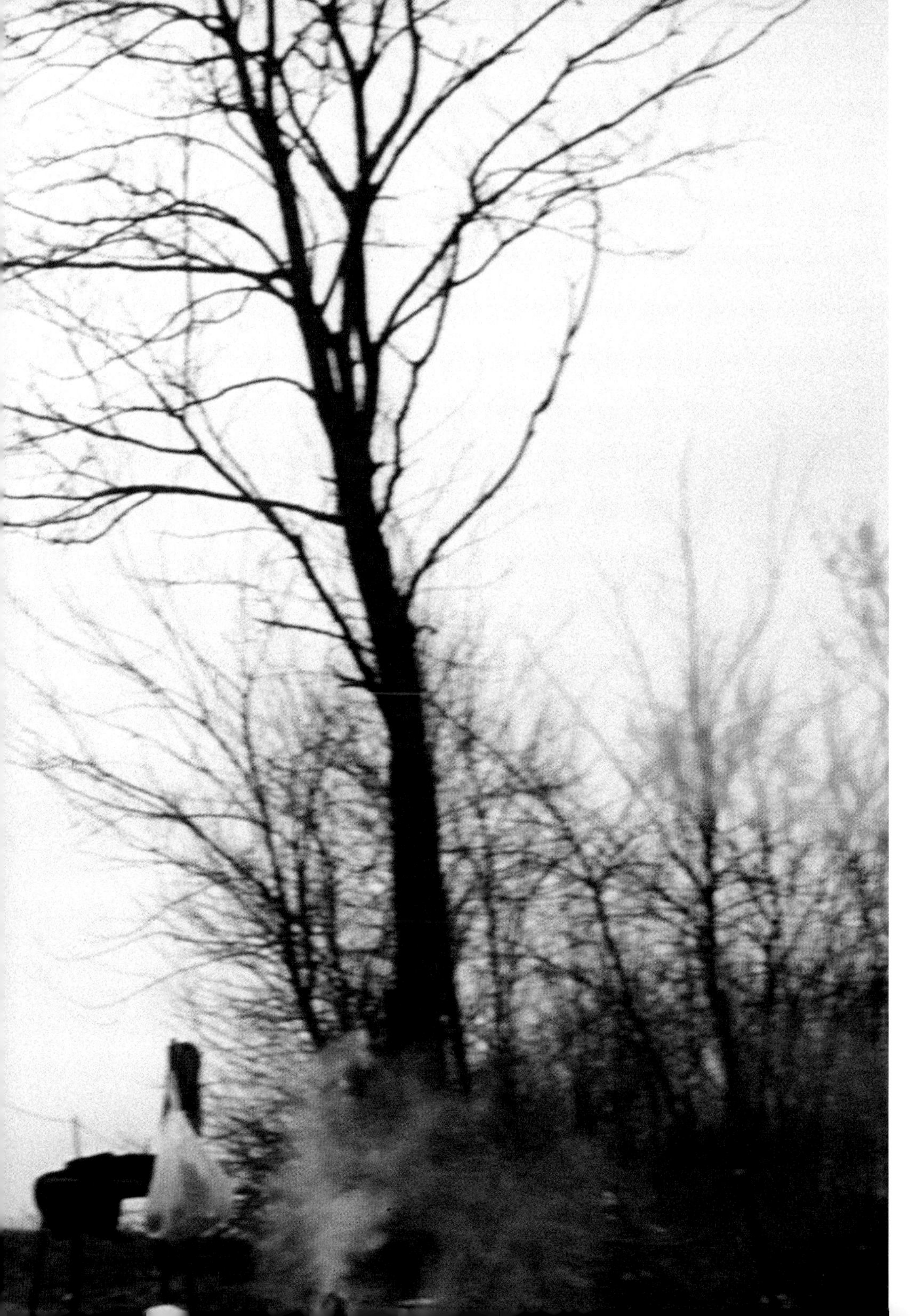

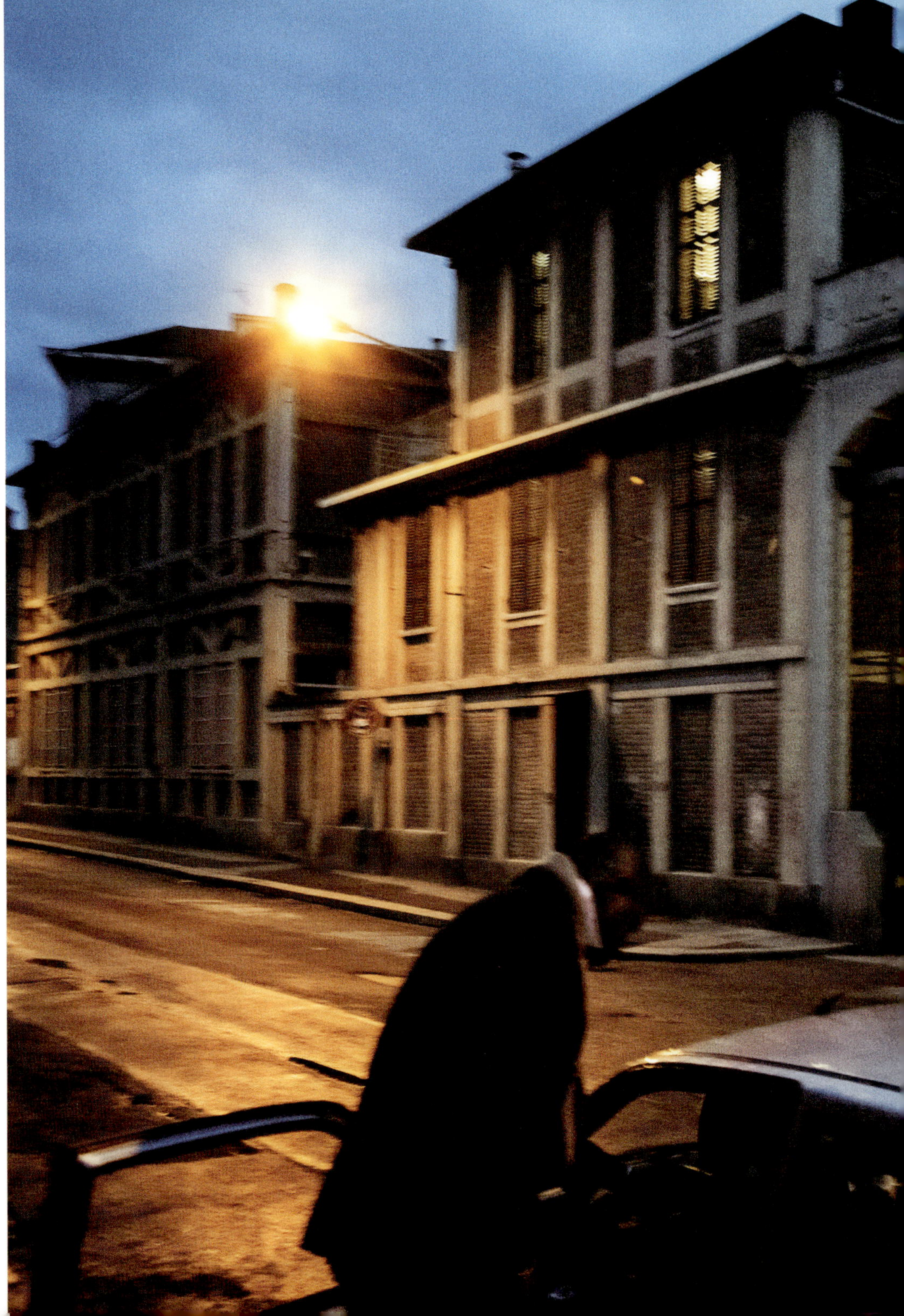

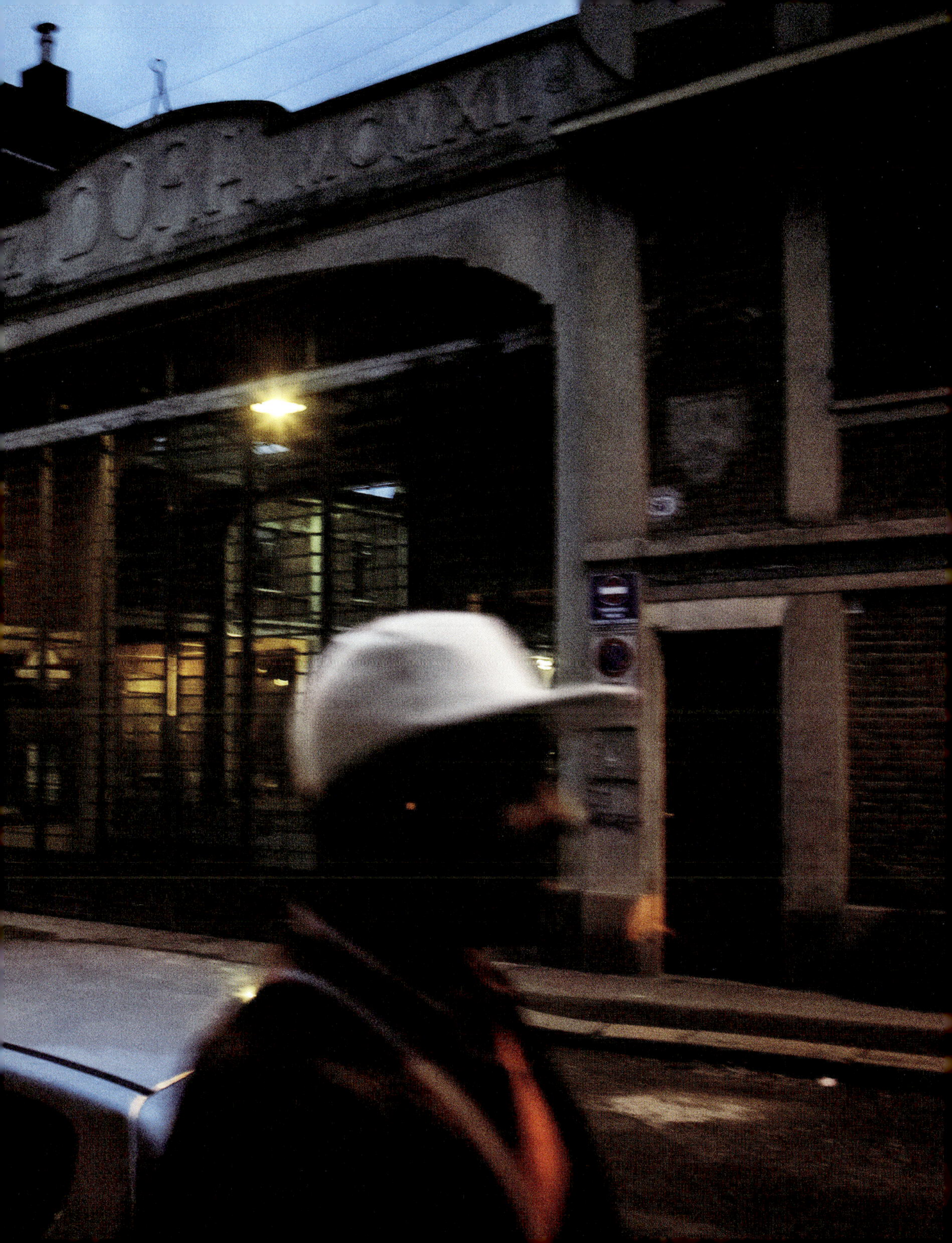

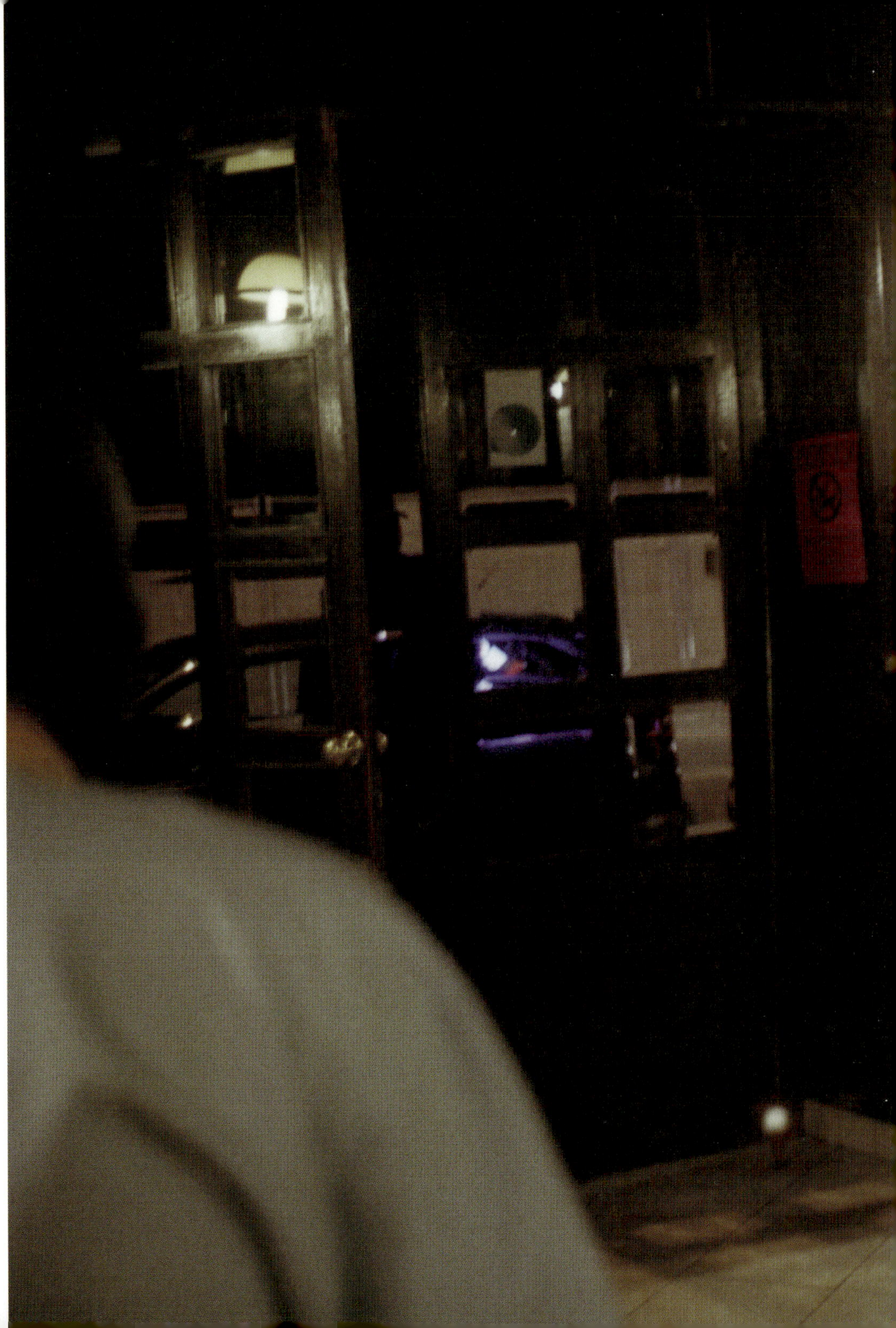

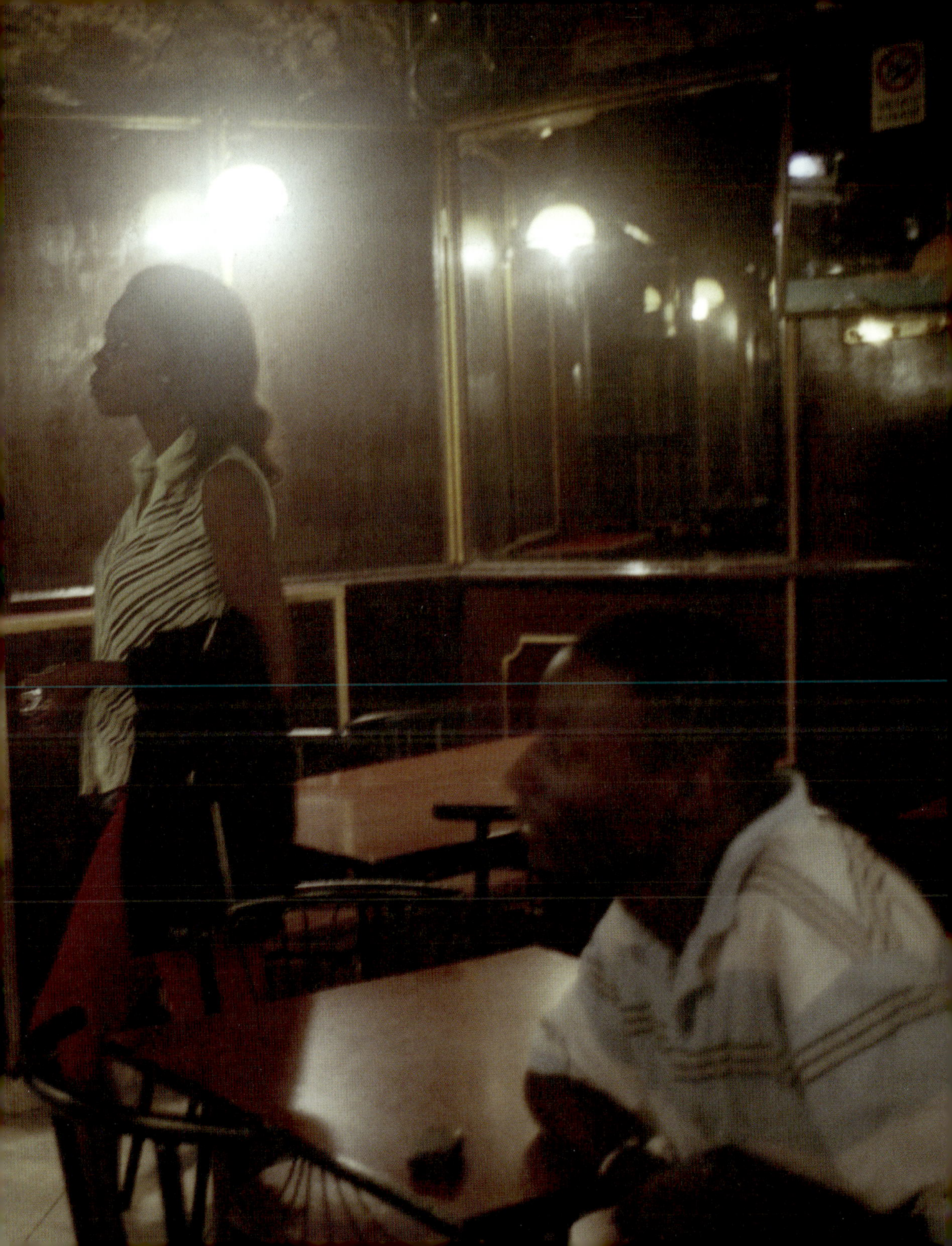

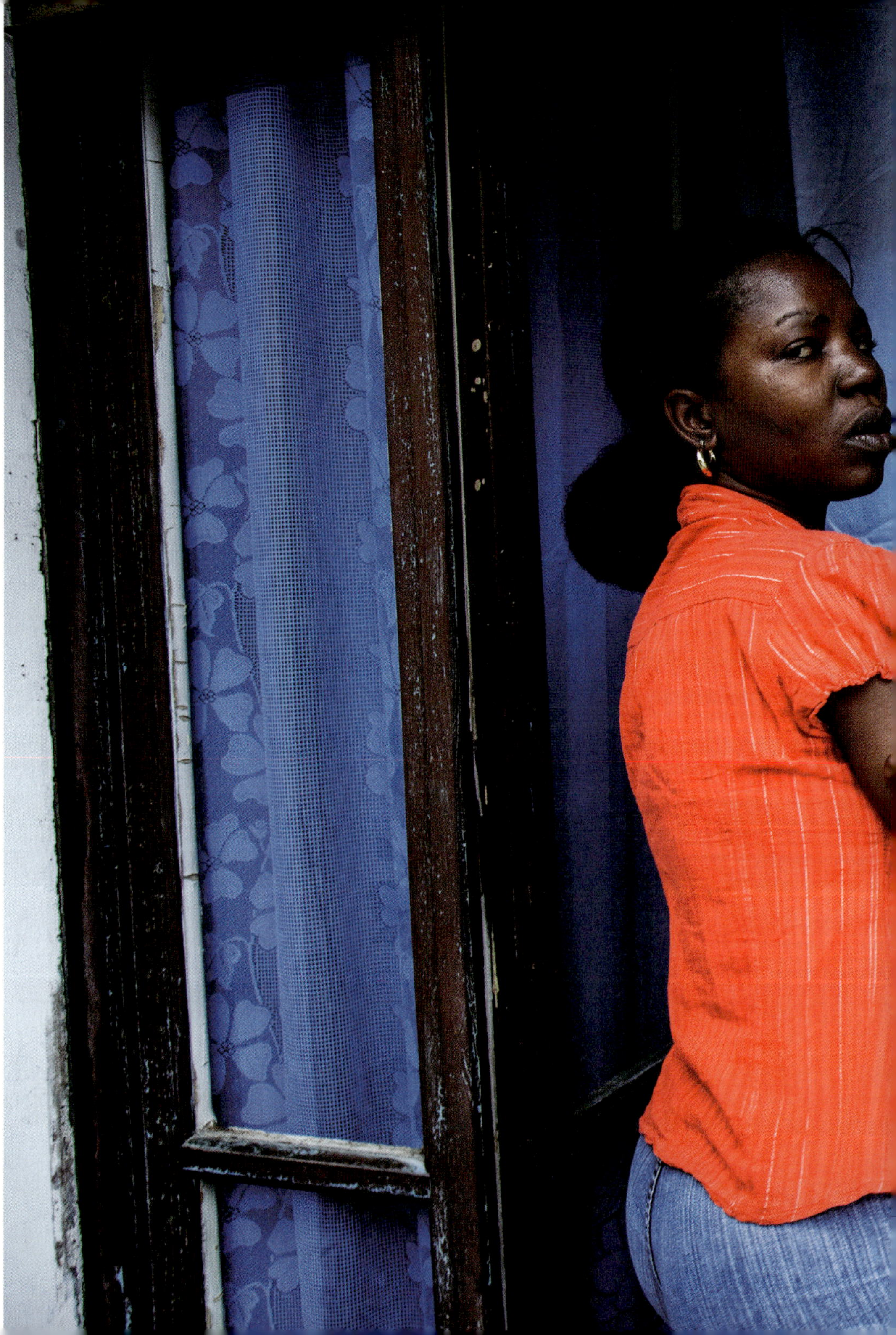

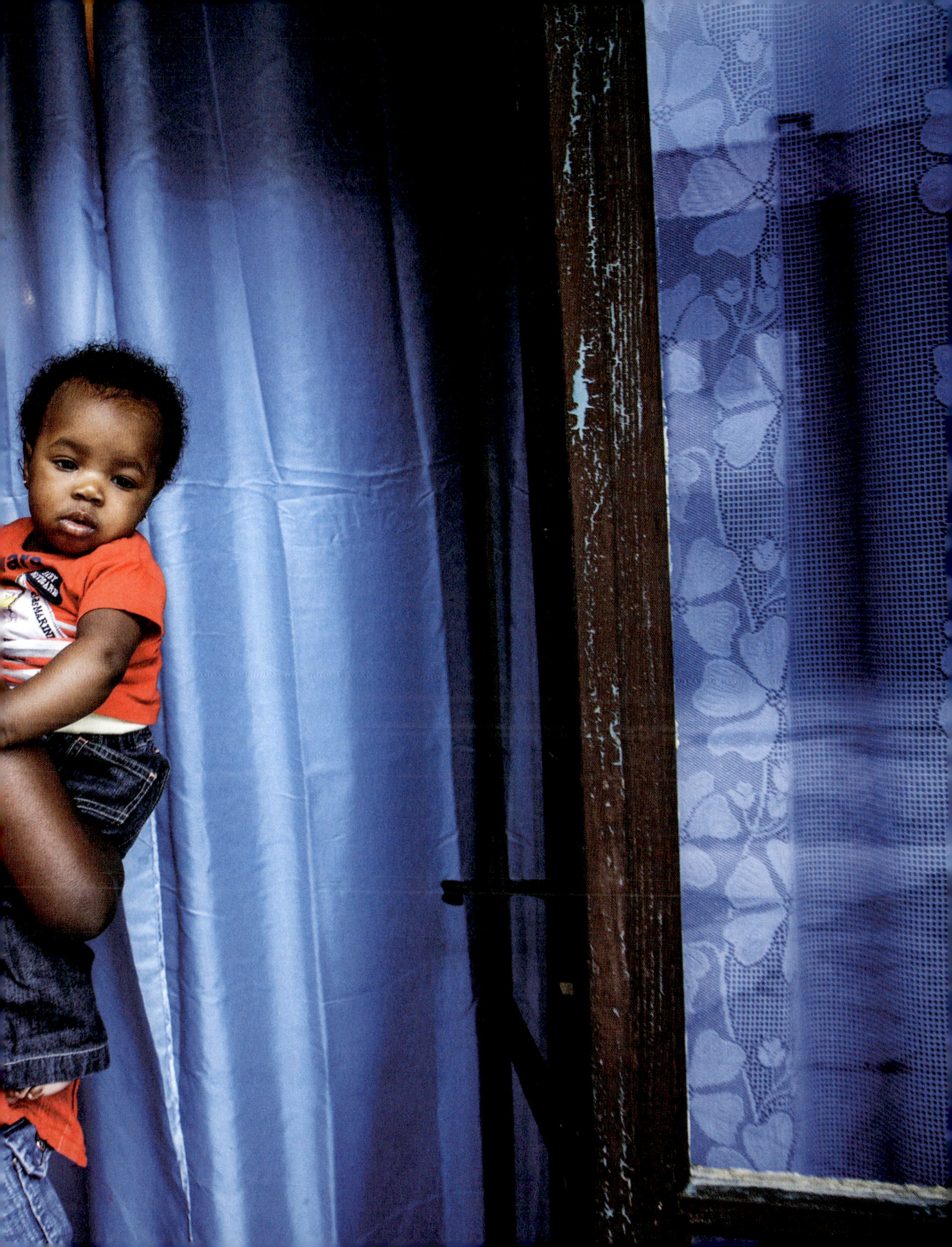

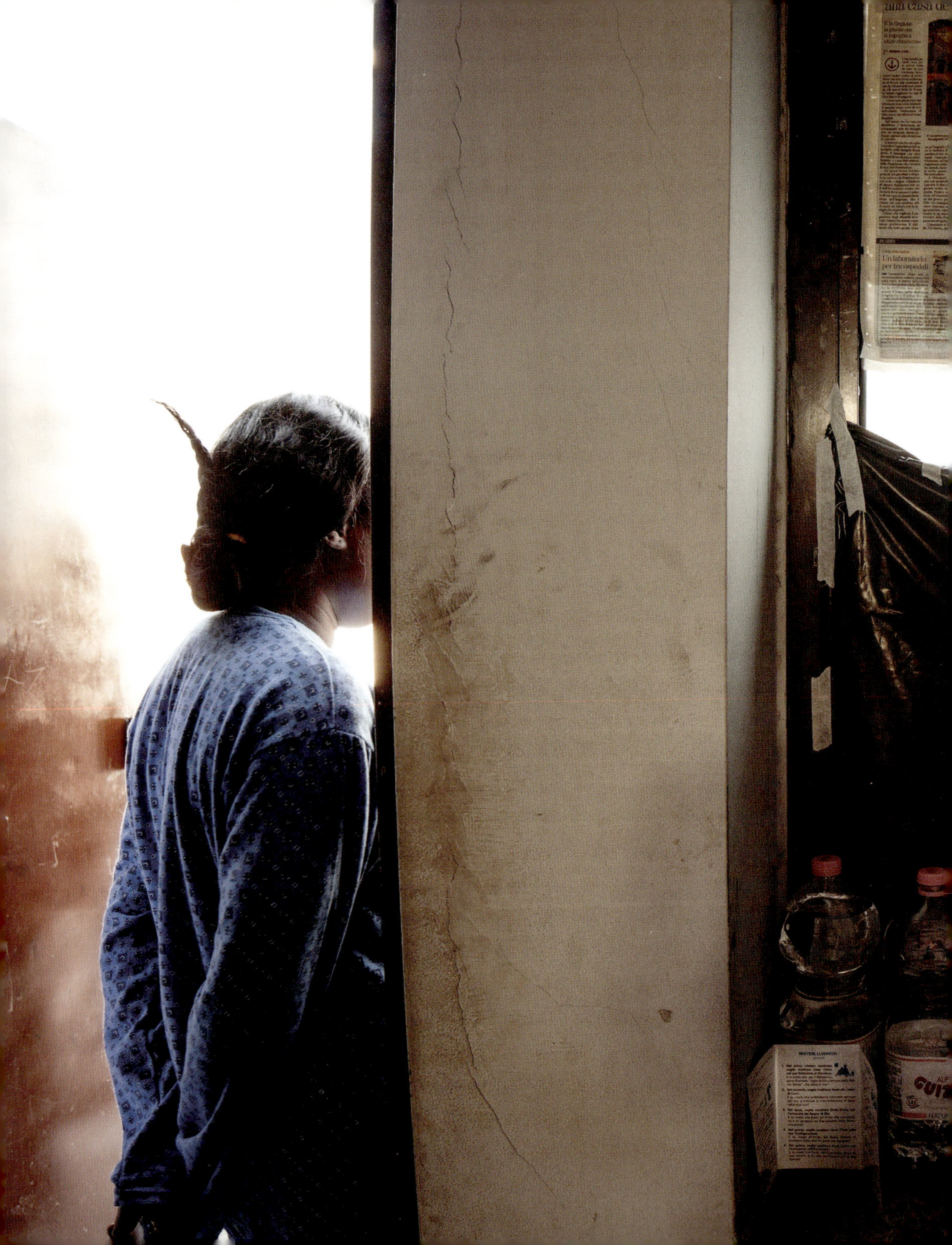

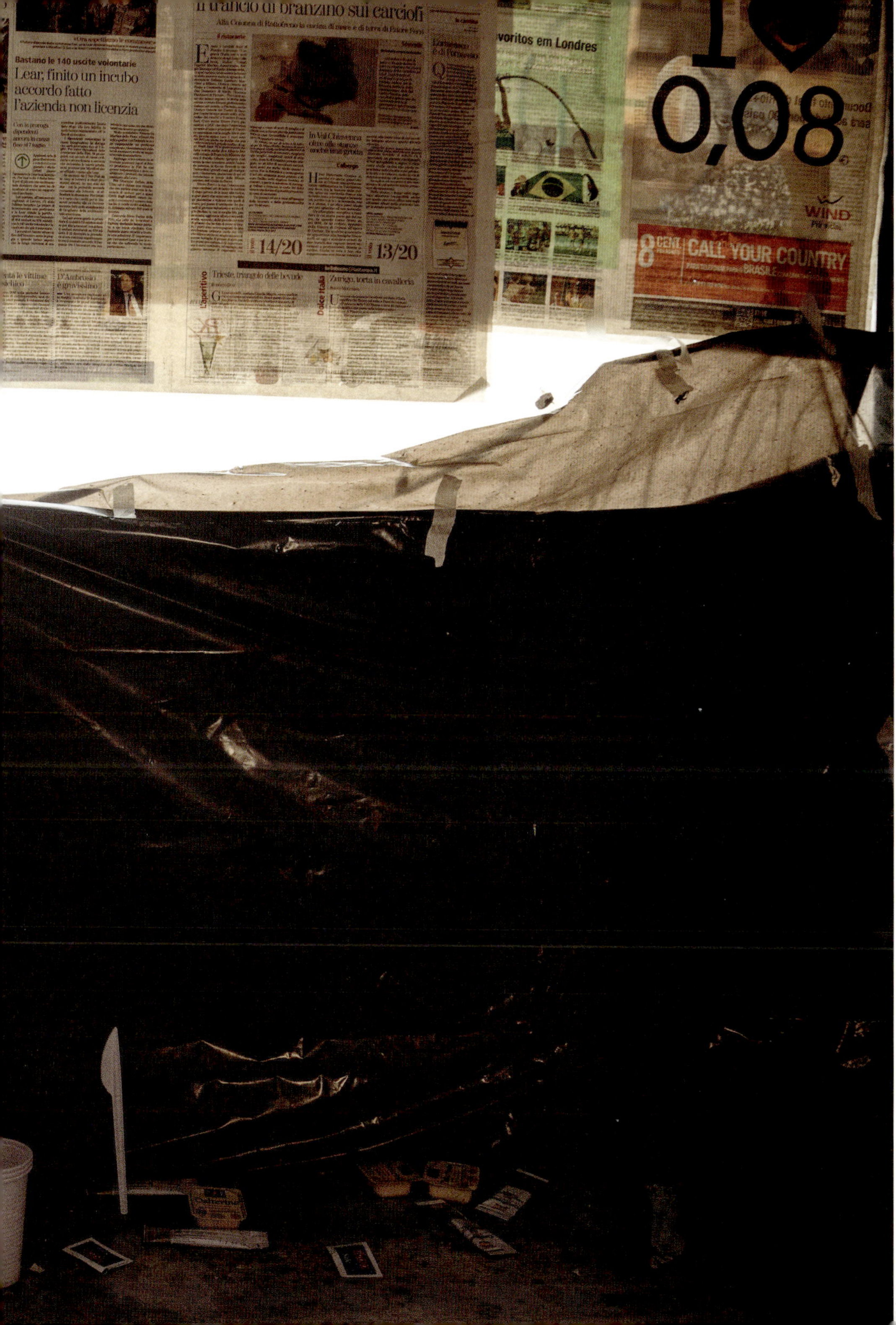

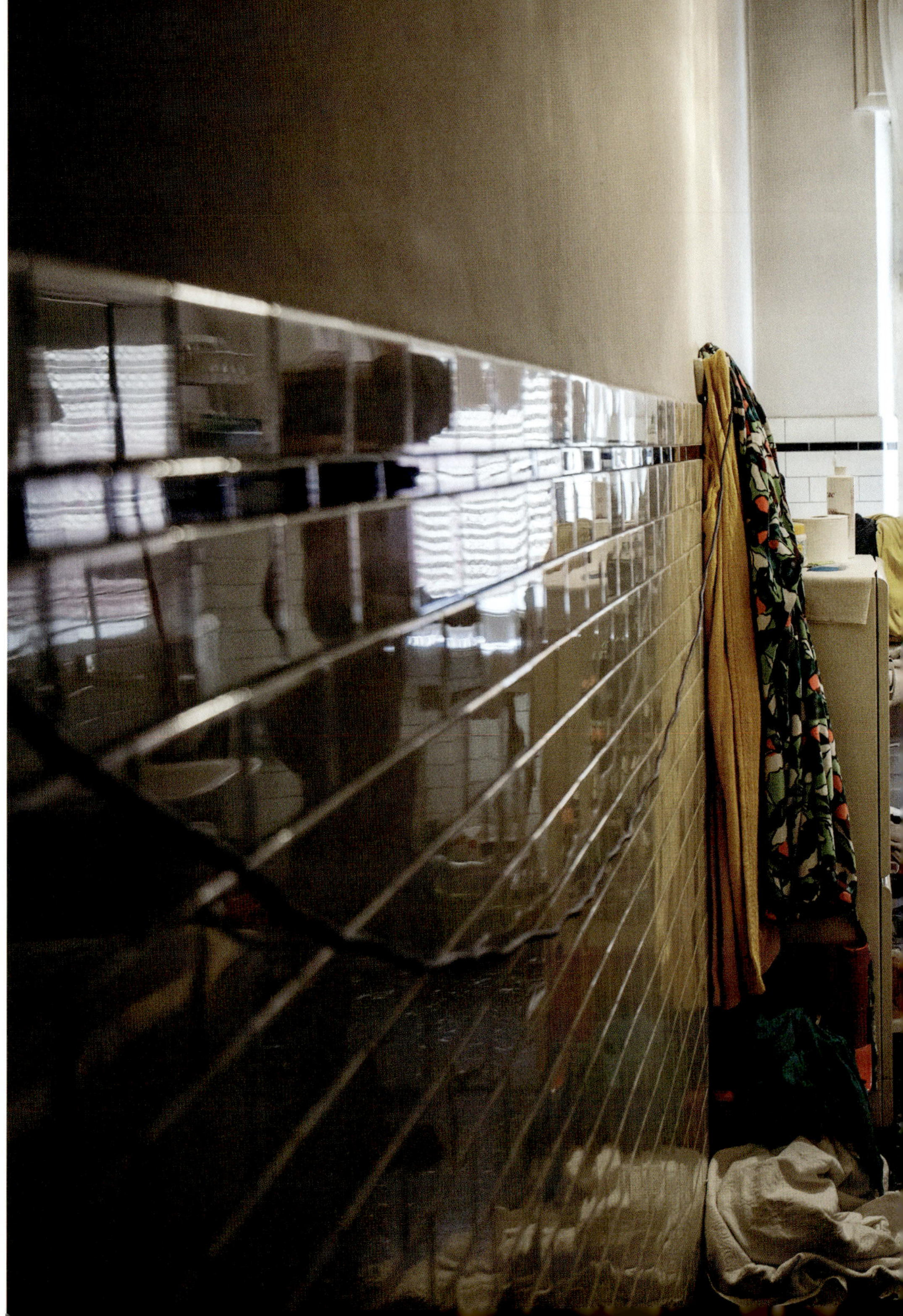

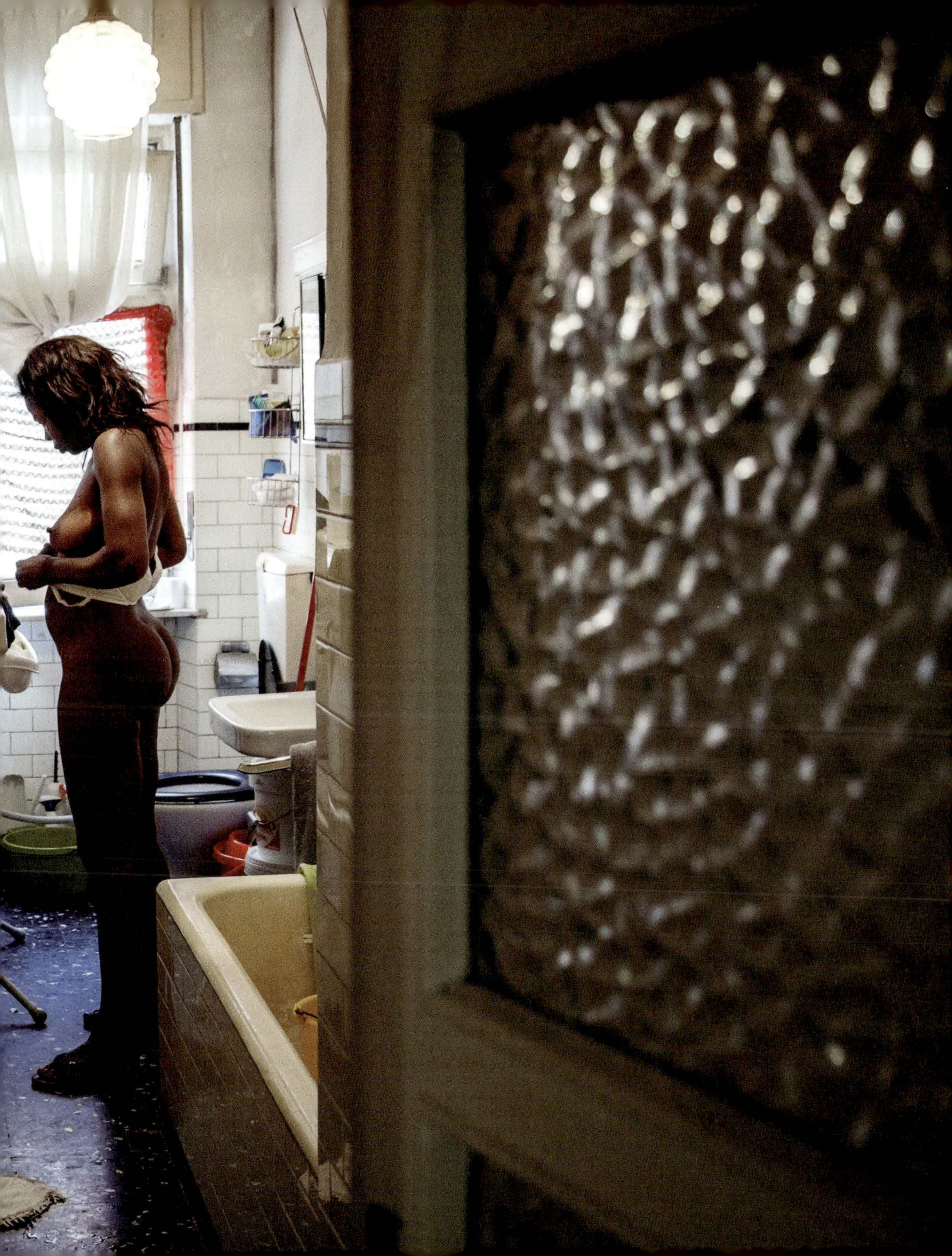

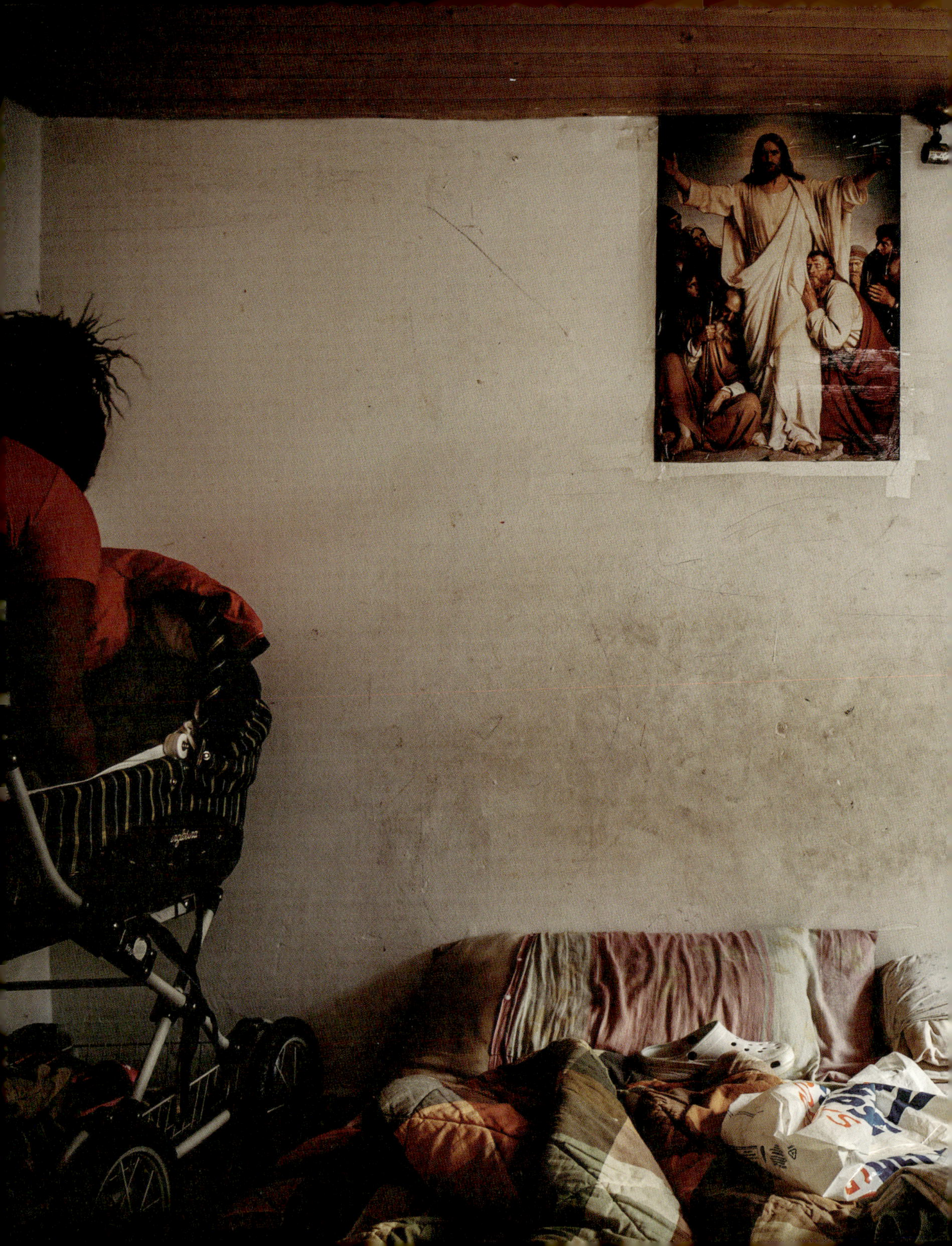

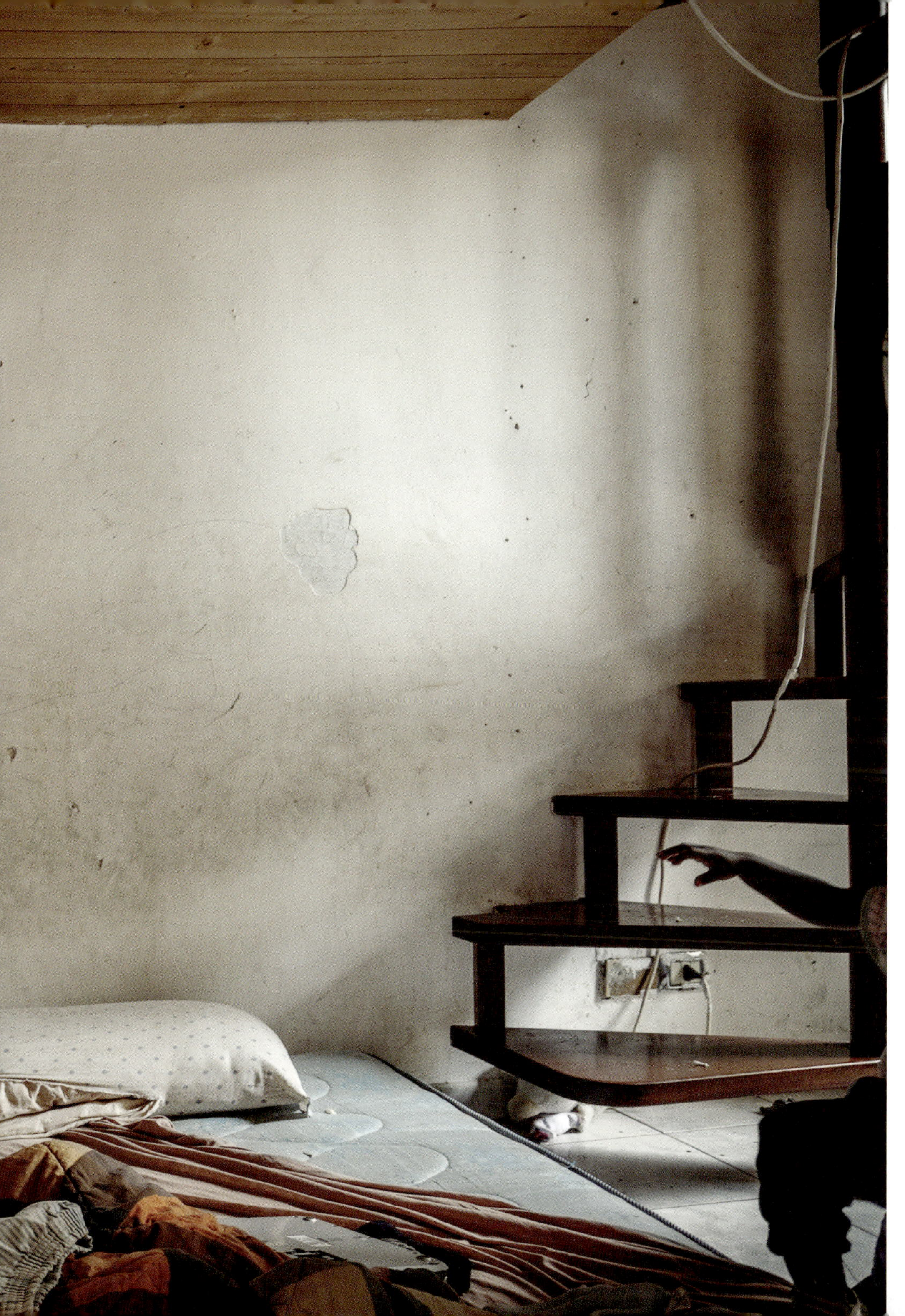

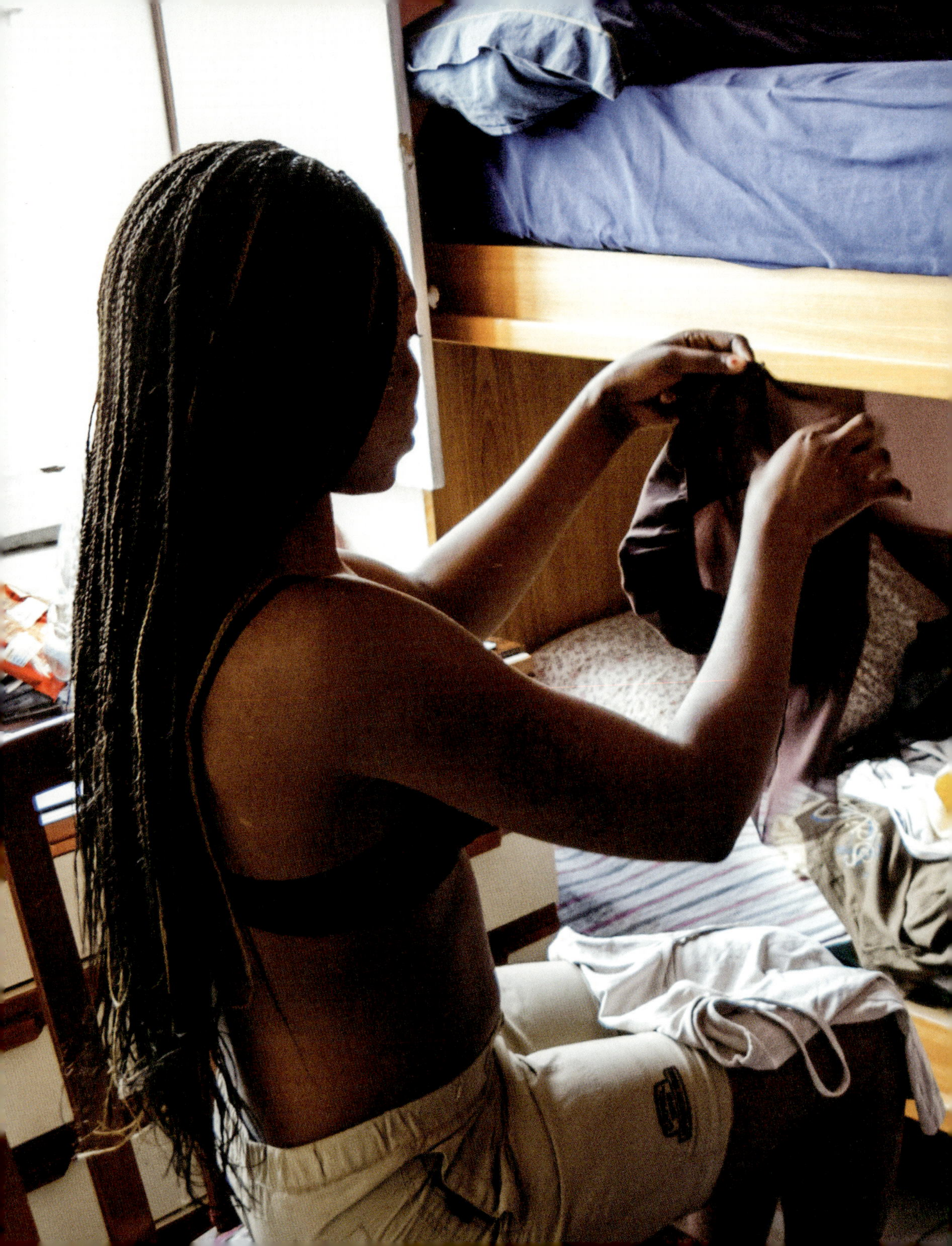

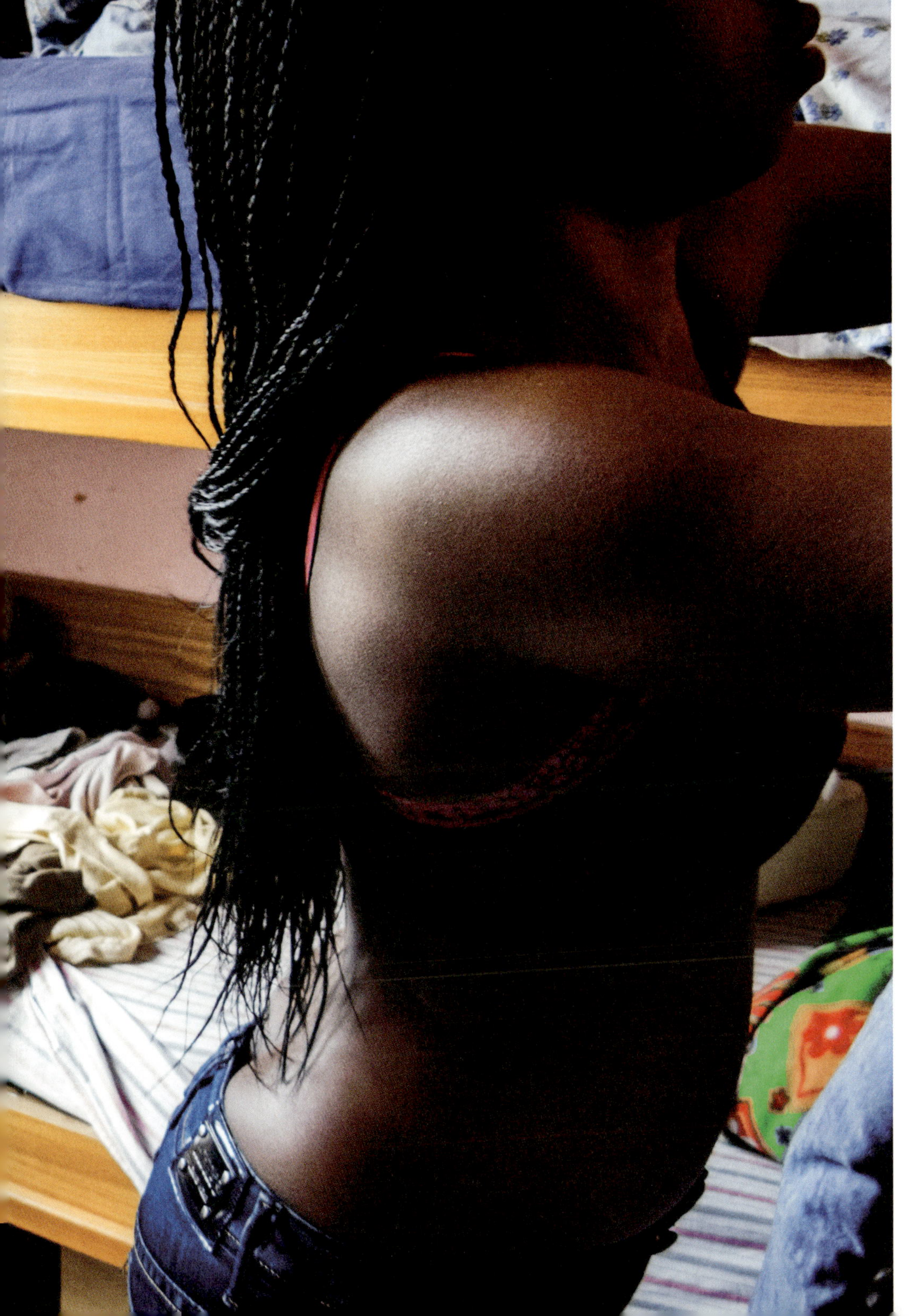

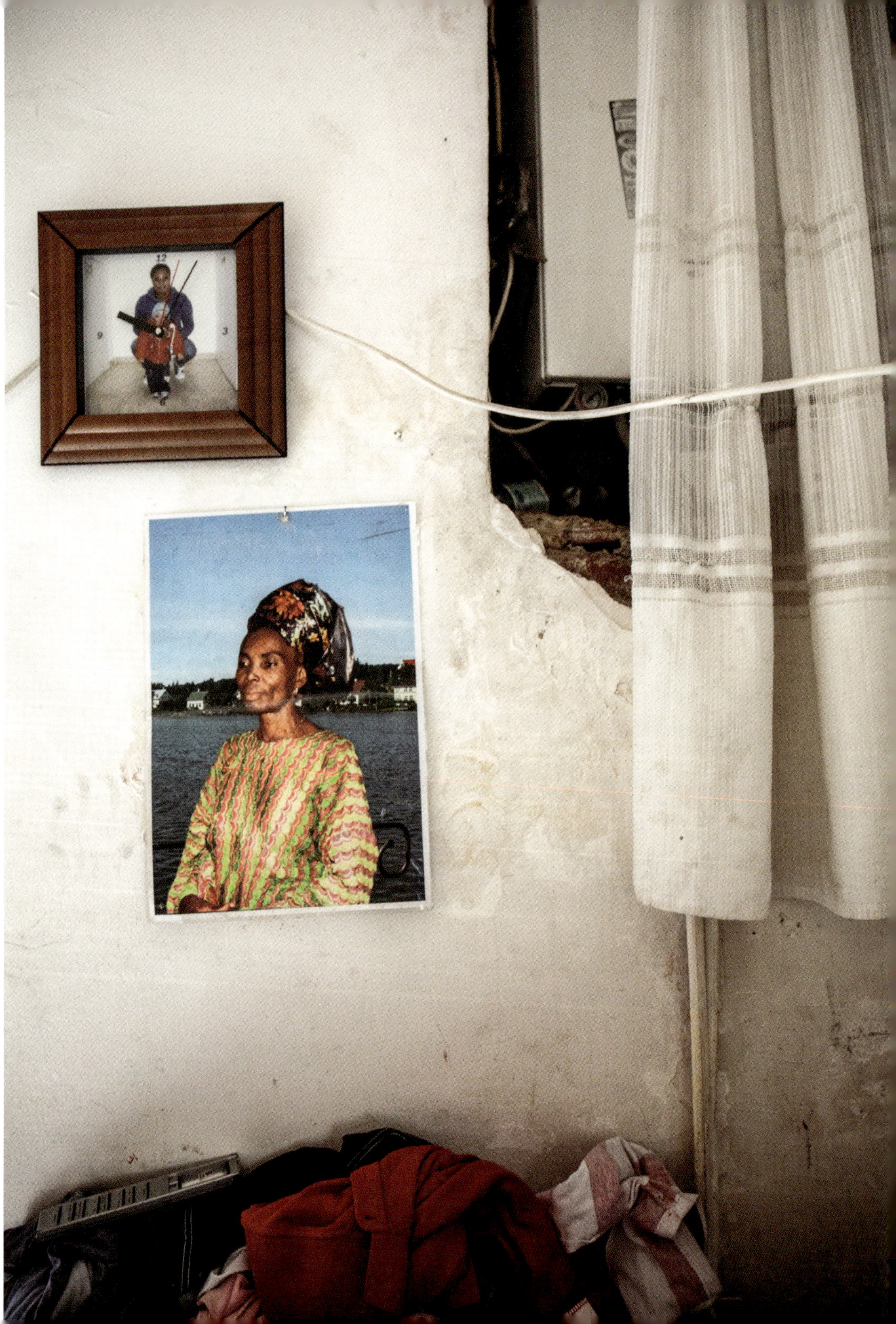

Cristiana Giordano
*Migrants in Translation. Caring and the
Logics of Difference in Contemporary Italy*

University of California Press, Berkeley, 2014

In 2000, Pia Covre, an Italian sex worker and
co-founder of the Italian Committee for the
Civil Rights of Prostitutes, gave the opening
speech at an international seminar on social
exclusion in Geneva. She said:

The migrant prostitute is the paradigmatic
figure of exclusion. [...] For the State, which
confers rights, the migrant prostitute is an
emblematic figure of singularity [...], she
embodies something extra, which is indigest-
ible, an immeasurable difference that no
prostitution policy wants to remove or
mitigate.

This quote speaks to the fact that the migrant
prostitute embodies the conundrum of
difference that doesn't have a language of its
own and therefore creates a rupture within
the dominant discourse of the law. In 1998,
Italy passed a law allowing victims of human
trafficking the right to temporary and renewable residence permits in order to escape from
situations of violence and abuse, on the
condition that they pursue criminal action
against their exploiters and that they participate in a rehabilitation program. I want to
reflect on Covre's words, and the paradoxical
logics of recognition at the heart of programs
of protection and rehabilitation of victims.
Over the course of my research in Northern
Italy, while I was mapping migrants' experiences through various institutional settings
that could grant them legal status, I listened
to different versions of migrants' stories

produced for the various purposes of their
physical and psychological integration into
Italian social and political life. I approached
the production of migrant stories as the
translation of the migrant's alterity into the
languages of various institutions (the police
department, the shelter, the clinic). Institutional vocabularies are complex nexuses of
bureaucratic, medical and legal discourses that
enable migrants to receive forms of recognition (legal documents, rights, services) and,
simultaneously, erase the singularity of voices
and individual biographies.

[...] The main goals of the rehabilitation
process for victims of human trafficking are
the training, the support, and the professional orientation of the women. According to the
various phases, women must attend Italian
classes, sessions aimed at professional
development such as taking care of the
elderly, cooking Italian dishes, learning how
to housekeep "Italian style," and doing
internships sponsored by the local government in factories, restaurants, and other
work places where there is a possibility for
long-term employment. [...] They are required
to spend a period of time during which they
depend on the assistance of social workers,
mental health practitioners, religious people,
and volunteers who are in charge of accom-
panying them through the different phases
of the program, and who act as the gatekeep-
ers of rules and norms. [...]

Women who have entered the social protection program have to abandon hopes of
economic independence and of helping their
families back home through sex work. If the
institutions do not grant the documents of
recognition that they promise, the person
experiences a sense of social annihilation.

[...] In 1998 the law on immigration (Law #39), also known as the Martelli Law,[I] was revised and it became what is commonly referred to as the Turco-Napolitano Law (Law #40) [...]. In the spirit of improving previous legislation on matters related to immigration, Law #40 was conceptualized to better regulate flows of migration to Italy, to facilitate the regrouping of migrants' families, and to strengthen the programs aimed at integrating foreigners into Italian society. One of the new aspects of the revised legislation concerned the "provisions of a humanitarian nature," within which Article 18 declared that victims of human trafficking had a right to a temporary (six-month), renewable residence permit. This permit is granted to allow non-nationals to escape from situations of violence and abuse. According to the law, people who classify as victims and prove to have been forced into prostitution or to have been victims of violence can participate in a rehabilitation and social integration program. [...]

Although informal and less structured rehabilitation programs of victims of violence had been in place since the early 1990s, when foreign prostitution became an issue of concern for immigration policies both nationally and internationally, Article 18 legalized these processes in an attempt to change the arbitrary treatment of victims of human trade.[II] [...] Article 27 of the Regulation outlines two different procedures to obtain a residence permit: one is known as "percorso sociale" (social itinerary) and the other as "percorso giuridico" (juridical/legal itinerary). Both procedures share the prerequisite that the person involved must be in physical danger. [...] The social itinerary is "made available when the danger originates with the woman's (or man's) efforts to escape from the control of a criminal organization." [...] She is not required to pursue criminal action against her traffickers and it is the role of the association or legal agency to present a request to the Chief Constable, who may then issue a residence permit entirely at his own discretion. The legal itinerary, on the other hand, requires that the person collaborate with the police or legal authorities by filing criminal charges against traffickers (this process is called a *denuncia*, a formal juridical accusation). The distinction between the two procedures is somewhat slippery insofar as, when filing criminal charges, a woman is presumably always in a position of danger and vulnerability. It is unclear when this kind of danger is considered to be serious enough to exempt the woman from denouncing her exploiters. Therefore, the ambivalence of Article 18 lies in the fact that while on the one hand it figures as an instrument of protection and integration of foreigners into Italian society, on the other hand, it functions as a mere instrument to fight criminality.[III]

I interviewed several administrators and lay volunteers who worked either for the immigration office or for associations involved in the implementation of Article 18. They mostly complained about the fact that legal authorities rarely used the social itinerary and instead favoured the legal itinerary.

[...] The program instituted by Article 18 is organized into several phases. [...] The first step is to file criminal charges against one's own traffickers. In addition, women can leave their previous residence and live in a shelter for six months or up to a year. In Italy these kinds of shelters are usually run by Catholic associations; [...] two leading figures in the national debate about human trafficking and the implementation of Article 18, Luigi Ciotti and Lorenzo Trucco – a priest and a lawyer respectively – have summarized the core meaning of the program as follows: "among all these other goals, the most fundamental element of the program is the residence permit; without it, it is neither possible to 'raise your head again' nor to pursue the paths that lead to autonomy and legality."[IV] [...] As a tangible sign of state recognition, the residence permit paradoxically functions as a surreal object: instead of providing real jobs alternatives and access, it legalizes those who continue to work in prostitution with the benefit that they can often do it independently from their previous exploiters. Women often discover that although they could not do much without papers, they could hardly do more once they had obtained them. [...] As victims they are recognized as legal subjects but they hardly have access to better jobs; as prostitutes they are not included, but they work – although illegally – and make money. Hence, the residence permit's perverse function: it grants recognition without guaranteeing employment, meaning that, financially, women were better off when they worked as prostitutes.

[...] An activist who works for one of the most important non-profit associations in Turin involved in the implementation of programs for victims once explained to me that "the limits of Article 18 are that it makes promises of integration into Italian society – a job, a house, a residence permit, access to services and education – that the institutions are not capable of keeping." Nonetheless, [...] Article 18 is also referred to as a "normative oasis,"[V] or as an anchor of hope for those seeking legality under increasingly punitive and exclusionary rules. [...] Article 18 remains the only regulation that allows illegal foreigners who are already present in the country – and who are not eligible for refugee status or medical reasons – to apply for a residence permit. In other words, a foreigner cannot be recognized as an 'economic migrant' if s/he works in prostitution. In these cases, full legal recognition can only be granted through appeal to the law for the protection of victims.

In many conversations I had with women about the act of filing criminal charges, I often heard the same comments repeated time and again: "Now that we have told our stories to the police, how is it that we still have neither the permit, nor a job, nor a house of our own?" It was obvious to me that the residence permit, along with the right of access to services, was the long-awaited reward that made filing criminal charges a more bearable experience to face. The *denuncia* (filing charges) was a means of obtaining those benefits that illegality and working in the street did not grant them. I remember very vividly the frustration on the face of Grace [...] when she found out that the authorities had issued her a residence permit for medical reasons – based on the records of her hospitalizations – rather than for being a "victim." The latter allows women to work, while the former does not. Being a victim grants more rights than a permit granted for medical or humanitarian reasons. And, of course, it is more difficult to fake a medical condition than to craft a personal story with varying tones of victimhood that can be heard by the state.

[...] The case of the Article 18 program of rehabilitation is complex because it demonstrates that foreign prostitutes are not merely passive nor exclusively victims of networks of exploitation. The reality, as always, is more nuanced. [...] Women's discrepant narratives force us to deal with the fundamental issue of the relationship between freedom and prostitution, trafficking and migration, and to push beyond these dichotomies. The legislation sets the terms of the debates, and individual stories are made to fit those terms. In this way, women's choices and desires, decisions and free will are distorted and translated into portions of a victim story. [...] What challenges this binary mode of representing migration, prostitution, and trafficking are those cases that do not fit any of these dichotomies.

For example, Ife told me that she came to Italy because there was no future for her in Nigeria. In Italy she worked as a prostitute for several months, and this was an opportunity to make money and escape from a place that had nothing to offer her. She later decided to file criminal charges against her madam, not for moral issues, but practical ones. She needed a residence permit in order to stay in Italy and have access to health care. She was also tired of giving her madam most of her income. She wanted to send more money home, and keep the rest for herself. In her case, entering the rehabilitation program did not imply leaving prostitution, but breaking the ties and debts with her madams. Another woman, Peace, wanted to become a nurse but could only enter Europe with fake documents and through the prostitution networks between Nigeria and Italy. After working on the streets for a year, she decided to appeal to Article 18 and gain legal status. After receiving the papers, she was able to enrol in a nursing program. [...] For the state, the complexity of women's trajectories and stories – often punctuated by the support of family members and friends from the country of origin – is often completely erased or misrecognized. By instituting practices such as filing criminal charges against traffickers as the condition to receive a residence permit, laws against human trafficking induce women to constitute and re-present themselves as innocent victims who have been abused by criminal groups. As a consequence, these laws fail to address the structural and social conditions that may lead women to choose prostitution as a way to leave countries that offer no future prospects. Even more alarming is that these laws also fail to address the receiving country's lack of job opportunities for those who decide to leave prostitution. It is not uncommon to hear about ex-prostitutes who have turned into madams after going through the rehabilitation program. Or, as was pointed out by Amen, who worked for an NGO that helped women leave prostitution, some women leave their exploiters, file criminal charges against them, receive the legal papers, find nothing better, and return to prostitution, maybe in nightclubs rather than on the streets, and independent from any network. Therefore, the line drawn between the innocent victim and the wilful illegal migrant that determines protection or punishment is dangerous and inconsistent. [...] In most cases, foreign women involved in prostitution view their sexual activities as a temporary means to an income, and they resist an explicit identification with their work. Several women I encountered talked about sex work as a way to make a lot of money in a short period of time, after which

they imagined looking for other jobs. [...] It is
at the intersection of these different discur-
sive fields on trafficking, prostitution, and
migration that Article 18 has emerged as a
legal space, an 'oasis of legality', and as a
good practice aimed at dealing with the
question of integration and difference in
Italian society. [...]

It is not my intention to argue that women are
never exposed to serious risks, neither is it to
suggest that they do not experience violence
and abuse while involved in prostitution.[VI] On
the contrary, many women I met encountered
harsh conditions and dangerous situations
while working on the streets. At the same
time, I also want to stress that the discourse
on trafficking reproduces the marginalization
of women by constructing them as victims.
[...] The process of naming the victim confines
her disturbing presence within the security
of the language of the law. [...] In this way, the
state, the Church, and other institutions
recuperate some sort of relationship with the
rejected, and she is made into the object of
their practices of recognition. Thinking back
on Pia Covre's words at the beginning of this
article, her difference thus becomes visible
and "digestible".

I   Italy passed the first comprehensive immigration legislation since the 1940s in 1990 (Law #39). This law was named after its sponsor, the Socialist deputy Claudio Martelli. Law #39 concerns the entry, residence, and employment of foreign workers, refugees, and foreign students, and demands the expulsion of those who are illegally present in the country or those who have been convicted of crimes. It basically serves two purposes: on the one hand it facilitates the legal absorption of foreigners and, on the other hand, it closes the borders until further labourers are considered necessary.

II   Several activists in Turin remember how the Minister of Equal Opportunities, Livia Turco, paid numerous visits to Turin to see how the different associations and services were dealing with the issue of foreign prostitution at the time when the immigration law was being revised (1997-1998), and how her exchanges with them had influenced the drafting of Article 18. Turin was identified as one of the most advanced Italian cities as far as the discussion and implementation of immigration policies and programs of integration were concerned.

III   The debates which stress the ambivalence of this piece of legislation refer to the antecedent to Article 18, a decree introduced in 1995-1996 in the first comprehensive immigration law instituted in 1990 (Law #39). According to this decree, the foreign national who decides to collaborate with legal authorities to denounce criminal actions related to illegal immigration could be granted a residence permit (only for one year with no possibility for renewal) for social protection on the conditions that he or she was in danger for having filed criminal charges against traffickers, that he or she could not safely be repatriated, and that her/his testimony had made a substantial contribution to police investigations against the illegal trafficking. Those collaborating with the police to fight criminality were also known as "collaboratori di giustizia" (collaborators of/for justice). Before the institution of Article 18, foreign illegal women who worked in the sex trade and wanted to obtain legal status could only collaborate with the police under the umbrella of collaborators for justice. The kind of permit they would receive did not grant them the right to work. Article 18, however, grants a residence permit that is renewable after six months, and allows foreign residents to work; it therefore represents a way to establish, in time, permanent residence.

IV   In *Questa è la legge...Art. 18 e dintorni*, Pagine. Il sociale da fare e pensare, n.2/2001, Gruppo Abele, Turin, p. 5. Luigi Ciotti is the founder and president of the non-profit association *Gruppo Abele* based in Turin. This association is involved in several projects of support for different categories of marginalized groups: the homeless, the drug addict, the migrant prostitute, HIV/AIDS patients. It is also involved in projects of co-operation in Africa and Latin America. Luigi Ciotti is the spokesman of the association. Lorenzo Trucco is president of the *Associazione Studi Giuridici sull'Immigrazione* (Association of Juridical Studies on Immigration).

V   See for example Vincenzo Castelli, in *Articolo 18: Tutela delle vittima del traffico di esseri umani e lotta alla criminalità (l'Italia e gli scenari europei, Rapporto di ricerca*, On the Road Edizioni, 2002, p. 25.
3636

VI   Laura Agustin, referring to the work of Francesco Carchedi et al (2003), suggests three categories of "prostitution": 1) autonomous, 2) semi-autonomous or semi-voluntary, 3) coerced and/or slave-like. She also argues: "such schemes need considerable leeway to account for the mixed nature of many experiences. Some people start out doing domestic work but feel compelled to sell sex because of the differential pay; others feel psychologically obligated who actually could physically escape; some connive with and manipulate those obligating them; others find no room to maneuver at all" (Agustin 2005: 8).

A. Akinyoade, F.Carchedi
*Cases of severely exploited Nigerian
citizens and other forms of exploitation*

Ediesse, Roma, 2012

The most commonly investigated crimes for
Nigerians are exploitation of prostitution and
illegal cross-border trafficking of persons [...]
in addition to international drug trafficking,
mainly of cocaine and heroin. [...] According
to police sources there is a strong link between human trafficking and other crimes, at
least for money-laundering purposes, in the
Nigerian community[1]. Nigerian criminals
operating in Italy do not specialise in one
single area of activity but instead shift their
interests from one sector to another with
great ease[2]. Even the routes used to move
immigrants change continually, and respond
to the need to avoid border checks.

[...] The instruments developed to increase
the level of cooperation between Italy and
Nigeria are three bilateral agreements, signed
at the police and judicial levels, between the
two countries' various institutions. The
memoranda of understanding are geared
towards combating practices connected with
trafficking of persons and also regard,
indirectly, practices of forced, severely
exploited labour, laying the ground for
increasing prevention and countermeasures.
The first bilateral agreement was signed in
Abuja on 11 November 2003 [...] and lays the
groundwork for the creation and development of transnational cooperation in the fight
against human trafficking and other crimes
linked to it. [...] Specifically, the areas of future
cooperation between the two countries would
include: exchange of information, legal texts

and documents regarding human trafficking
and other related crimes; [...] the adoption of
the necessary measures for the prompt,
efficient execution of every request for
extradition; [...] the development of professional contacts and relations between members of the respective departments [...].

A second bilateral agreement was signed in
Abuja on 18 January 2009 by the chief of the
Nigerian police, the chief of the Italian police,
and the Interpol general secretary. The agreement [...] aims to strengthen the capacity of
the three parties to combat more effectively
not only human trafficking but also organised
crime and illegal immigration in Italy.

[...] Finally, the third agreement was signed in
Abuja in December 2010 by NAPTIP, the
Nigerian federal agency for combating
trafficking, and the Italian National Anti-Mafia Department. It is an important document
which specifically regards human trafficking,
and which brings together the two aspects of
protecting victims and combating crime. [...]

Despite the existence of these specific instruments, there still appears to be a low level of
police and judicial cooperation between the
two countries in terms of investigations. The
difficulties involved in applying these agreements are considerable. [...] The DNA Deputy
Public Prosecutor has observed that [...]: "it is
very difficult to cooperate with Nigeria"[3].

In Italy there is still no National Anti-Trafficking Plan or National Referral System
capable of coordinating an effective strategy
against trafficking and for linking up with
comparable instruments implemented in
other European countries and thus boosting
the capacity to counter the phenomenon on a

transnational basis. [...] At the judicial level, in the last ten years the Italian and Nigerian governments have backed four major projects aimed at reducing the trafficking of people between Nigeria and Italy. These projects were entirely or partly funded by the Italian Cooperation Department of the Ministry of Foreign Affairs. [...]

All of the Nigerian victims who broke off the relationship of exploitation confirmed the importance of the encounters that they had had with the police, social workers and ordinary citizens, both Nigerian and Italian, in helping them to make the qualitative leap towards their own liberation. Without this network, which is mobile and flexible but present and active at the same time, it would have been much more difficult for them to escape their condition of quasi-slavery. Strengthening social services, therefore, must remain a categorical imperative. What is more, this recommendation must not apply just to Italy, but also – with Italian cooperation instruments – a number of areas in Nigeria [...].

Against this background, a question arises which necessarily places Italy's and Nigeria's capacity for law enforcement at the centre, as well as their reciprocal capacity to link up their action to counter the crimes in question through the designated agencies (first of all Interpol). For this to be effective, in our view, a number of basic conditions need to be established. [...]

a. The ability to identify trafficking victims with complete confidence, as in order to enter Italy they often use false passports given to them by the criminal organisation which has arranged to transfer them abroad. This aspect calls into question Nigeria's system for issuing passports. [...] The Nigerian Embassy in this regard must be able to correct victims' passports when requested by the social services or by the local police headquarters. This would improve the cooperation of victims with the judicial authorities.

b. For several years, Nigeria has had a national agency for victim protection and countering criminal organisations specialising in human trafficking: NAPTIP. This agency must be able to communicate directly with the Department for Equal Opportunities – which is responsible for assistance and social protection for victims – and vice versa, while with regard to law enforcement issues it needs to communicate with the National Anti-Mafia Department (via Interpol).

c. With regard to the social protection aspect it will be necessary to set up a "specialist task group" on Nigerian trafficking [...] which is capable of working together with the Nigerian Embassy (regarding victims' identity documents), with NAPTIP (in Nigeria) and the non-governmental organisations that operate in Italy on behalf of Nigerian women and in Nigeria in the same field, in order to create constant, continuous "relational bridges", and at the same time to develop – where the mechanisms have a hard time "getting off the ground" – cooperation projects designed to get such mechanisms up and running again smoothly.

---

1   Interview no. 56 and 57, cit.
2   Ibidem.
3   Ibidem.

Interview with Claudio Magnabosco

(Journalist, communications expert and former official of the European Parliament)

Claudio, you have studied the issue of prostitutes' clients for a long time and your book on the situation in Italy is about to be published. Can you tell us something about it?
The book *10 milioni di clienti. I maschi italiani nella realtà della tratta e della prostituzione* (10 million clients. Italian men, trafficking and prostitution) talks about the challenging work done in men's awareness groups, initially comprising clients and former clients who have experienced and described the sex industry as one of the many forms of violence men exert against women.
For the victims, being forced into prostitution means being raped constantly for money, and violence is indeed the main element of the power relationship that men seek en masse when they go to prostitutes. Awareness groups, on the other hand, seek to reverse the trend, opening men's eyes: they show that there is a big difference between trafficking and prostitution, and explain how the clients effectively contribute to the enslavement of trafficked women.
The book talks about the difficult process of bringing together these men's groups and women's organisations, and between these groups and the associations that work on an institutional level to combat trafficking: it reports on the attempts to forge a dialogue between these different worlds and does not criminalise the clients, rather showing that initiatives focusing on information, education and prevention can reduce the number of clients and contribute to men's awareness, which is basically about combating sexism, on a peer to peer basis.

Nigerian trafficking has been an issue for twenty years now. What changes have there been in Italy?
The women are still coming: they are younger than ever and arrive here with massive debts to pay off. They are forced into prostitution and are now increasingly reinventing themselves as madams or working for the traffickers, also trafficking men, children for adoptions and

organs and drug-dealing. These are the activities of the powerful Nigerian mafia, which is also involved in arms dealing.
What has changed is that the madams are now less violent towards the girls, having understood that if they mistreat them, the girls run away: the girls forced into the sex industry now get to keep a little of the money they earn and this makes their lives a little bit more tolerable. As they cannot find a real way out, they get used to life as prostitutes and prostitution becomes their only source of income.

What does the association "Le ragazze di Benin City" (The Girls of Benin City) do?
We have been working with Nigerian women for over ten years on a peer to peer basis; our projects are self-directed and self-financed. Little by little this initiative has grown, and other women have started to do what Isoke did, taking in trafficked women or hosting them in accommodation rented for the purpose. At present, around Italy there are various Nigerian women who are helping others. New families have formed, along with a special kind of support: trafficked women are taken in by families who decide to help them, like a sort of sponsorship program. More than 80% of these initiatives have been successful.

What do you think of the way in which the Italian institutions have responded to the phenomenon?
The data available shows that one Nigerian woman in ten has received some kind of assistance. You sometimes come across the figure of 10,000 girls having used the service in around ten years. With the means and the budget made available, the number of women reached by these official, funded services should be at least five times that. Many women have left their illegal status behind, but continue to be victims of trafficking: many of them have a residence permit but are still working as prostitutes. As the system has failed to get them out of that situation, people are now saying they should be safeguarded as prostitutes, calling for brothels to be reinstated and a law on prostitution to be passed, basically setting the seal on a human and humanitarian failure. The only valid response to this, first and foremost, is that a clear distinction needs to be made between trafficking and prostitution.

Are there some positive aspects, or best practices to highlight?
There is great work being done by various associations and individuals: *Piam* in Asti, for example, which is run by a couple, an Italian man and a trafficked Nigerian woman, who operate dynamically within the system, and *Gatta Dedalus* in Naples, where the Nigerian cultural mediators play a key role and those working with Andrea Morniroli have great freedom of action.

Then there is *Be Free* in Rome, where Oria and her co-workers face a complex situation, beleaguered by the problems in the Ponte Galeria Immigration Detention Centre. And *On the Road*, set up by Vincenzo Castelli, an intelligence association which has come up with strategies like confiscating the possessions of traffickers and providing compensation to the victims, to all the religious associations working across Italy, to the recent *Coordinamento Antitratta (Anti-trafficking organisation)* set up in Palermo. Best practices? I wouldn't use that term, given that the phenomenon has been going on for 20 years and has led to too many women being abused and killed.

Interview with Paolo Borgna

(Magistrate / Deputy Prosecutor, Turin)

*From the legislative point of view, what has changed in the way
Italy combats Nigerian trafficking?*
When Article 18 came into force in Italy, the positive effects were felt
immediately. In 1997 at the Prosecutor's Office in Turin there were 27
trials for crimes against Nigerian women. In 2000, with Article 18 in
force, there were 111 trials held for crimes against Nigerian women. The
number of crimes reported had increased fourfold. In the years that
followed, this growth trend continued.

Over the years the madams found ways to get around Article 18, which
was very advantageous to the girls who reported crimes: they were able
to get out from the madam's clutches and above all they got a residence
permit and a work bursary. Article 18 offered a very strong incentive to
women to report crimes.

The madams discovered that by applying for political asylum, the girls
could circulate freely throughout Italy and Europe for a long period of
time before the application, as happens in most cases, was rejected. The
right to asylum was therefore exploited, with "heterogony of ends", to
stop the girls from reporting their captors.

In the early 2000s, and prior to that with the Consolidated Act on Immigration (the Turco/Napolitano Act) of 1998, Italian legislation did much
to combat trafficking. Article 12 states that bringing people into the
country illegally for the purposes of prostitution is a very serious crime,
and sanctions were increased under the controversial Bossi/Fini law
(2002).

In the first decade of 2000, the articles of the Criminal Code regarding
enslavement and trafficking were rewritten (Art. 600 of the Criminal
Code). Enslavement means holding a person in conditions that are

comparable to slavery, whether for the purposes of sexual exploitation
or forced labour. Trafficking is trading in these people. The two crimes
are very similar, and usually reported simultaneously. They both fig-
ured in the Italian Criminal Code (1930) but the articles were originally
written with slaves from the Italian colonies in mind and hardly ever
applied. In 2003 the Italian parliament and government rewrote the two
articles. They kept the structure of the article in the 1930 code but adapt-
ed the contents to the present-day phenomenon of slavery: "Whoever
exerts on any other person powers and rights corresponding to owner-
ship; places or holds any other person in conditions of continuing
enslavement, sexually exploiting said person, imposing coerced labour
or forcing said person into begging, or exploiting him/her in any other
way, shall be punished with imprisonment from eight to twenty years."
In particular: "Placing or holding a person in a position of slavery oc-
curs when use is made of violence, deceit, or abuse of power; or when
anyone takes advantage of a situation of physical or mental inferiority
or poverty; or when money is promised, payments are made or other
kinds of benefits are promised to those who are responsible for the
person in question."
The difference here is that enslavement now applies not only to physical coercion, but exploiting the victim's poverty. The new article, which
was introduced in 2003, follows the definition of enslavement present
in the Protocol of the Palermo Convention of 2000 almost to the letter.

*What still needs to be changed to combat this transnational criminal
phenomenon?*
One aspect that has not been sufficiently strengthened – more due to
the overall weakness of Europe rather than Italy – is that of operative
agreements with the countries these women come from aimed at
protecting the victims' families. Thanks to a fantastic support network, and the assistance of Catholic and lay volunteers, the girls who
go to the police are protected, and immediately removed from the
street. What we are not able to tackle is the problem of the families
left behind in their home countries. Behind every girl who goes to the
police, in the home country there are families, parents, children to
support, who are often threatened, attacked or kidnapped. We, the
Italian Police, can do nothing. But Italy as a nation can, with specific

agreements, ask the countries in question to offer protection to the victims' families. Various conventions have been signed: in 2003 in Abuja, the capital of Nigeria, we signed a Memorandum of Understanding on trafficking with Nigeria, which entailed offering protection to the families of trafficked women. But it's one thing to sign a convention and make a commitment on paper, and another to get international judicial and police cooperation mechanisms up and running when the systems in place in these countries do not actually function. At this stage we do not have enough power to make a stand: only Europe wields that kind of power. Many countries present a high level of disorder internally, and do not have a specific political authority we can interface with. Take Libya for example. Everything gets very complicated. The new frontier we need to work on in the coming years is constructing an efficient international protection network for the families of the women who report these crimes to the police: to prevent the traffickers intimidating their victims by threatening to harm family members back in their home countries.

F.Carchedi
Trafficking of Nigerian Girls in Italy.

The Data, the Stories, the Social Services,
UNICRI, Turin, 2010

[...] Four interconnected factors are at the core of the system exploiting Nigerian women and girls. First, the instrumental and often criminal way that the *maman* and her collaborators/recruiters put in place in exploiting the tendency to migrate of many Nigerian young people, i.e. the psychological and actual propensity of many young people to accept proposals for migrating in order to improve their living conditions[26]. [...] The second factor is linked to the need to find enough money for travelling abroad, in our case in Italy. This necessity pushes the person into the hands of people – and almost inevitably with organizations specialized in transferring migrants abroad – that lend money (i.e. *sponsors*), know the legal and often illegal ins and outs for acquiring the necessary documents, and know how to make a binding contract with the people they send abroad. The third factor is of symbolic and ritual significance. The woman or girl must swear in front of the sponsor[27] (the maman or her helpers), i.e. those lending her the money and organizing the journey, that she will pay back to the organization the amount previously established and written in the contract. [...] The ways used for subjugating these women once they arrive in Italy is the fourth factor to be taken into account.

[...] The debt, which holds an economic, moral and psychological obligation,[32] is usually very high [...]. It is a system that still works on older women who are generally more aware of the risk of falling into the prostitution rings. It should therefore not come as a surprise if many young girls, who are much less aware of what could become of them once they arrive at their destination, fall into the trap. It is even harder for these young girls to understand the hidden implications of such an operation when family members are the ones that organize the journey[35].

[...]The exploitation process (recruitment, journey and trip, passing the border(s), settling in the new country and coercion into the prostitution rings) penalises young girls more than older women since their age easily makes them potential victims of criminals that enrich themselves thanks to their victims. Richard Sennet states that in the Ibo culture (one of the ethnic groups more involved in trafficking in human beings for sexual exploitation)[38] to be under age does not grant any extra protection to the young, who are considered as a subject not only by the family but of society as well[39].

[...] Women older than 18 – even 20 or 25 – suddenly become under-age during the recruiting stage and, vice versa, very young girls may suddenly become older, if the *maman* thinks that this is the right thing to do for ensuring their expatriation at any point in time. [...] Once in Italy, the age may change again. Their real or falsified documents are then withheld, and they are personally brought back or sent to Nigeria. [...] Two the reasons for doing so: first, to deprive the girl of her identity, making her feel isolated and with no links to the outside world, and as such beginning the depersonalisation/dehumanization pro-

26   UNICRI, 2004, cit. , p. 334.

27   UNICRI, 2004, cit. , p. 355.

32   Carchedi F., 2003, cit, II Section, p. 9. "The monetary debt between the potential victim and the maman – says the Report – seems almost accidental and of little importance if compared to the moral one". Beneluce R. in his Breve dizionario di etnopsichiatria, says "the debt has an economic and psychological feature from which the victim's dependence derives", Rome: Carocci, 2008, p.131

35   E ghafona K. A., The bane of female trafficking in Nigeria: an examination of the role of the family in the Benin City society, in Awaritefe A., Toward a sane society, Benin City: Roma Publication - Ambik Press Ltd, 2009, p. 13.

38   Nigerian women, both adults and minors, come from the Igbo (o Ibo), the Yoruba, the Bini and, the Edo Communities. Senato della Repubbli-ca – Camera dei Deputati, Comitato per la Sicurezza della Repubblica, 2009, cit., p. 35.

39   In his book Authority (cit.) R Sennett writes that the Ibo child does not have any authority, he/she is a considered a subject. T. Falola and M. M. Heaton express the opinion that in modern Nigeria, especially in the Southern Delta States, the age subdivision of society still represents the local community main hierarchi-cal order. UNICRI, 2004, cit. p. 355.

45   UNICRI, 2004, cit. p. 35.

49   The condition of human pawn is transitory and limited to the time it takes for the money to be paid back. The parents still consider her their child and the *maman* knows that the human pawn will be free the minute the debt is fully settled. The mamans are not interested in owning a person for ever, they want to make sure that the money will come back. F. Viti in his book *Schiavi, servi e dipendenti* (op. cit.) states that paying back the entire amount is a point of honour for the debtor and that the final settlement immediately frees the human pawn. The creditor cannot change this rule under any circumstance. Falola T., Heaton M. M. in *A history of Nigeria*, New York, Cambridge University Press, 2008, p. 4, affirm that "the persons that are usually given as human pawn are the most pliant to the new conditions and readier to integrate in a new environment... minors are better suited than adults... they have more energy. This is why they cost more and are better paid".

cess; second, to reuse the documents for
other travellers. [...]

Generally speaking, there is a tendency to
raise the potential victim's age during the
journey to Italy, thus stressing the consensu-
al and voluntary aspect of the journey[45]. By
contrast, there is a tendency to lower the age
when the woman is working as a prostitute,
since this may attract a broader clientele.

[...] The condition of the Nigerian girls who
are sexually exploited is made even more
dramatic by their young age, putting them in a
very weak social position and making them
fully dependent on a number of people. [...]
The young girl may feel very excited by her
parents' decision to send her abroad since she
is the one entrusted to improve the family
living conditions. But in reality the parents,
even if involuntarily, place the child outside
the family, preventing her from enjoying the
solidarity that is naturally given to the other
family members. [...] In the first "model", the
father, with the mother as the second-lead, is
the main actor (considering that they often are
de facto polygamous families). The prestige
that the father, as head of the family, holds
within the men's family circle gives solemnity
to the child's choice to emigrate, a choice that
may seem autonomous but is strongly moti-
vated by the father. She feels honoured to be
given the role: to contribute to the improve-
ment of the family living conditions. [...] In the
second "model" the father is absent [...] and it
is the mother who takes the lead, becoming
the pivot of the entire transaction. In such
cases the mothers usually belong to family
lines within polygamous groups.

[...] In both "models", notwithstanding the
different reference persons, it is the daughter
that takes the full responsibility for the
family's debt since she is the one leaving the
family even if only fulfilling a migratory
project that has been planned collectively. [...]
These girls are not expected to contribute to
settle the debt according to their abilities, i.e.
proportionally to the hierarchical role they
have within the family, but are asked to settle
it by themselves, compromising – willingly
or not – their psychological and physical
integrity. [...]
On the one hand, the parents momentarily
abandon the child and, on the other hand, the
girl becomes a "human pawn" to the *maman/
sponsor*, as guarantee that the debt will be
repaid[49] and as a productive "tool" able to
acquire the needed resources in order to
honour the pact.

Acknowledgments

This book was made possible with the generous support of:

Open Society Foundations;
Fondazione Cassa di Risparmio di Cuneo.

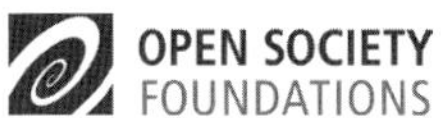

Thanks
To the following people who helped at various stages in making the book: Francesca Bosco, Ivano Dal Conte, Marta Costantino, Andrea Deaglio, Davide Dutto, Paolo Putti, Cristiana Giordano, Faith Jackson, Angelo Bagnasacco, Paolo Borgna, Claudio Magnabosco, Isoke Aikpitanyi, Francesco Carchedi, Giuseppe Carrisi, Maria Teresa Falzone, Maria Rosa Scala, Andrea Torre, Centro Studi Medi', Be Free, Francesca De Masi, Salvatore Fachile, Alberto Barbieri, Carmen Bertolazzi, Cooperativa Dedalus, Andrea Morniroli, Enrica Di Nanni, Fatima and Elizabeth, Valter Negro, Squadra Volante - Questura di Torino, Diego Orlando, Stefanella Campana, Roberta Alberotanza, Associazione Pellegrino della terra, Padre Vivian Wiwoloku, Valerio Costanzia, Marta Benedetto, Enrico Sabena, Davide Sannazzaro, Marco Bonfiglioli, Maria Franchitti, Panta Rei, Stanley Greene, Christopher Morris, Maria Louise & Maarten Schilt, André Frère, Miriam Anati, Teun van der Heijden, Sandra van der Doelen, the crowd-funding financial supporters from Kickstarter, Philipp Leube, my family and especially Emma.

A special thanks to all the Nigerian women portrayed in the book for giving me their trust and teaching me what dignity means.

This book is dedicated to Piero and Rosangela for always being there, no matter what.